DICTIONARY OF

Obsolete English

DICTIONARY OF

Obsolete English

BY

RICHARD CHENEVIX TRENCH, D.D.

ARCHBISHOP OF DUBLIN.

'Res fugiunt, vocabula manent'

PHILOSOPHICAL LIBRARY

New York

ISBN 978-0-8065-3042-1

PREFACE

THIS VOLUME is intended to be a contribution, I am aware a very slight one, to a special branch of the study of our own language. It proposes to trace in a popular manner and for general readers the changes of meaning which so many of its words have undergone ; words which, as current with us as they were with our forefathers, yet meant something different on their lips from what they mean on ours. Of my success in carrying out the scheme which I had set before myself, it does not become me to speak, except to say that I have fallen a good deal below my hopes, and infinitely below my desires. But of the scheme itself I have no doubts. I feel sure that, if only adequately carried out, few works of the same compass could embrace matter of more manifold instruction, or in a region of knowledge which it would be more desirable to occupy. In the present condition of education in England, above all with the pressure upon young men, which is ever increasing, to complete their educational course at the earliest possible date, the number of those enjoying the inestimable advantages, mental and moral, which more than any other languages the Latin and the Greek supply, must ever be growing smaller. It becomes therefore a duty to seek elsewhere the best substitutes within reach for that discipline of the faculties which these languages would better than any other have afforded. And I believe, when these two are set aside, our own language and literature will furnish the best substitutes; which, even though they may not satisfy perfectly, are not therefore to be rejected. I am persuaded that in the *decomposition*, word by word, of small portions of our best poetry and prose, the compensations which we look for are most capable of being found; even as I have little doubt that in many of our higher English schools compensations of the kind are already oftentimes obtained. *Lycidas* suggests itself to me, in the amount of *resistance* which it would offer, as in verse furnishing more exactly what I seek than any other poem, perhaps some of Bacon's *Essays* in prose.

In such a decomposition, to be followed by a reconstruction, of some small portions of a great English Classic, matters almost innumerable, and pressing on the attention from every side, would claim to be noticed ; but certainly not last nor least the changes in meaning which, on close examination, would be seen to have past on many of the words employed. It is to point out some of these changes ; to suggest how many more there may be, there certainly are, which have not been noticed in these pages ; to show how slight and subtle, while yet most real, how easily therefore evading detection, unless constant vigilance is used, these changes often have been ; to trace here and there the progressive steps by which the old meaning has been put off, and the new put on, the exact road which a word has travelled ; this has been my purpose here ; and I have desired by such means to render some small assistance to those who are disposed to regard this as a serviceable discipline in the training of their own minds or the minds of others.

The book is, as its name declares, a *Select* Glossary. There would have been no difficulty whatever in doubling or trebling the number of articles admitted into it. But my purpose being rather to arouse curiosity than fully to gratify it, to lead others themselves to take note of changes,

and to account for them, rather than to take altogether this pleasant labour out of their hands and
to do for them what they could more profitably
do for themselves, I have consciously left much of
the work undone, even as unconsciously no doubt
I have left a great deal more. At the same
time it has not been mere caprice which has induced the particular selection of words which has
been actually made. Various motives, but in
almost every case such as I could give account of
to myself, have ruled this selection. Sometimes
the past use of a word has been noted and compared with the present, as usefully exercising the
mind in the tracing of minute differences and
fine distinctions ; or again, as helpful to the understanding of our earlier authors, and likely to
deliver the readers of them from misapprehensions
into which they might very easily fall ; or, once
more, as opening out a curious chapter in the
history of manners, or as involving some interesting piece of history, or some singular
superstition ; or, again, as witnessing for the
good or for the evil which have been unconsciously at work in the minds and hearts of
those who insensibly have modified in part or
changed altogether the meaning of some word ;
or, lastly and more generally, as illustrating well
under one aspect or another those permanent

laws which are everywhere affecting and modifying human speech.

And as the words brought forward have been selected with some care, and according to certain rules which have for the most part indicated their selection, so also has it been with the passages adduced in proof of the changes of meaning which they have undergone. A principal value which such a volume as the present can possess, must consist in the happiness with which these have been chosen. Not every passage, which really contains evidence of the assertion made, will for all this serve to be adduced in proof, and this I presently discovered in the many which for one cause or another it was necessary to set aside. There are various excellencies which ought to meet in such passages, but which will not by any means be found in all.

In the first place they ought to be such passages as will tell their own story, will prove the point which they are cited to prove, quite independently of the uncited context, to which it will very often happen that many readers cannot, and of those who can, that the larger number will not, refer. They should bear too upon their front that amount of triumphant proof, which will carry conviction not merely to the student who by a careful observation of many like passages, and a previous knowledge of what was a word's prevailing use in the time of the writer, is prepared to receive this conviction, but to him also, to whom all this is presented now for the first time, who has no predisposition to believe, but is disposed rather to be incredulous in the matter. Then again, they should, if possible, be passages capable of being detached from their context without the necessity of drawing a large amount of this context after them to make them intelligible ; like trees which will endure to be transplanted without carrying with them a huge and cumbrous bulk of earth, clinging to their roots. Once more, they should, if possible, be such as have a certain intrinsic worth and value of their own, independent of their value as illustrative of the point in language directly to be proved—some weight of thought, or beauty of expression, or merit of some other kind, that so the reader may be making a second gain by the way. I can by no means claim this for all, or nearly all, of mine. Indeed it would have been absurd to seek it in a book of which the primary aim is quite other than that of the bringing together a collection of striking quotations ; any merit of this kind must continually be subordinated, and, where needful, wholly sacrificed, to the purposes more immediately in view. Still there will be many citations found in these pages which, while they fulfil the primary intention with which they were quoted, are not wanting also in this secondary worth.

In my citations I have throughout acted on the principle that 'Enough is as good as a feast:' and that this same 'Enough,' as the proverb might well be completed, 'is better than a surfeit.' So soon as that earlier meaning, from which our present is a departure, or which once subsisted side by side with our present, however it has now disappeared, has been sufficiently established, I have held my hand, and not brought further quotations in proof. In most cases indeed it has seemed desirable to adduce passages from several authors ; without which a suspicion may always remain in the mind, that we are bringing forward the exceptional peculiarity of a single writer, who even in his day stood alone. I do not feel confident that in some, though rare, instances I have not adduced exceptional uses of this kind.

One value I may claim for my book, that whatever may be wanting to it, it is with the very most trifling exceptions an entirely independent and original collection of passages illustrative of the history of our language. Of my citations, I believe about a thousand in all, I may owe some twenty at the most to existing

Dictionaries or Glossaries, to Nares or Johnson or Todd or Richardson. In perhaps some twenty cases more I have lighted upon and selected a passage by one of them selected before, and have not thought it desirable, or have not found it possible, to dismiss this and choose some other in its room. These excepted, the collection is entirely independent of all those which have previously been made ; and in a multitude of cases notes uses and meanings of words which have never been noted before.

ABANDON. 'Bann,' a word common to all the Germanic languages, and surviving in our 'banns of marriage,' is open proclamation. In low Latin it takes the forms of 'bannus,' 'bannum,' edict or interdict; while in early French we have 'bandon,' almost always with the particle à prefixed, 'à bandon;' thus 'vendre à bandon,' to sell by outcry. From this we have the verb 'abandonare,' which has passed into all the Romance languages; it is to proclaim, announce, but more often denounce, a bandit ('bandetto') being a denounced man, a proclaimed outlaw. Here is the point of contact between the present use of 'abandon' and the past. What you denounce, you loosen all ties which bind you to it, you detach yourself from it, you forsake, in our modern sense of the word, you 'abandon' it.

Blessed shall ye be when men shall hate you, and *abandon* your name as evil [et *ejecerint* nomen vestrum tanquam malum, Vulg.] for the Son of man's sake.—*Luke* vi. 22.   Rheims.

> *Beggar.* Madame wife, they say that I have dreamed
> And slept above some fifteen years or more.
> *Lady.* Aye, and the time seems thirty unto me,
> Being all this time *abandoned* from thy bed.
> SHAKESPEARE, *The Taming of the Shrew*, act i. sc. I.

ACHIEVEMENT. This fuller form of the word is seldom if ever used now, as it was often of old, where ' hatchment ' is intended.

As if a herald in the *achievement* of a king should commit the indecorum to set his helmet sideways and close; not full-faced and open, as the posture of direction and command.—MILTON, *Tetrachordon.*

ACT. The verb ' to actuate ' seems of comparatively late introduction into the language. The first example of it which our Dictionaries give is drawn from the works of the Latinist, Sir Thomas Browne, of Norwich. I have also met it in Jeremy Taylor. But even for some time after ' actuate ' was introduced—as late, we see, as Pope,—' act ' did often the work which ' actuate ' alone does now.

Within, perhaps, they are as proud as Lucifer, as covetous as Demas, as false as Judas, and in the whole course of their conversation act and are *acted*, not by devotion, but design.—SOUTH, *Sermons*, 1737, vol. ii. p. 391.

Many offer at the effects of friendship; but they do not last. They are promising at the beginning, but they fail and jade and tire in the prosecution. For most people in the world are *acted* by levity and humour, and by strange and irrational changes.— Id. *ib.* vol. ii. p. 73.

Self-love, the spring of motion, *acts* the soul.
POPE, *Essay on Man*, ep. 2.

ADAMANT. It is difficult to trace the exact motives which induced the transferring of this name to the lodestone; but it is common enough in our best English writers, thus in Chaucer, Bacon, and Shakespeare; as is ' aimant ' in French, and ' iman ' in Spanish. See 'Diamond,' and the art. 'Adamant' in *Appendix* A to the *Dictionary of the Bible.*

Right as an *adamant* ywis
Can drawen to him subtelly
The yron that is laid thereby,
So draweth folkes hearts ywis
Silver and gold that yeven is.

> Chaucer, *Romaunt of the Rose*, 1182.

Demetrius. Hence, get thee gone, and follow me no more.
Helena. You draw me, you hard-hearted *adamant*;
And yet you draw not iron, for my heart
Is true as steel.

> Shakespeare, *Midsummer Night's Dream*, act ii. sc. 1.

If you will have a young man to put his travel in little room, when he stayeth in one city or town, let him change his lodging from one end and part of the town to another; which is a great *adamant* of acquaintance.—Bacon, *Essays*, 18.

ADMIRAL. This was a title often given in the seventeenth century to the principal and leading vessel in a fleet; the ' admiral-galley ' North (*Plutarch's Lives*) calls it.

Falstaff (to Bardolph). Thou art our *admiral*; thou bearest the lantern in the poop—but 'tis the nose of thee; thou art the knight of the Burning Lamp.—Shakespeare, 1 *Henry IV.*, act iii. sc. 3.

Lincoln spake what was fit for comfort, and did what he was able for redress. He looked like the lanthorn in the *admiral*, by which the rest of the fleet did steer their course.—Hacket, *Life of Archbishop Williams*, part ii. p. 143.

His spear—to equal which the tallest pine
Hewn on Norwegian hills, to be the mast
Of some great *ammiral*, were but a wand—
He walked with, to support uneasy steps
Over the burning marle.

> Milton, *Paradise Lost*, b. i.

The *admiral* of the Spanish Armada was a Flemish ship.—Hawkins, *Observations* &c., 1622, p. 9.

ADMIRE,   ⎫ It now always implies to wonder
ADMIRABLE,   ⎬ *with approval*; but was by no means
ADMIRATION.   ⎭ restrained to this wonder *in bonam*
partem of old.

Neither is it to be *admired* that Henry [the Fourth], who was
a wise as well as a valiant prince, should be pleased to have the
greatest wit of those times in his interests, and to be the trumpet
of his praises.—DRYDEN, *Preface to the Fables.*

> Let none *admire*
> That riches grow in hell; that soil may best
> Deserve the precious bane.
>
> MILTON, *Paradise Lost*, b. i.

In man there is nothing *admirable* but his ignorance and
weakness.—J. TAYLOR, *Dissuasive from Popery*, part ii. b. i. § 7.

And I saw the woman drunken with the blood of the saints
. . . and when I saw her I wondered with great *admiration.*—
Rev. xvii. 6. Authorized Version.

ALCHYMY. By this we always understand now the
pretended art of transmuting other metals into gold;
but it was often used to express itself a certain mixed
metal, which having the appearance of gold, was yet
mainly composed of brass. Thus the notion of false-
ness, of show and semblance not borne out by reality,
frequently underlay the earlier uses of the word.

As for those gildings and paintings that were in the palace
of Alcyna, though the show of it were glorious, the substance of
it was dross, and nothing but *alchymy* and cosenage.—Sir J.
HARINGTON, *A brief Allegory of Orlando Furioso.*

Whereupon out of most deep divinity it was concluded, that
they should not celebrate the sacrament in glass, for the brittle-
ness of it; nor in wood, for the sponginess of it, which would
suck up the blood; nor in *alchymy*, because it was subject to
rusting; nor in copper, because that would provoke vomiting;
but in chalices of latten, which belike was a metal without exception.—FULLER, *The Holy War*, b. iii. c. 13.

Towards the four winds four speedy cherubim
Put to their mouths the sounding *alchymy.*
MILTON, *Paradise Lost*, b. ii.

ALLOW,   'To allow,' from the French 'allouer,'
ALLOWANCE, and through it from the Latin 'allau-
ALLOWABLE. dare,' and not to be confounded with
another ' allow,' derived from another ' allouer,' the
Latin 'allocare,' had once a sense very often of praise
or approval, which may now be said to have departed
from it altogether. Thus in Cotgrave's *French and
English Dictionary*, an invaluable witness of the
force and meanings which words had two centuries
ago, ' allow ' is rendered by 'allouer,' 'gréer,' 'ap-
proauver,' ' accepter,' and ' allowable ' by ' louable.'

Mine enemy, say they, is not worthy to have gentle words or
deeds, being so full of malice or frowardness. The less he is
worthy, the more art thou therefore *allowed* of God, and the
more art thou commended of Christ.—*Homilies ; Against Contention.*

The hospitality and alms of abbeys is not altogether to be *allowed*, or dispraised.—PILKINGTON, *The Burning of Paul's*, § 12.

Truly ye bear witness that ye *allow* [συνευδοκεῖτε] the deeds of
your fathers.—*Luke* xi. 48. Authorized Version.

A stirring dwarf we do *allowance* give
Before a sleeping giant.
SHAKESPEARE, *Troilus and Cressida*, act ii. sc. 3.

Though I deplore your schism from the Catholic Church, yet I
should bear false witness if I did not confess your decency,
which I discerned at the holy duty, was very *allowable* in the
consecrators and receivers.—HACKET, *Life of Archbishop Williams*, part ii. p. 211.

AMIABLE. This and ' lovely ' have been so far
differentiated that ' amiable ' never expresses now any
other than *moral* loveliness; which in ' lovely ' is
seldom or never implied. There was a time when

'amiable' had no such restricted use, when it and 'lovely' were absolutely synonymous, as, etymologically, they might claim still to be.

> Come sit thee down upon this flow'ry bed,
> While I thy *amiable* cheeks do coy.
>> SHAKESPEARE, *Midsummer Night's Dream*, act iv. sc. 1.

How *amiable* are thy tabernacles, O Lord of Hosts.—*Ps.* lxxxiv. 1. Authorized Version.

> Groves whose rich trees wept odorous gums and balm,
> Others whose fruit, burnished with golden rind,
> Hung *amiable*.   MILTON, *Paradise Lost*, b. iv.

AMUSE, } The attempt which Coleridge makes
AMUSEMENT. } to bring 'amuse' into some connection with the Muses is certainly an error; from whence we have obtained the word is harder to say. For two suggestions about it, see Diez, *Wört. d. Roman. Sprachen*, p. 236, and *Proceedings of the Philological Society*, vol. v. p. 82. Sufficient here to observe that the notion of diversion, entertainment, is comparatively of recent introduction into the word. ' To amuse ' was to cause to muse, to occupy or engage, and in this sense indeed to *divert*, the thoughts and attention. The quotation from Phillips shows the word in transition to its present meaning.

Camillus set upon the Gauls, when they were *amused* in receiving their gold.—HOLLAND, *Livy*, p. 223.

Being *amused* with grief, fear, and fright, he could not find a house in London (otherwise well known to him), whither he intended to go.—FULLER, *Church History of Britain*, b. ix. § 44.

A siege of Maestricht or Wesel (so garrisoned and resolutely defended) might not only have *amused*, but endangered the French armies.—Sir W. TEMPLE, *Observations on the United Provinces*, c. 8.

To *amuse*, to stop or stay one with a trifling story, to make him lose his time, to feed with vain expectations, to hold in play. —PHILLIPS, *New World of Words.*

In a just way it is lawful to deceive the unjust enemy, but not to lie ; that is, by stratagems and semblances of motions, by *amusements* and intrigues of actions, by ambushes and wit, by simulation and dissimulation.—J. TAYLOR, *Ductor Dubitantium*, b. iii. c. 2.

ANATOMY. Now the act of dissection, but it was often used by our elder writers for the thing or object dissected, and then, as this was stripped of its flesh, for what we now call a skeleton. ' Skeleton,' which see, had then another meaning.

Here will be some need of assistants in this live, and to the quick, dissection, to deliver me from the violence of the *anatomy*. —WHITLOCK, *Zootomia,* p. 249.

Antiquity held too light thoughts from objects of mortality, while some drew provocatives of mirth from *anatomies,* and jugglers showed tricks with skeletons.—Sir T. BROWNE, *Hydriotaphia.*

ANIMOSITY. While 'animosus' belongs to the best period of Latin literature, ' animositas ' is of quite the later silver age. It was used in two senses ; in that, first, of spiritedness or courage ('equi *animositas,*' the courage of a horse), and then, secondly, as this spiritedness in one particular direction, in that, namely, of a vigorous and active enmity or hatred (*Heb.* xi. 27, Vulg.). Of these two meanings the latter is the only one which our 'animosity' has retained ; yet there was a time when it also had the other as well.

When her [the crocodile's] young be newly hatched, such as give some proof of *animosity*, audacity, and execution, those she loveth, those she cherisheth.—HOLLAND, *Plutarch's Morals,* p. 977.

Doubtless such as are of a high-flown *animosity* affect *fortunas laciniosas*, as one calls it, a fortune that sits not strait and close to the body, but like a loose and a flowing garment.—HACKET, *Life of Archbishop Williams*, part i. p. 30.

In these cases consent were conspiracy; and open contestation is not faction or schism, but due Christian *animosity*.—HALES, *Tract concerning Schism*.

Cato, before he durst give the fatal stroke, spent part of the night in reading the Immortality of Plato, thereby confirming his wavering hand unto the *animosity* of that attempt.—Sir T. BROWNE, *Hydriotaphia*.

ANNOY,   ⎫ Now rather to vex and disquiet than
ANNOYANCE. ⎬ seriously to hurt and harm.   But
until comparatively a late day, it was true to its etymology, and admitted no such mitigation of meaning.

For the Lord Almygti *anoyede* [*nocuit*, Vulg.] hym, and bitook him into the hondes of a womman.—*Judith* xvi. 7. WICLIF.

Than cometh malignitee, thrugh which a man *annoieth* his neeghbour, as for to brenne his house prively, or enpoison him, or sle his bestes, and semblable things.—CHAUCER, *The Persones Tale*.

> Against the Capitol I met a lion,
> Which glared upon me, and went surly by,
> Without *annoying* me.
> > SHAKESPEARE, *Julius Cæsar*, act i. sc. 3.

> Look after her,
> Remove from her the means of all *annoyance*,
> And still keep eyes upon her.
> > Id. *Macbeth*, act v. sc. 1.

ANTICS.   Strange gestures now, but the makers of these strange gestures once.

> Behold, destruction, fury, and amazement,
> Like witless *antics*, one another meet.
> > SHAKESPEARE, *Troilus and Cressida*, act v. sc. 4.

> Have they not sword-players, and every sort
> Of gymnic artists, wrestlers, riders, runners,
> Jugglers and dancers, *antics*, mummers, mimics?
> MILTON, *Samson Agonistes.*

APPARENT,⎱ With the exception of the one phrase
APPARENTLY.⎰ 'heir *apparent*,' meaning heir evident, manifest, undoubted, we do not any longer employ 'apparent' for that which appears, because it *is*, but always either for that which appears and is not, or for that which appears, leaving in doubt whether it is or no. Thus we might say with truth in the modern sense of the word, that there are *apparent* contradictions in Scripture; we could not say it in the earlier sense without denying its inspiration.

> It is *apparent* foul play; and 'tis shame
> That greatness should so grossly offer it.
> SHAKESPEARE, *King John*, act iv. sc. 2.

At that time Cicero had vehement suspicions of Cæsar, but no *apparent* proof to convince him.—NORTH, *Plutarch's Lives*, p. 718.

The laws of God cannot without breach of Christian liberty, and the *apparent* injury of God's servants, be hid from them in a strange language, so depriving them of their best defence against Satan's temptations.—FULLER, *Twelve Sermons concerning Christ's Temptations*, p. 59.

> Love was not in their looks, either to God
> Or to each other, but *apparent* guilt,
> And shame and perturbation and despair.
> MILTON, *Paradise Lost*, b. x.

At that time [at the resurrection of the last day], as the Scripture doth most *apparently* testify, the dead shall be restored to their own bodies, flesh and bones.—*Articles of the Church* (1552).

APPREHENSIVE. As there is nothing which persons lay hold of more readily than that aspect of a subject

in which it presents matter for fear, ' to apprehend '
has acquired the sense of to regard with fear; yet not
so as that this use has excluded its earlier; but it *has*
done so in respect of ' apprehensive,' which has now
no other meaning than that of fearful, a meaning
once quite foreign to it.

> See their odds in death:
> Appius died like a Roman gentleman,
> And a man both ways knowing; but this slave
> Is only sensible of vicious living,
> Not *apprehensive* of a noble death.
>> WEBSTER, *Appius and Virginius*, act v. sc. 3.

She, being an handsome, witty, and bold maid, was both
apprehensive of the plot, and very active to prosecute it.—FULLER,
The Profane State, b. v. c. 5.

> My father would oft speak
> Your worth and virtue; and as I did grow
> More and more *apprehensive*, I did thirst
> To see the man so praised.
>> BEAUMONT AND FLETCHER, *Philaster*, act v. sc. 1.

ARTIFICIAL, ⎫ That was 'artificial' once which
ARTIFICIALLY. ⎭ wrought, or which was wrought,
according to the true principles of art. The word
has descended into quite a lower sphere of meaning;
such, indeed, as the quotation from Bacon shows, it
could occupy formerly, though not then exactly the
same which it occupies now.

Queen Elizabeth's verses, some extant in the elegant, witty,
and *artificial* book of *The Art of English Poetry*, are princely as
her prose.—BOLTON, *Hypercritica*.

> We, Hermia, like two *artificial* gods,*
> Have with our neelds created both one flower.
>> SHAKESPEARE, *Midsummer Night's Dream*, act iii. sc. 2.

---

* Deabus *artificibus* similes, as S. WALKER (*Criticisms on
Shakespeare*, vol. i. p. 96) gives it well.

This is a demonstration that we are not in the right way, that we do not enquire wisely, that our method is not *artificial*. If men did fall upon the right way, it were impossible that so many learned men should be engaged in contrary parties and opinions.—J. TAYLOR, *A Sermon preached before the University of Dublin.*

This he did the rather, because having at his coming out of Britain given *artificially*, for serving his own turn, some hopes in case he obtained the kingdom, to marry Anne, inheritress to the duchy of Britany.—BACON, *History of Henry VII.*

ARTILLERY. Leaving the perplexed question of the derivation of this word, it will be sufficient to observe, that while it is now only applied to the heavy ordnance of modern warfare, in earlier use any engines for the projecting of missiles, even to the bow and arrows, would have been included under this term.

The Parthians, having all their hope in *artillery*, overcame the Romans ofter than the Romans them.—ASCHAM, *Toxophilus*, 1761, p. 106.

So the Philistines, the better to keep the Jews thrall and in subjection, utterly bereaved them of all manner of weapon and *artillery*, and left them naked.—JEWEL, *Reply to Mr. Harding*, article xv.

> The Gods forbid, quoth he, one shaft of thine
> Should be discharged 'gainst that uncourteous knight;
> His heart unworthy is, shootress divine,
> Of thine *artillery* to feel the might.
>
> FAIRFAX, *Tasso*, b. 17, s. 49.

And Jonathan gave his *artillery* unto his lad, and said unto him, Go, carry them to the city.—1 *Sam.* xx. 40. Authorized Version.

ARTISAN, ARTIST, ARTFUL. 'Artisan' is no longer either in English or in French used of him who cultivates one of the *fine* arts, but only those of common life. The fine arts, losing this word, have now claimed 'artist' for their exclusive property; which yet was far from belonging to them always. An 'artist' in its earlier acceptation was one who cultivated, not the *fine*, but the *liberal* arts. The classical scholar was eminently the 'artist.' 'Artful' did not any more than 'cunning,' which see, imply art which had degenerated into artifice or trick.

He was mightily abashed, and like an honest-minded man yielded the victory unto his adversary, saying withal, Zeuxis hath beguiled poor birds, but Parrhasius hath deceived Zeuxis, a professed *artisan.*—HOLLAND, *Pliny*, vol. ii. p. 535.

> Rare *artisan*, whose pencil moves
> Not our delights alone, but loves!
> > WALLER, *Lines to Van Dyck.*

> For then, the bold and coward,
> The wise and fool, the *artist* and *unread*,
> The hard and soft, seem all affined and kin.
> > SHAKESPEARE, *Troilus and Cressida*, act i. sc. 3.

Nor would I dissuade any *artist* well grounded in Aristotle from perusing the most learned works any Romanist hath written in this argument. In other controversies between them and us it is dangerous, I must confess, even for well-grounded *artists* to begin with their writings, not so in this.—JACKSON, *Blasphemous Positions of Jesuits*, Preface.

Some will make me the pattern of ignorance for making this Scaliger [Julius] the pattern of the general *artist*, whose own son Joseph might have been his father in many *arts*.—FULLER, *The Holy State*, b. ii. c. 8.

> Stupendous pile! not reared by mortal hands;
> Whate'er proud Rome or *artful* Greece beheld,
> Or elder Babylon its fame excelled.
> > POPE, *Temple of Fame.*

ASCERTAIN. Now to acquire a certain knowledge of a thing, but once to render the thing itself certain. Thus, when Swift wrote a pamphlet having this title, 'A Proposal for correcting, improving, and *ascertain-*

ing the English Tongue,' he did not propose to obtain a subjective certainty of what the English language was, but to give to the language itself an objective certainty and fixedness.

> Sometimes an evil or an obnoxious person hath so secured and *ascertained* a mischief to himself, that he that stays in his company or his traffic must also share in his punishment.—J. TAYLOR, *The Return of Prayers.*

> Success is intended him [the wicked man] only as a curse, as the very greatest of curses, and the readiest way, by hardening him in his sin, to *ascertain* his destruction. —SOUTH, *Sermons*, vol. v. p. 286.

ASPERSION. Now only used figuratively, and in an evil sense; being that which one *sprinkles* on another to spot, stain, or hurt him: but subject to none of these limitations of old.

> The book of Job, and many places of the prophets, have great *aspersion* of natural philosophy.—BACON, *Filum Labyrinthi.*

> No sweet *aspersion* shall the heavens let fall
> To make this contract grow.
> > SHAKESPEARE, *Tempest*, act iv. sc. 1.

ASSASSINATE. Once used, by Milton at least, as is now the French ' assassiner,' the Italian ' assassinare,' in the sense of to assault, treacherously and with murderous intent, even where the murderous purpose is not accomplished; and then, secondly, to extremely maltreat.

> As for the custom that some parents and guardians have of forcing marriages, it will be better to say nothing of such a savage inhumanity, but only thus, that the law which gives not all freedom of divorce to any creature endued with reason, so *assassinated*, is next in cruelty.—MILTON, *The Doctrine and Discipline of Divorce*, b. i. c. 12.

Such usage as your honourable lords
Afford me, *assassinated* and betrayed.

Id. Samson Agonistes.

ASSURE, ⎫ Used often in our elder writers in the
ASSURANCE. ⎭ sense of ' to betroth,' or ' to affiance.'
See ' Ensure,' ' Sure.'

King Philip. Young princes, close your hands.
Austria. And your lips too; for I am well assured
That I did so, when I was first *assured.*

SHAKESPEARE, King John, act ii. sc. 2.

I myself have seen Lollia Paulina, only when she was to go
unto a wedding supper, or rather to a feast when the *assurance*
was made, so beset and bedeckt all over with emeralds and pearls.
—HOLLAND, *Pliny*, vol. i. p. 256.

But though few days were before the day of *assurance* appointed,
yet Love, that saw he had a great journey to make in a short time,
hasted so himself, that before her word could tie her to Dema-
goras, her heart hath vowed her to Argalus.—Sir PHILIP SIDNEY,
Arcadia, p. 17.

ASTONISH. ' To astonish ' has now loosened itself
altogether from its etymology, 'attonare' and 'attoni-
tus.' The man 'astonished' can now be hardly said
to be ' thunderstruck,' either in a literal or a figurative sense. But continually in our early literature
we shall quite fall below the writer's intention unless
we read this meaning into the word.

Stone-still, *astonished* with this deadly deed,
Stood Collatine and all his lordly crew.

SHAKESPEARE, Lucrece.

The knaves that lay in wait behind rose up and rolled down
two huge stones, whereof the one smote the king upon the head,
the other *astonished* his shoulder.—HOLLAND, *Livy*, p. 1124.

The cramp-fish [the torpedo] knoweth her own force and power,
and being herself not benumbed, is able to *astonish* others.—
Id. *Pliny*, vol. i. p. 261.

In matters of religion, blind, *astonished*, and struck with superstition as with a planet; in one word, monks.—MILTON, *History
of England*, b. ii.

ASTROLOGY,⎱ As 'chemist' only little by little dis-
ASTROLOGER.⎰ engaged itself from 'alchemist,' and
that, whether we have respect to the thing itself, or
the name of the thing, so 'astronomer' from 'astrologer,' 'astronomy' from 'astrology.' It was long
before the broad distinction between the lying art
and the true science was recognized and fixed in
words.

If any enchantress should come unto her, and make promise
to draw down the moon from heaven, she would mock these
women and laugh at their gross ignorance, who suffer themselves
to be persuaded for to believe the same, as having learned somewhat in *astrology*.—HOLLAND, *Plutarch's Morals*, p. 324.

The *astrologer* is he that knoweth the course and motion of
the heavens, and teacheth the same; which is a virtue if it pass
not his bounds, and become of an *astrologer* an *astronomer*, who
taketh upon him to give judgment and censure of these motions
and courses of the heavens, what they prognosticate and destiny
unto the creature.—HOOPER, *Early Writings*, Parker Society's
Edition, p. 331.

ASTRONOMY,⎱ See 'Astrology.'
ASTRONOMER.⎰

> Not from the stars do I my judgment pluck,
> And yet, methinks, I have *astronomy*,
> But not to tell of good or evil luck,
> Of plagues, of dearths, of seasons' quality.
>
> SHAKESPEARE, *Sonnets*, 14.

Bowe ye not to *astronomyers*, neither axe ye onything of fals
dyvynours.—*Levit.* xix. 31. WICLIF.

If *astronomers* say true, every man at his birth by his constellation hath divers things and desires appointed him.—PILKING
TON, *Exposition upon the Prophet Aggeus*, c. i.

ATONE,　　　The notion of *satisfaction* lies now in
ATONEMENT.　these words rather than that of *reconciliation*.　An 'atonement' is the *satisfaction* of a
wrong which one party has committed against another,
not the *reconciliation* of two estranged parties.　This
last, however, was its earlier meaning ; and is in harmony with its etymology ; for which see the quotation from Bishop Hall.

> He and Aufidius can no more *atone*
> Than violentest contrarieties.
>
> > SHAKESPEARE, *Coriolanus*, act iv. sc. 6.

His first essay succeeded so well, Moses would adventure on
a second design, to *atone* two Israelites at variance.—FULLER,
A Pisgah Sight of Palestine, vol. ii. p. 92.

Having more regard to their old variance than their new *atonement*.—Sir T. MORE, *History of King Richard III.*

> Ye witless gallants I beshrew your hearts,
> That set such discord twixt agreeing parts
> Which never can be set *at onement* more.
>
> > Bishop HALL, *Sat.* 3.7.

If Sir John Falstaff have committed disparagements unto you,
I am of the Church, and will be glad to do my benevolence, to
make *atonements* and compromises between you.—SHAKSPEARE,
Merry Wives of Windsor, act i. sc. 1.

ATTIRE.　Properly bandeau or *head*-dress, the
French 'atours,' but not now restricted to this any
more.　'Attired with stars' in Milton's beautiful
lines *On Time* is not, *clothed* with stars, but, *crowned*
with them ; compare Rev. xii. 1 : 'upon her head a
crown of twelve stars.'

She tore her *attire* from her head, and rent her golden hair.—
The Seven Champions, b. ii. c. 13.

And with the linen mitre shall he be *attired*.—*Lev.* xvi. 4.
Authorized Version.

ATTORNEY. Seldom used now except of the attorney
at law; being one, according to Blackstone's definition,
'who is put in the place, stead, or *turn* of another to
manage his matters of law;' and even in this sense it
is going out of honour, and giving way to 'solicitor.'
But formerly any who in any cause acted in the room,
behalf, or turn of another would be called his 'attorney:' thus Phillips (*New World of Words*) defines attorney, 'one appointed by another man to do anything
in his stead, or to take upon him the charge of his
business in his absence;' and in proof of what honourable use the word might have, I need but refer to the
quotation which immediately follows:

Our everlasting and only High Bishop; our only *attorney*,
only medjator, only peacemaker between God and men.—*A Short
Catechism*, 1553.

> *Attorneys* are denied me,
> And therefore *personally* I lay my claim
> To my inheritance of free descent.
> SHAKESPEARE, *King Richard II.* act ii. sc. 3.

Tertullian seems to understand this baptism for the dead
[1 Cor. xv. 29] de vicario baptismate, of baptism by an *attorney*,
by a proxy, which should be baptized for me when I am dead.—
DONNE, *Sermons*, 1640, p. 794.

AUTHENTIC. A distinction drawn by Bishop Wat-
son between 'genuine' and 'authentic' has been often
quoted: 'A *genuine* book is that which was written by
the person whose name it bears as the author of it.
An *authentic* book is that which relates matters of
fact as they really happened.' Of 'authentic' he has
certainly not seized the true force, neither do the uses
of it by good writers bear him out. The true opposite to αὐθεντικός in Greek is ἀδέσποτος, and 'au-

thentic' is properly having an author, and thus coming with authority, authoritative; the connexion of 'author' and 'authority' in our own language giving us the key to its successive meanings. Thus, an 'authentic' document is, in its first meaning, a document written by the proper hand of him from whom it professes to proceed. In all the passages which follow it will be observed that the word might be exchanged for 'authoritative.'

> As doubted tenures, which long pleadings try,
> *Authentic* grow by being much withstood.
>
> DAVENANT, *Gondibert*, b. ii.

Should men be admitted to read Galen or Hippocrates, and yet the monopoly of medicines permitted to some one empiric or apothecary, not liable to any account, there might be a greater danger of poisoning than if these grand physicians had never written ; for that might be prescribed them by such an *authentic* mountebank as a cordial, which the other had detected for poison.

JACKSON, *The Eternal Truth of Scriptures*, b. ii. c. 23.

Which letter *in the copy* his lordship read over, and carried the *authentic* with him.—HACKET, *Life of Archbishop Williams*, part ii. p. 24.

It were extreme partiality and injustice, the flat denial and overthrow of herself [i. e. of Justice], to put her own *authentic* sword into the hand of an unjust and wicked man.—MILTON, Εἰκονοκλάστης, c. 28.

[A father] to instil the rudiments of vice into the unwary flexible years of his poor children, poisoning their tender minds with the irresistible *authentic* venom of his base example !—SOUTH, *Sermons*, vol. ii. p. 190; cf. vol. viii. p. 171.

Men ought to fly all pedantisms, and not rashly to use all words that are met with in every English writer, whether *authentic* or not.—PHILLIPS, *New World of Words*, Preface.

AWFUL,　} This used once to be often employed AWFULNESS. } of that which *felt* awe ; it is only employed now of that which *inspires* it.

The kings sat still with *awful* eye,
As if they surely knew their sovran Lord was by.
> Milton, *On the Morning of Christ's Nativity.*

The highest flames are the most tremulous, and so are the most holy and eminent religious persons more full of *awfulness*, of fear and modesty and humility.—J. Taylor, *Life of Christ*, part i. § 5.

AWKWARD. In its present signification, unhandy, ungainly, maladroit; but formerly untoward, and that, whether morally or physically, perverse, contrary, sinister, unlucky.

With *awkward* wind and with sore tempest driven
To fall on shore.
> Marlowe, *Edward II.* act iv. sc. 7.

The beast long struggled, as being like to prove
An *awkward* sacrifice,* but by the horns
The quick priest pulled him on his knees and slew him.
> Id., *The First Book of Lucan.*

Was I for this nigh wrecked upon the sea,
And twice by *awkward* wind from England's bank
Drove back again unto my native clime?
> Shakespeare, 1 *Henry VI.* act iii. sc. 2.

But time hath rooted out my parentage,
And to the world and *awkward* casualties
Bound me in servitude.
> *Pericles, Prince of Tyre*, act v. sc. 1.

BABE, } 'Doll' is of late introduction into the
BABY. } English language, is certainly later than Dryden. 'Babe,' 'baby,' or 'puppet' supplied its place.

True religion standeth not in making, setting up, painting, gilding, clothing, and decking of dumb and dead images, which be but great puppets and *babies* for old fools, in dotage and

---

* 'Non grati victima sacri.'

wicked idolatry, to dally and play with.—*Homilies; Against Peril of Idolatry.*

> But all as a poor pedlar did he wend,
> Bearing a truss of trifles at his back,
> As bells, and *babes*, and glasses, in his pack.
>> SPENSER, *The Shepherd's Calendar, May.*

Think you that the child hath any notion of the strong contents of riper age? or can he possibly imagine there are any such delights as those his *babies* and rattles afford him?—ALLESTREE, *Sermons*, part ii. p. 148.

BACCHANAL. Used now only of the votaress of Bacchus; but it was once more accurately applied to the ' bacchanalia,' or orgies celebrated in his honour.

Do not ye, like those heathen in their *bacchanals*, inflame yourselves with wine.—HAMMOND, *Paraphrase on the N. T.*, Ephes. v. 18.

So *bacchanals* of drunken riot were kept too much in London and Westminster, which offended many, that the thanks due only to God should be paid to the devil.—HACKET, *Life of Archbishop Williams*, part i. p. 165.

> Well, I could wish that still in lordly domes
> Some beasts were killed, though not whole hecatombs;
> That both extremes were banished from their walls,
> Carthusian fasts, and fulsome *bacchanals*.
>> POPE, *Satires of Dr. Donne.*

BAFFLE. Now to counterwork and to defeat; but once not this so much as to mock and put to shame, and, in the technical language of chivalry, it expressed a ceremony of open scorn with which a recreant or perjured knight was visited.

> First he his beard did shave and foully shent,
> Then from him reft his shield, and it reversed,
> And blotted out his arms with falsehood blent,
> And himself *baffled*, and his arms unhersed,
> And broke his sword in twain, and all his armour spersed.
>> SPENSER, *Fairy Queen*, v. 3, 37.

He that suffers himself to be ridden, or through pusillanimity or sottishness will let every man *baffle* him, shall be a common laughing-stock to flout at.—BURTON, *Anatomy of Melancholy*, part ii. sec. 3.

> Alas, poor fool, how have they *baffled* thee!
> SHAKESPEARE, *Twelfth Night*, act v. sc. 1.

BANQUET. At present the entire course of any solemn or splendid entertainment; but 'banquet' (the Italian 'banchetto' a small bench or table), used generally to be restrained to the lighter and ornamental dessert or refection with wine, which followed the more substantial repast.

I durst not venture to sit *at supper* with you; should I have received you then, coming as you did with armed men to *banquet* with me? [*Convivam* me tibi committere ausus non sum; *comissatorem* te cum armatis venientem recipiam?]—HOLLAND, *Livy*, p. 1066.

Then was the banqueting-chamber in the tilt-yard at Greenwich furnished for the entertainment of these strangers, where they did both sup and *banquet*.—CAVENDISH, *Life of Cardinal Wolsey*.

> We'll *dine* in the great room; but let the music
> And *banquet* be prepared here.
> MASSINGER, *The Unnatural Combat*, act iii. sc. 1.

BASE, }
BASENESS. } The aristocratic tendencies of speech (tendencies illustrated by the word 'aristocracy' itself), which reappear in a thousand shapes, on the one side in such words, and their usages, as καλοκἀγαθός, ἐπιεικής, 'noble,' on the other in such as 'villain,' 'boor,' 'knave,' and in this 'base,' are well worthy of accurate observation. Thus 'base' always now implies moral unworthiness; but did not so once. 'Base' men were no more than men of humble birth and low degree.

> But virtuous women wisely understand
> That they were born to *base* humility,
> Unless the heavens them lift to lawful sovereignty.
> SPENSER, *Fairy Queen*, v. 5, 25.

He that is ashamed of *base* and simple attire, will be proud of gorgeous apparel, if he may get it.—*Homilies ; Against Excess of Apparel.*

By this means we imitate the Lord Himself, who hath abased Himself to the lowest degree of *baseness* in this kind, emptying Himself (Phil. ii. 8), that He might be equal to them of greatest *baseness.*—ROGERS, *Naaman the Syrian*, p. 461.

BATTLE.   Used, not as now, of the hostile shock of armies; but often of the army itself; or sometimes in a more special sense, of the main body of the army, as distinguished from the van and rear.

> Each *battle* sees the other's umbered face.
> SHAKESPEARE, *King Henry V.* act iv. Chorus.

Richard led the vanguard of English; Duke Odo commanded in the main *battle* over his French; James of Auvergne brought on the Flemings and Brabanters in the rear.—FULLER, *The Holy War*, b. iii. c. 11.

Where divine blessing leads up the van, and man's valour brings up the *battle*, must not victory needs follow in the rear?— Id., *A Pisgah Sight of Palestine*, vol. i. p. 174.

BAWD.   Not confined once to one sex only, but could have been applied to pandar and pandaress alike.

> He was, if I shall yeven him his laud,
> A theef, and eke a sompnour and a *baud*.
> CHAUCER, *The Freres Tale.*

One Lamb, a notorious impostor, a fortune-teller, and an employed *bawd*.—HACKET, *Life of Archbishop Williams*, part ii. p. 81.

A carrion crow he [the flatterer] is, a gaping grave,
The rich coat's moth, the court's bane, trencher's slave,
Sin's and hell's winning *bawd*, the devil's factoring knave.
　　　　　　P. FLETCHER, *The Purple Island*, c. viii.

BEASTLY, ⎫ We translate σῶμα ψυχικόν (1 Cor.
BEASTLINESS. ⎭ xv. 44) ' a *natural* body;' some
have regretted that it was not rendered ' an *animal*
body.' This is exactly what Wiclif meant when he
translated the ' corpus animale ' which he found in
his Vulgate, ' a *beastly* body.' The word had then no
ethical tinge; nor, when it first acquired such, had it
exactly that which it now possesses; in it was rather
implied the absence of reason, the prerogative distinguishing man from beast.

It is sowun a *beestli* bodi; it shal ryse a spiritual bodi.—1 Cor.
xv. 44. WICLIF.

These ben, whiche departen hernself, *beestli* men, not havynge
spirit.—Jude 18. WICLIF.

Where they should have made head with the whole army upon
the Parthians, they sent him aid by small companies; and when
they were slain, they sent him others also. So that by their
beastliness and lack of consideration they had like to have made
all the army fly.—NORTH, *Plutarch's Lives*, p. 769.

BENEFICE, ⎫ It is only in later English that ' bene-
BENEFICIAL. ⎭ fice ' and ' benefit ' have been desynonymized. The same holds good of ' beneficial '
and ' beneficent.' Persons are not now ' beneficial,'
which word is reserved for things, but ' beneficent.'

The *benefices* that God did tham here
Sal tham accuse on sere manere.
RICHARD ROLLE DE HAMPOLE, *Pricke of Conscience*, 5582.

The proper nature of God is always to be helpful and *beneficial*.
—HOLLAND, *Plutarch's Morals*, p. 600.

> I wonder
> That such a keech can with his very bulk
> Take up the rays of the *beneficial* sun,
> And keep it from the earth.
>
> SHAKESPEARE, *Henry VIII.* act i. sc. 1.

Bring my soul out of prison, that I may praise thy name ; then shall the righteous come about me when Thou art *beneficial* unto me.—Ps. cxlii. 7. Geneva.

BLACKGUARD. The scullions and other meaner retainers in a great household, who, when progress was made from one residence to another, accompanied and protected the pots, pans, and other kitchen utensils, riding among them and being smutted by them, were contemptuously styled the 'black guard.' It is easy to trace the subsequent history of the word. With a slight forgetfulness of its origin, he is now called a 'blackguard,' who would have been once said to belong to the 'black guard.'

Close unto the front of the chariot marcheth all the sort of weavers and embroiderers; next unto whom goeth the *black guard* and kitchenry.—HOLLAND, *Ammianus*, p. 12.

A lousy slave, that within this twenty years rode with the *black guard* in the Duke's carriage, 'mongst spits and dripping-pans ! —WEBSTER, *The White Devil.*

Thieves and murderers took upon them the cross to escape the gallows ; adulterers did penance in their armour. A lamentable case that the devil's *black guard* should be God's soldiers !—FULLER, *The Holy War*, b. i. c. 12.

Where the apologist meets with this *black guard*, these factors for error and sin, these agitators for the Prince of darkness, God forbid he should give place to them, or not charge them home, and resist them to the face. — GAUDEN, *Hieraspistes*, To the Reader.

Dukes, earls, and lords, great commanders in war, common soldiers and kitchen boys were glad to trudge it on foot in the mire hand in hand, a duke or earl not disdaining to support or help up one of the *black guard* ready to fall, lest he himself might fall into the mire, and have none to help him.—JACKSON, *A Treatise of the Divine Essence and Attributes*, b. vi. c. 28.

We have neither school nor hospital for the distressed children, called the *black guard.*—NELSON, *Address to Persons of Quality*, p. 214.

BLEAK. This, the German ' bleich,' pale, colourless, comes out clearly in its original identity with ' bleach ' in the following quotations.

When she came out, she looked as pale and as *bleak* as one that were laid out dead.—FOXE, *Book of Martyrs ; The Escape of Agnes Wardall.*

And as I looked forth, I beheld a pale horse, whom I took for the universal synagogue of hypocrites, pale as men without health, and *bleak* as men without that fresh spirit of life which is in Christ Jesus.—BALE, *The Image of Both Churches*, P.S. p. 321.

BLUNDERBUSS. ' Primarily a man who blunders in his work, does it in a boisterous violent way ; subsequently applied to a short, wide-mouthed, noisy gun.'—Wedgwood, *Dictionary of English Etymology.*

We could now wish we had a discreet and intelligent adversary, and not such a hare-brained *blunderbuss* as you, to deal with.— MILTON, *A Defence of the People of England*, Preface.

> Jacob, the scourge of grammar, mark with awe,
> Nor less revere him, *blunderbuss* of law.
>
> POPE, *Dunciad*, b. iii.

BOISTEROUS. The sense of noisy, turbulent, blustering, is a later superaddition on ' boisterous,' or ' boistous,' as was its earlier form. Of old it meant no more than rude, rough, strong, uncompliant ; thus the ' boisterous wind ' of Matt. xiv. 30, is simply a violent wind, ἄνεμος ἰσχυρός in the original.

No man putteth a clout of *buystous* cloth [panni rudis, Vulg.] into an elde clothing.—*Matt.* ix. 16. WICLIF.

O Clifford, *boisterous* * Clifford, thou hast slain
The flower of Europe for his chivalry.

SHAKESPEARE, 3 *Henry VI.* act ii. sc. 1.

His *boistrous* body shines in burnished steel.

SYLVESTER, *Dubartas' Weeks, The Magnificence,* p. 460.

The greatest danger indeed is from those that are *stolide feroces,* full of those *boisterous,* rude, and brutish passions, which grow as bristles upon hogs' backs, from ignorance, pride, rusticity, and prejudice.—GAUDEN, *Hieraspistes,* To the Reader.

The leathern outside, *boisterous* as it was,
Gave way, and bent beneath her strict embrace.

DRYDEN, *Sigismunda and Guiscardo,* 159, 160.

The other thing in debate seemed very hard and *boisterous* to his Majesty, that sundry leaders in the House of Commons would provoke him to proclaim open war with Spain.—HACKET, *Life of Archbishop Williams,* part i. p. 79.

BOMBAST. Now inflated diction, words which, sounding lofty and big, have no real substance about them. This, which is now the sole meaning, was once only the secondary and the figurative, 'bombast' being literally the cotton wadding with which garments are stuffed out and lined, and often so used by our writers of the Elizabethan period, and then by a vigorous image transferred to what now it exclusively means.

Certain I am there was never any kind of apparel ever invented, that could more disproportion the body of man than these doublets, stuffed with four, five, or six pound of *bombast* at the least.—STUBS, *Anatomy of Abuses,* p. 23.

We have received your letters full of love ;
Your favours, the ambassadors of love ;
And, in our maiden council, rated them
At courtship, pleasant jest, and courtesy,
As *bombast,* and as lining to the time.

SHAKESPEARE, *Love's Labour's Lost,* act v. sc. 2.

---

* '*Rough* Clifford' he is called a few lines before.

Bombast, the cotton-plant growing in Asia.—Phillips, *New World of Words.*

Boot. Not the luggage, but the chief persons, used once to ride in the 'boot,' or rather the boots, of a carriage, for they were two. Projecting from the sides of the carriage and open to the air, they derived, no doubt, their name from their shape.

His coach being come, he causeth him to be laid in softly, and so he in one *boot,* and the two chirurgeons in the other, they drive away to the very next country house.—Reynolds, *God's Revenge against Murder,* b. i. hist. 1.

He [James the First] received his son into the coach, and found a slight errand to leave Buckingham behind, as he was putting his foot in the *boot.*—Hacket, *Life of Archbishop Williams,* part i. p. 196.

Bounty. The tendency to accept freedom of giving in lieu of all other virtues, or at least to regard it as the chiefest of all, the same which has brought 'charity' to be for many identical with almsgiving, displays itself in our present use of 'bounty,' which, like the French 'bonté,' meant goodness once.

> For God it woot that childer ofte been
>   Unlik her worthy eldrie hem before ;
> *Bounte* cometh al of God, nought of the streen,
>   Of which thay been engendrid and i-bore.
>   Chaucer, *Canterbury Tales,* 8031.

Nourishing meats and drinks in a sick body do lose their *bounty,* and augmenteth malady.—Sir T. Elyot, *The Governor,* b. ii. c. 7.

Brat. The same word as 'brood,' it is now used always in contempt, but was not so once.

> O Israel, O household of the Lord,
> O Abraham's *brats,* O brood of blessed seed,
> O chosen sheep that loved the Lord indeed.
>   Gascoigne, *De Profundis.*

> Take heed how thou layest the bane for the rats,
> For poisoning thy servant, thyself, and thy *brats.*
> > Tusser, *Points of Good Husbandry.*

BRAVE,
BRAVERY. } The derivation of 'brave' is altogether uncertain (Diez, *Wört. d. Roman. Sprachen*, p. 67) ; we obtained it in the sixteenth century, the Germans in the seventeenth, (Grimm [*s. v.* 'brav'] says during the Thirty Years' War,) from one or other of the Romance languages. I do not very clearly trace by what steps it obtained the meaning of showy, gaudy, rich, which once it so frequently had, in addition to that meaning which it still retains.

His clothes [St. Augustine's] were neither *brave,* nor base, but comely.—Fuller, *The Holy State,* b. iv. c. 10.

If he [the good yeoman] chance to appear in clothes above his rank, it is to grace some great man with his service, and then he blusheth at his own *bravery.*—Id. *ib.* b. ii. c. 18.

Man is a noble animal, splendid in ashes, and pompous in the grave, solemnizing nativities and deaths with equal lustre, not omitting ceremonies of *bravery* in the infamy of his nature.— Sir T. Browne, *Hydriotaphia.*

There is a great festival now drawing on, a festival designed chiefly for the acts of a joyful piety, but generally made only an occasion of *bravery.*—South, *Sermons,* vol. ii. p. 285.

BRIBE.
BRIBERY. } 'To bribe' was to rob, a 'bribour' a robber, and 'bribery' robbery, once. For an ingenious history of the steps by which the words left their former meaning, and acquired their present, see Marsh, *Lectures on the English Language,* 1st Series, p. 249.

They that delight in superfluity of gorgeous apparel and dainty fare, commonly do deceive the needy, *bribe,* and pill from them. —Cranmer, *Instruction of Prayer.*

Woe be to you, scribes and pharisees, hypocrites, for ye make clean the utter side of the cup and of the platter; but within they are full of *bribery* [ἁρπαγῆς, and in the E. V. 'extortion'] and excess.—*Matt.* xxiii. 25. Geneva Version.

BRITAIN,⎫ The distinction between these is per-
BRITANY. ⎰ fectly established now: by the first we always intend *Great* Britain; by the second, the French duchy, corresponding to the ancient Armorica. But it was long before this usage was accurately settled and accepted by all. By 'Britany' Great Britain was frequently intended, and *vice versâ*. Thus, in each of the passages which follow, the other word than that which actually is used would be now employed.

He [Henry VII.] was not so averse from a war, but that he was resolved to choose it, rather than to have *Britain* carried by France, being so great and opulent a duchy, and situate so opportunely to annoy England, either for coast or trade.—BACON, *History of King Henry VII.*

The letter of Quintus Cicero, which he wrote in answer to that of his brother Marcus, desiring of him an account of *Britany.*—Sir T. BROWNE, *Musæum Clausum.*

> And is it this, alas! which we
> (O irony of words!) do call *Great Britany?*
>   COWLEY, *The Extasy.*

BROOK. This, identical with the German 'brauchen,' to use, has now obtained a special limitation, meaning not so much, as once it did, to use, as to endure to use.

> But none of all those curses overtook
> The warlike maid, the ensample of that might;
> But fairly well she thrived, and well did *brook*
> Her noble deeds, ne her right course for ought forsook.
>   SPENSER, *Fairy Queen*, iii. 4, 44.

Forasmuch as many *brooked* divers and many laudable ceremonies and rites heretofore used and accustomed in the Church
of England, not yet abrogated by the king's authority, his
Majesty charged and commanded all his subjects to observe and
keep them.—STRYPE, *Memorials of Archbishop Cranmer*, vol. i.
p. 412.

And, as a German writer well observes, the French kings
might well *brook* that title of *Christianissimi* from that admirable exploit of Carolus Martellus, the next means under God's
providence that other parts of Europe had not Saracen tyrants
instead of Christian princes.—JACKSON, *The Eternal Truth of
Scriptures*, b. i. c. 26.

> Let us *bruik* the present hour,
> Let us pou' the fleeting flouir,
> Youthheid is love's holiday,
> Let us use it, when we may.
> > PINKERTON, *Scotch Comic Ballads*, p. 149.

BULLION. We are indebted to Mr. Wedgwood
(*Dictionary of English Etymology*, s. v.) for the first
accurate history of ' bullion,' and explanation of the
fact that this, which was once equivalent to the
French 'billon' ('toute matière d'or ou d'argent
décriée, et qui se trouve à plus bas titre que celui
d'ordonnance,') is now applied to the precious metals,
uncoined indeed and unstamped, but with no suggestion, indeed the contrary rather, that this bullion is
below the recognised standard of purity. The ' bullion ' (' nostre bullione,' as it is called in a statute of
Edward III., see Cowell's *Interpreter*, s. v.) was the
Royal Mint, so called from the ' bulla,' the impress
seal or die with which money was stamped. All
gold and silver which had not the standard purity
or weight was to be brought to this that it might be
melted ; ' monnaie de billon ' it was called in French,
and ' bullion ' in the English of Elizabeth and

James. Gradually, however, not the comparative inferiority which it had *before* it passed through the Mint, but the recognition which it obtained *after*, became the predominant idea ; and here is the explanation of the present use of the word.

> Base *bullion* for the stamp's sake we allow.
> > MARLOWE, *Hero and Leander. First Sestyad.*

> Words, whilom flourishing,
> Pass now no more, but, banished from the court,
> Dwell with disgrace among the vulgar sort ;
> And those which eld's strict doom did disallow,
> And damn for *bullion*, go for current now.
> > SYLVESTER, *Dubartas' Weeks, Babylon.*

> Nigh on the plain, in many cells prepared,
> That underneath had veins of liquid fire
> Sluiced from the lake, a second multitude
> With wondrous art founded the massy ore,
> Severing each kind, and scummed the *bullion* dross.
> > MILTON, *Paradise Lost*, b. i.

BUXOM. The modern spelling of ' buxom ' (it was somewhat, though not much better, when it was spelt ' bucksome ') has quite hidden its identity with the German ' biegsam,' ' beugsam,' bendable, pliable, and so obedient. Ignorant of the history of the word, and trusting to the feeling and impression which it conveyed to their minds, men spoke of ' *buxom* health ' and the like, meaning by this, having a cheerful comeliness. The epithet in this application is Gray's, and Johnson justly finds fault with it. Milton when, he joins ' buxom ' with ' blithe and debonair,' and Crashaw, in his otherwise beautiful line,

> ' I am born
> Again a fresh child of the *buxom* morn,'

show that already for them the true meaning of the word, common enough in our earlier writers, was passing away; yet Milton still uses it in its proper sense in *Paradise Lost,*—' winnowing the *buxom* air,' that is, the *yielding* air.

I submit myself unto this holy Church of Christ, to be ever *buxom* and obedient to the ordinance of it, after my knowledge and power, by the help of God.—FOXE, *Book of Martyrs; Examination of William Thorpe.*

Buxom, kind, tractable, and pliable one to the other.—HOLLAND, *Plutarch's Morals*, 316.

> [Love] tyrannizeth in the bitter smarts
> Of them that to him *buxom* are and prone.
> > SPENSER, *Fairy Queen*, iii. 2, 23.

BY. The first clause in the quotation which follows from the Authorized Version of the Bible must often either fail to convey any meaning, or must convey a wrong meaning, to the English reader of the present day. The 'nil conscire sibi' is what the Apostle would claim for himself; and the other passages quoted show that this idiomatic use of 'by,' as equivalent to 'concerning' (it is related to ἀμφί), but with also a suggestion of 'against,' was not peculiar to our Translators.

I think S. Paul spake these words ['who mind earthly things'] *by* the clergymen that will take upon them the spiritual office of preaching, and yet meddle in worldly matters too, contrary to their calling.—LATIMER, *Sermons*, p. 529.

Thou hast spoken evil words *by* the Queen.
No man living upon earth can prove any such things *by* me.
> FOXE, *Book of Martyrs; Examination of Elizabeth Young by Martin Hussie.*

This angry prior told the archbishop to his face, in a good audience, concerning what he had preached of the bishop of

Rome's vices, that he knew no vices *by* none of the bishops of Rome.—Strype, *Memorials of Archbishop Cranmer*, b. i. c. 8.

> For all the wealth that ever I did see,
> I would not have him know so much *by* me.
>> Shakespeare, *Love's Labour's Lost*, act iv. sc. 3.

I know nothing *by* myself [οὐδὲν ἐμαυτῷ σύνοιδα]; yet am I not hereby justified; but He that judgeth me is the Lord.— 1 *Cor.* iv. 4. Authorized Version.

God is said to be greater than our hearts, and knoweth all things. He knows more *by* us than we *by* ourselves.—Gurnall, *The Christian in Complete Armour*, iii. 2, 8.

By and by. Now a future more or less remote; but when our Version of the Bible was made, the nearest possible future. The inveterate procrastination of men has put ' by and by ' farther and farther off. Already in Barrow's time it had acquired its present meaning.

And some counselled the archbishop to burn me *by and by*, and some other counselled him to drown me in the sea, for it is near hand there.—Foxe, *Book of Martyrs; Examination of William Thorpe.*

Give me *by and by* [ἐξαυτῆς] in a charger the head of John the Baptist.—*Mark* vi. 25. Authorized Version.

These things must first come to pass; but the end is not *by and by* [εὐθέως].—*Luke* xxi. 9. Authorized Version.

When Demophantus fell to the ground, his soldiers fled *by and by* [εὐθὺς ἔφυγον] upon it.—North, *Plutarch's Lives*, p. 308.

Caitiff. The same word as ' captive; ' the only difference being that ' captive ' is derived directly from the Latin, ' caitiff ' through the interposition of the Norman-French; it had once the same meaning with it. The deep-felt conviction of men that slavery breaks down the moral character, a chief argument against it, but unhappily also a chief difficulty in removing it, this, so grandly unfolded by Horace (*Carm.* iii. 5), and speaking out in the Italian ' cattivo,' in the French 'chétif,' speaks out with no less distinctness in the change of meaning which ' caitiff' has undergone, signifying, as it now does, one of a base, abject disposition, while there was a time when it had nothing of this in it.

Aristark, myne evene *caytyf* [concaptivus meus, Vulg.], greetith you wel.—*Col.* iv. 10. WICLIF.

The riche Crœsus, *caitif* in servage.
CHAUCER, *The Knightes Tale.*

Avarice doth tyrannize over her *caitiff* and slave, not suffering him to use what she commanded him to win.—HOLLAND, *Plutarch's Morals*, p. 208.

CAPITULATE. There is no reason why the reducing of any agreement to certain heads or 'capitula' should not be called to ' capitulate,' the victor thus ' capitulating' as well as the vanquished ; and the present limitation of the word's use, by which it means to surrender on certain specified terms, is quite of modern introduction.

Gelon the tyrant, after he had defeated the Carthaginians near to the city Himera, when he made peace with them, *capitulated*, among other articles of treaty, that they should no more sacrifice any infants to Saturn.—HOLLAND, *Plutarch's Morals*, p. 405.

He [the Emperor Charles V.] makes a voyage into England, and there *capitulates* with the King, among other things, to take to wife his daughter Mary.—HEYLIN, *History of the Reformation.*

Wonder He will condescend to it ! To *capitulate* with dust and ashes ! To article with his own creature, with whom He may do what He will.—HOWE, *The Redeemer's Dominion*, &c.

CAPTIVATE. This is not used any longer in a literal, but always in a more or less allegorical sense.

They that are wise had rather have their judgments at liberty in differences of readings, than to be *captivated* to the one when it may be the other.—*The Translators* [*of the Authorized Version*] *to the Reader.*

> How ill beseeming is it in thy sex
> To triumph, like an Amazonian trull,
> Upon their woes whom Fortune *captivates.*
> SHAKESPEARE, 3 *Henry VI.* act i. sc. 4.

CAREFUL. Now full of diligence and attention; but once of anxiety.

The stretes of Sion mourn; her priests make lamentacions, her maydens are *carefull,* and she herself is in great hevynesse. —*Lament.* i. 4. COVERDALE.

He shall be as a tree planted by the waters, . . . and shall not be *careful* in the year of drought.—*Jer.* xvii. 8. Authorized Version.

> Pale as he is, here lay him down,
> Oh, lay his cold head on my pillow;
> Take off, take off, these bridal weeds,
> And crown my *careful* head with willow.
> HAMILTON, *The Braes of Yarrow.*

CARP. The *Promptorium* gives 'fabulor,' 'confabulor,' 'garrulo' as Latin equivalents; nor do we anywhere in early English find the subaudition of fault-finding or detraction, which now is ever implied in the word.

Ac to *carpe* moore of Crist, and how He come to that name, Faithly for to speke his firste name was Jhesus.
Piers Ploughman, 13088.

Now we leven the kyng, and of Joseph *carpen.*—*Joseph of Arimathie,* 212.

> So gone thei forthe, *carpende* fast
> On this, on that.
> GOWER, *Confessio Amantis,* l. 7.

CARPET. The covering of floors only at present,
but once of tables as well. It was in this sense that a
matter was ' on the carpet.' For the etymology see
Transactions of the Philological Society, 1859, p. 77.

In the fray one of their spurs engaged into a *carpet* upon
which stood a very fair looking-glass and two noble pieces of
porcelain, drew all to the ground, broke the glass.—*Harleian
Miscellany*, vol. x. p. 189.

Private men's halls were hung with altar-cloths ; their *tables*
and beds covered with copes, instead of *carpets* and coverlets.—
FULLER, *Church History of Britain*, b. vii. § 2, 1.

And might not these [copes] be handsomely converted into
private uses, to serve as *carpets* for their tables, coverlids to
their beds, or cushions to their chairs or windows ?—HEYLIN,
History of the Reformation, To the Reader.

CARRIAGE. Now, that which carries, or the act of
carrying; but once, that which was carried, and thus
baggage. From ignorance of this, the Authorized
Translation, at Acts xxi. 15, has been often found
fault with, but unjustly. See the quotation from
Webster, *s. v.* ' Blackguard.'

Spartacus charged his [Lentulus'] lieutenants that led the
army, gave them battle, overthrew them, and took all their
carriage [τὴν ἀποσκευὴν ἄπασαν].—NORTH, *Plutarch's Lives*,
p. 470.

And David left his *carriage* [τὰ σκεύη αὐτοῦ, LXX.] in the
hand of the keeper of the *carriage.*—1 *Sam.* xvii. 22. Authorized
Version.

An index is a necessary implement, and no impediment of a
book, except in the same sense in which the *carriages* of an
army are termed *impedimenta.*—FULLER, *Worthies of England :
Norfolk.*

CATTLE. This and 'chattel' are only different
forms of the same word. At a time when wealth

mainly consisted in the number of *heads* of cattle
(*capita, capitalia*), the word which designated *them*
easily came to signify all other kinds of property as
well. (Note the well-known parallel in ' pecus ' and
' pecunia ; ' in ' multa' which meant originally a fine
in ' cattle,' and then in money ; in ' fee ' and ' vieh.')
At a later day this was found to have its. incon-
veniences ; which some of the writers of the Elizabethan age sought to remedy by using the term
'*quick* cattle ' when they intended live stock ; so Sir
J. Harington (*Epigrams*, i. 91), and Puttenham (*Art
of English Poesy*, b. i. c. 18). The distinction, however, was more effectually asserted by the appropri-
ating of the several forms ' cattle ' and ' chattel,' one
to the living, the other to the dead.

Though a man give al the *catel* of his hous [omnem *substantiam* domûs suæ, Vulg.] for love, he schal despise that *catel* as
nought.—*Cant.* viii. 7. WICLIF.

A womman that hadde a flux of blood twelve yeer, and hadde
spendid all hir *catel* [omnem *substantiam* suam, Vulg.] in
leechis.—*Luke* viii. 43, 44. WICLIF.

The avaricious man hath more hope in his *catel* than in Jesu
Christ.—CHAUCER, *The Persones Tale*.

CENSURE. It speaks ill for the charity of men's
judgments, that ' censure,' which designated once
favourable and unfavourable judgments alike, is now
restricted to unfavourable ; for it must be that the
latter, being by far the most frequent, have in this
way appropriated the word exclusively to themselves.

Take each man's *censure*, but reserve thy judgment.
SHAKESPEARE, *Hamlet*, act i. sc. 3.

His [Richard, Earl of Cornwall's] voyage was variously *censured*; the Templars, who consented not to the peace, flouted

thereat, as if all this while he had laboured about a difficult nothing ; others thought he had abundantly satisfied any rational expectation.—FULLER, *The Holy War*, b. iv. c. 8.

Which could.not be past over without this *censure*; for it is an ill thrift to be parsimonious in the praise of that which is very good.—HACKET, *Life of Archbishop Williams*, part ii. p. 13.

CHAFFER. Once, to buy, to make a bargain, to higgle or dispute about the making of a bargain, it has at length seen the buying or bargaining quite disappear from it ; so that ' to chaffer ' is now to talk much and idly.

That no man overgo, nether disceyve his brother in *chaffaringe* [in negotio, Vulg.].—1 *Thess.* iv. 6. WICLIF.

He comaundid his servauntis to be clepid, to whiche he hadde geve money : to witte how myche ech had wonne by *chaffarynge*. —*Luke* xix. 15. WICLIF.

> Where is the fair flock thou was wont to lead ?
> Or been they *chaffred*, or at mischief dead ?
> SPENSER, *Shepherd's Calendar*, Ecl. 9.

CHAOS. The earliest meaning of χάος in Greek, of ' chaos ' in Latin, was empty infinite space, the *yawning* kingdom of darkness ; only a secondary, that which we have now adopted, namely, the rude, confused, indigested, unorganized matter out of which the universe according to the heathen cosmogony was formed. But the primary use of ' chaos ' was not strange to the literature of the sixteenth and seventeenth century.

Beside all these things, between us and you there is fixed a great *chaos*, that they which will pass from hence to you may not. —*Luke* xvi. 26. Rheims.

And look what other thing soever besides cometh within the *chaos* of this monster's mouth, be it beast, boat, or stone, down it goeth incontinently that foul great swallow of his.—HOLLAND, *Plutarch's Morals*, p. 975.

> To the brow of heaven
> Pursuing, drive them out from God and bliss
> Into their place of punishment, the gulf
> Of Tartarus, which ready opens wide
> His fiery *chaos* to receive their fall.
> MILTON, *Paradise Lost*, b. 6.

CHEAT, ⎫ The steps by which 'escheat' has yielded
CHEATER. ⎭ 'cheat,' and 'escheatour' ' cheater,' are interesting to trace. The ' escheatour ' was an officer in each county who took notice of fines and forfeitures technically called ' escheats ' on the royal manors which had *fallen in* to the Crown, and certified these to the Exchequer. But he commonly allowed himself in so much fraud and concussion in the execution of his office, that by an only too natural transition the ' escheatour' passed into the ' cheater,' and ' escheat ' into ' cheat.' The quotation from Gurnall is curious as marking the word in the very act of this transition.

And yet the taking off these vessels was not the best and goodliest *cheat* of their victory; but this passed all, that with one light skirmish they became lords of all the sea along those coasts.—HOLLAND, *Livy*, p. 444.

This man who otherwise beforetime was but poor and needy, by these windfalls and unexpected *cheats* became very wealthy. —Id. *Plutarch's Morals*, p. 1237.

Falstaff. Here's another letter to her. She bears the purse too ; she is a region in Guiana, all gold and bounty. I will be *cheaters* to them both, and they shall be exchequers to me.— SHAKESPEARE, *Merry Wives of Windsor*, act i. sc. 2.

By this impudence they may abuse credulous souls into a belief of what they say, as a *cheater* may pick the purses of innocent people, by showing them something like the King's broad seal, which was indeed his own forgery.—GURNALL, *Christian Armour*, 1639, vol. ii. p. 201.

CHEER. Cicero, who loves to bring out superiorities, where he can find them, of the Latin language over the Greek, urges this as one, that the Greek has no equivalent to the Latin 'vultus' (*Leg.* i. 9, 27); the countenance, that is, ethically regarded, as the ever-varying index and exponent of the sentiments and emotions of the soul ('imago animi vultus est,' *De Orat.* iii. 59, 221). Perhaps it may be charged on the English, that it too is now without such a word. But 'cheer,' in its earlier uses, of which vestiges still survive, was exactly such.

In swoot of thi *cheer* thou schalt ete thi breed, till thou turne ayen in to the erthe of which thou art takun.—*Gen.* iii. 19. WICLIF.

And Cayn was wrooth greetli, and his *cheer* felde doun.—*Gen.* iv. 5. WICLIF.

Each froward threatening *cheer* of fortune makes us plain ;
And every pleasant show revives our woful hearts again.
                                        SURREY, *Ecclesiastes*, c. 3.

CHEMIST, } The distinction between the alchemist
CHEMISTRY.} and the chemist, that the first is the fond searcher after the philosopher's stone or the elixir vitæ, the other the follower of a true and scientific method in a particular region of nature, is of comparatively recent introduction into the language. 'Chemist' is='alchemist' in the quotations which follow.

Five sorts of persons he [Sir Edward Coke] used to foredesign to misery and poverty ; *chemists*, monopolizers, concealers,* pro-

---

* ' Concealers be such as find out concealed lands, that is such lands as privily are kept from the king by common persons, having nothing to shew for them.'—COWELL, *The Interpreter*, s. v.

moters, and rythming poets.—FULLER, *Worthies of England, Norfolk.*

I have observed generally of *chymists* and theosophists, as of several other men more palpably mad, that their thoughts are carried much to astrology.—H. MORE, *A Brief Discourse of Enthusiasm*, sect. 45.

> Visions and inspirations some expect,
>   Their course here to direct ;
> Like senseless *chemists* their own wealth destroy,
>   Imaginary wealth to enjoy.
>> COWLEY, *Use of Reason in Divine Matters.*

> Hence the fool's paradise, the statesman's scheme,
> The air-built castle, and the golden dream,
> The maid's romantic wish, the *chemist's* flame,
> The poet's vision of eternal fame.
>> POPE, *The Dunciad*, b. iii. 9–12.

He that follows *chemistry* must have riches to throw away upon the study of it ; whatever he gets ʋy it, those furnaces must be fed with gold.—SOUTH, *Sermons*, 1644, vol. ix. p. 277.

CHEST. I am not aware that ' cista ' was ever used in the sense of a coffin, but ' chest ' is continually so used in our early English ; and ' to chest,' for to place in a coffin, occurs in the heading of a chapter in our Bibles, *Gen.* l. 26 : ' He [Joseph] dieth, and is *chested.*'

> He is now ded, and nailed in his *cheste.*
>> CHAUCER, *The Clerkes Prologue.*

> Your body is now wrapt in *chest,*
> I pray to God to give your soul good rest.
>> HAWES, *Pastime of Pleasure*, cap. 14.

CHIMNEY. This, which means now the gorge or vent of a furnace or fire, was once in frequent use for the furnace itself ; in this more true to its origin ; being derived from the Greek κάμινος, as it passed into the Latin ' caminus,' and the French ' cheminée,'

The fact that it is the 'chimney,' in the modern use'of
the word, which, creating a draught, alone gives
activity or fierceness to the flame, probably explains
the present limitation of the meaning of the word.
In Scotland 'chimney' still is, or lately was, 'the
grate, or iron frame that holds the fire.' (*Scoticisms*,
Edinburgh, 1787.)

And his feet [were] like to latoun as in a brennynge *chymeney.*
—*Rev.* i. 15. WICLIF.

The Son of Man shall send his angels, and shall gather all
hindrances out of his kingdom and all that worketh unlawfulness,
and shall cast them into the *chimney* of fire.—*Matt.* xiii. 50.
Sir JOHN CHEKE.

CHIVALRY.   It is a striking evidence of the extent
to which in the feudal times the men-at-arms, the
mounted knights, were esteemed as the army, while
the footmen were regarded as little better than a
supernumerary rabble,—another record of this contempt probably surviving in the word 'infantry,'—
that 'chivalry,' which of course is but a different
form of 'cavalry,' could once be used as convertible
with army.   It needed more than one Agincourt to
teach that this was so no longer.

Abymalach forsothe aroos, and Phicol, the prince of his
chyvalrye [princeps *exercitûs* ejus, Vulg.], and turneden ayen into
the loond of Palestynes.—*Gen.* xxi. 33. WICLIF.

CHOUSE.   The history of the introduction of this
word into the popular, or at all events the schoolboy,
language of England, and the quarter from whence
derived, are now sufficiently well-known.   A 'chiaus,'
or interpreter, attached to the Turkish Embassy, in
1609 succeeded in defrauding the Turkish and Per-

sian merchants resident in England of 4,000*l.* From
the vast dimensions of the fraud, vast, that is, as
men counted fraudulent 'vastness' then, and the noto-
riety it acquired, a chiaus (presently spelt 'chouse' to
look more English) became equivalent to a swindler,
and somewhat later to the act of swindling. It is
curious that a correspondent of Skinner (*Etymologicon*, 1671), though quite ignorant of this story,
suggests a connection between chouse and the
Turkish 'chiaus.' The quotation from Ben Jonson
gives us the word in its passage from the old meaning
to the new.

About this time the Turks proposed at the instigation of the
French ambassador to send a *chiaus* into France, England and
Holland, to acquaint those princes with the advancement of
Sultan Solyman to the throne.—RYCAUT, *History of the Turks,*
vol. iii. p. 261.

> *Dapper.* What do you think of me,
> That I am a *chiaus*?
> *Face.* What's that?
> *Dapper.* The Turk was here;
> As one would say, do you think I am a Turk?
> BEN JONSON, *The Alchemist*, act i. sc. 1.

CHRISTEN, ⎫ By 'Christendom' we now under-
CHRISTENDOM. ⎭ stand that portion of the world
which makes profession of the faith of Christ, as
contradistinguished from all heathen and Mahomedan
lands. But it was often used by our early writers as
itself the profession of Christ's faith, or sometimes
for baptism, inasmuch as in that this profession was
made ; which is also the explanation of the use of
'christen' as equivalent to 'christianize' below. In
Shakespeare our present use of 'Christendom' very

much predominates, but once or twice he uses it in
its earlier sense, as do authors much later than he.

Most part of England in the reign of King Ethelbert was
christened, Kent only excepted, which remained long after in
misbelief and *unchristened.*—E. K., *Gloss. to Spenser's Shepherd's Calendar, September.*

Sothli we ben togidere biried with him bi *christendom* [per
baptismum, Vulg.] in to death.—*Rom.* vi. 4. WICLIF.

He that might have his body wrapped in one of their old
coats at the houre of death, it were as good to him as his
christendom.—TYNDALE, *Exposition upon Matthew VI.*

> They all do come to him with friendly face,
> When of his *christendom* they understand.
> 　　　Sir J. HARINGTON, *Orlando Furioso,* b. xliii. c. 189.

The draughts of intemperance would wash off the water of my
christendom; every unclean lust does as it were bemire and wipe
out my contract with my Lord.—ALLESTREE, *Sermons,* vol. ii.
p. 161.

CHURCH.　Our Translators are often taxed with an
oversight that they have allowed 'robbers of *churches*'
to remain at *Acts* xix. 37, as the rendering of ἱεροσύλους,
sounding, as it does, like an anachronism on the lips
of the town-clerk of Ephesus.　Doubtless ' spoilers
of *temples*,' or some such phrase, would have been
preferable ; yet was there not any oversight here.
The title of ' church,' which we with a fit reverence
restrain to a Christian place of worship, was in
earlier English not refused to the Jewish, or, as in
that place, even to a heathen, temple as well.

And, lo, the veil of the *church* was torn in two parts from the
top downwards.—*Matt.* xxvii. 51. Sir JOHN CHEKE.

> To all the gods devoutly she did offer frankincense,
> But most above them all the *church* of Juno she did cense.
> 　　　GOLDING, *Ovid's Metamorphosis,* b. xi.

> These troops should soon pull down the *church* of Jove.
> 　　　MARLOWE, *First Book of Lucan.*

CIVIL,
CIVILITY,
CIVILIAN.
} The tendency which there is in the meaning of words to run to the surface, till they lose and leave behind all their deeper significance, is well exemplified in ' civil ' and ' civility '—words of how deep an import once, how slight and shallow now. A *civil* man now is one observant of slight external courtesies in the intercourse between man and man; a *civil* man once was one who fulfilled all the duties and obligations flowing from his position as a ' civis,' and his relations to the other members of that ' civitas ' to which he belonged, and ' civility ' the condition in which those were recognized and observed. The gradual departure of all deeper significance from ' civility ' has obliged the creation of another word, ' civilization,' which only came up toward the conclusion of the last century. Johnson does not know it in his Dictionary, except as a technical legal term to express the turning of a criminal process into a civil one ; and, according to Boswell, altogether disallowed it in the sense which it has now acquired. A ' civilian ' in the language of the Puritans was one who, despising the righteousness of Christ, did yet follow after a certain civil righteousness, a ' justitia civilis ' of his own.

That wise and *civil* Roman, Julius Agricola, preferred the natural wits of Britain before the laboured studies of the French. —MILTON, *Areopagitica*.

As for the Scythian wandering Nomades, temples sorted not with their condition, as wanting both *civility* and settledness.— FULLER, *The Holy State*, b. iii. c. 24.

Then were the Roman fashions imitated and the gown ; after a while the incitements also and materials of vice and voluptuous life, proud buildings, baths, and the elegance of banquetings ; **which the foolisher sort called** *civility*, **but was** indeed a secret art to prepare them for bondage.—MILTON, *History of England*, b. ii.

Let us remember also that *civility* and fair customs were but in a narrow circle till the Greeks and Romans beat the world into better manners.—J. TAYLOR, *Ductor Dubitantium*, b. ii. c. I, § 19.

The last step in this [spiritual] death is the death of *civility*. *Civil* men come nearer the saints of God than others, they come within a step or two of heaven, and yet are shut out.—PRESTON, *Of Spiritual Death and Life*, 1636, p. 59.

I proceed to the second, that is to the mere naturalist or *civilian*; by whom I mean such an one as lives upon dregs, the very reliques and ruins of the image of God decayed.—ROGERS, *Naaman the Syrian*, p. 104.

CLERGY.   The use of ' clergy ' in the abstract for learning or for a learned profession, is, it needs hardly be said, the result of the same conditions which made ' clerk ' equivalent to scholar.

> Ne alle the clerkes that ever had witte
> Sen the world bigan, ne that lyfes yit,
> Couth never telle bi *clergy* ne arte
> Of these payns of helle the thousand parte.
>   RICHARD ROLLE DE HAMPOLE, *Pricke of Conscience*, 4832.

> Was not Aristotle, for all his *clergy*,
> For a woman wrapt in love so marvellously,
> That all his cunning he had soon forgotten?
>   HAWES, *Pastime of Pleasure*.

Also that every of the said landlords put their second sons to learn some *clergy*, or some craft, whereby they may live honestly. —*State Papers, State of Ireland*, 1515, vol. ii. p. 30.

CLUMSY.   A word about which little satisfactory has as yet found its way into our dictionaries; but although of no very frequent use in our early litera- ture (it does not once occur in Shakespeare), neither can it be said to be very rare; and where it occurs,

it is in a sense going before its present, namely, in
that of stiff, rigid, *clumped* and contracted with cold.
It is familiar to all how 'clumsy,' in our modern use
of the word, the fingers are when in this condition,
and thus it is easy to trace the growing of the
modern meaning out of the old. On its probable
etymology see the *Proceedings of the Philological
Society*, vol. v. p. 146.

Rigido ; Stark, stiffe, or num through cold, *clumzie.*—FLORIO,
New World of Words.

Havi de froid ; Stiffe, *clumpse*, benummed.—COTGRAVE, *A
French and English Dictionary.*

The Carthaginians followed the enemies in chase as far as
Trebia, and there gave over ; and returned into the camp so
clumsy and frozen [ita *torpentes gelu*] as scarcely they felt the
joy of their victory.—HOLLAND, *Livy*, p. 425.

This bloom of budding beauty loves not to be handled by such
nummed and so *clomsie* hands.—FLORIO, *Montaigne's Essays*,
b. iii. c. 5.

CLIMATE. At present the temperature of a region,
but once the region itself, the region, however, con-
templated in its *slope* or *inclination* from the equator
toward the pole, and therefore, by involved consequence, in respect of its temperature ; which circumstance is the point of contact between the present
meaning of ' climate ' and the past. We have derived
the word from the mathematical geographers of
antiquity. They were wont to run imaginary parallel
lines, or such at least as they intended should be
parallel, to the equator ; and the successive 'climates'
(κλίματα) of the earth were the spaces and regions
between these lines. See Holland's *Pliny*, vol.
p. 150.

The longitude of a *clymat* ys a lyne ymagined fro est to west, illike distant by-twene them alle.—CHAUCER, *Treatise on the Astrolabe*, 2, 39, 3.

> Almost five *climates* henceward to the south,
> Between the mainland and the ocean's mouth
> Two islands lie.
>
> *The Funerals of King Edward VI.*

> When these prodigies
> Do so conjointly meet, let not men say,
> 'These are their causes—they are natural;'
> For, I believe, they are portentous things
> Unto the *climate* that they point upon.
>
> SHAKESPEARE, *Julius Cæsar*, act i. sc. 3.

This *climate* of Gaul [hanc Galliarum *plagam*] is enclosed on every side with fences that environ it naturally.—HOLLAND, *Ammianus*, p. 47.

Climate, a portion of the earth contained between two circles parallel to the equator.—PHILLIPS, *New World of Words*.

COMFORT, } The verb 'comfortare,' not found in
COMFORTABLE. } classical Latin, but so frequent in the Vulgate, is first, as is plain from the 'fortis' which it embodies, to make strong, to corroborate, and only in a secondary sense, to console. We often find it in our early literature employed in that its proper sense.

And the child wexed, and was *counfortid* [confortabatur, Vulg.] in spirit.—*Luke* i. 80. WICLIF.

And there appeared an angel unto Him from heaven, *comforting* Him [ἐνισχύων αὐτόν].—*Luke* xxii. 43. TYNDALE.

Thy conceit is nearer death than thy powers ; for my sake, be *comfortable*; hold death awhile at the arm's end.—SHAKESPEARE, *As you like it*, act ii. sc. 6.

COMMON-SENSE. The manner is very curious in which the metaphysical or theological speculations, to which the busy world is indifferent, or from which

it is entirely averse, do yet in their results descend
to it, and are adopted by it; while it remains quite
unconscious of the source from which they spring,
and counts that it has created them for itself and
out of its own resources. Thus, many would wonder
if asked the parentage of this phrase 'common-sense,'
would count it the most natural thing in the world
that such a phrase should have been formed, that it
demanded no ingenuity to form it, that the uses to
which it is now put are the same which it has served
from the first. Indeed, neither Reid, Beattie, nor
Stewart seem to have assumed anything else. But
in truth this phrase, 'common-sense,' meant once
something very different from that plain wisdom, the
common heritage of men, which now we call by this
name; having been bequeathed to us by a very complex theory of the senses, and of a *sense* which was
the *common* bond of them all, and which passed its
verdicts on the reports which they severally made to
it. This theory of a κοινὸς νοῦς, familiar to the Greek
metaphysicians, see Cicero, *Tusc. Quæst.* i. 20, is sufficiently explained by the interesting quotations from
Henry More and Burton. In Hawes' *Pastime of
Pleasure* (cap. 24) the relation between the 'common wit' and the 'five wits' is at large set forth.
For an interesting history of the phrase, see Sir
William Hamilton's edition of Reid's *Works*, appendix A, especially pp. 757, &c.; and for some classical
uses of it Horace, *Sat.* i. 3. 65; Juvenal, 8. 73; Seneca,
Ep. 5. 3; 105. 4; *De Benef.* i. 12. 3; Quintilian,
i. 2. 20.

The senses receive indifferently, without discretion and judgement, white and black, sweet and sour, soft and hard; for their

E

office is only to admit their several objects, and to carry and refer the judgement thereof to the *common sense.*—NORTH, *Plutarch's Lives*, p. 732.

But for fear to exceed the commission of an historian (who with the outward senses may only bring in the species, and barely relate facts, not with the *common sense* pass verdict or censure on them), I would say they had better have built in some other place, especially having room enough besides, and left this floor, where the Temple stood, alone in her desolations. —FULLER, *The Holy War*, b. i. c. 4.

That there is some particular or restrained seat of the *common sense* is an opinion that even all philosophers and physicians are agreed upon. And it is an ordinary comparison amongst them, that the external senses and the *common sense* considered together are like a circle with five lines drawn from the circumference to the centre. Wherefore, as it has been obvious for them to find out particular organs for the external senses, so they have also attempted to assign some distinct part of the body to be an organ of the *common sense*; that is to say, as they discovered sight to be seated in the eye, hearing in the ear, smelling in the nose, &c., so they conceived that there is some part of the body wherein seeing, hearing, and all other perceptions meet together, as the lines of a circle in the centre, and that there the soul does also judge and discern of the difference of the objects of the outward senses.—H. MORE, *Immortality of the Soul*, b. iii. c. 13.

Inner senses are three in number, so called because they be within the brain-pan, as *common sense*, phantasy, memory. Their objects are not only things present, but they perceive the sensible species of things to come, past, absent, such as were before in the sense. This *common sense* is the judge or moderator of the rest, by whom we discern all differences of objects; for by mine eye I do not know that I see, or by mine ear that I hear, but by my *common sense*, who judgeth of sounds and colours; they are but the organs to bring the species to be censured; so that all their objects are his, and all the offices are his. The fore part of the brain is his organ or seat.—BURTON, *Anatomy of Melancholy*, part i. sect. 2.

COMPANION. This had once the same contemptuous use which its synonyme 'fellow' still retains (for a curious use of this see 2 *Pet.* ii. 14, Geneva Version), and which 'gadeling,' a word of the same meaning, had, so long as it survived in the language. The notion originally involved in companionship, or accompaniment, would appear to have been rather that of inferiority than of equality. A companion (or *comes*) was an attendant.

> What should the wars do with these jigging fools?
> *Companion*, hence.
> > SHAKESPEARE, *Julius Cæsar*, act iv. sc. 3.

As that empty barren *companion* in St. James who bids the poor be warm and fed and clothed (as if he were all made of mercy), yet neither clothes, feeds, nor warms his back, belly, or flesh, so fares it with these lovers.—ROGERS, *Naaman the Syrian*, p. 391.

The young ladies, who thought themselves too much concerned to contain themselves any longer, set up their throats all together against my protector. 'Scurvy *companion!* saucy tarpaulin! rude, impertinent fellow! did he think to prescribe to grand-papa!'—SMOLLETT, *Roderick Random*, vol. i. c. 3.

CONCEITED, } 'Conceit' is so entirely and irre-
CONCEITEDLY. } coverably lost to the language of philosophy, that it would be well if 'concept,' used often by our earlier philosophical writers, were revived. Yet 'conceit' has not so totally forsaken all its former meanings (for there are still '*happy* conceits' in poetry), as have 'conceited,' which once meant well conceived, and 'conceitedly.'

> Oft did she heave her napkin to her eyne,
> Which had on it *conceited* characters.
> > SHAKESPEARE, *A Lover's Complaint.*

E 2

> Triumphal arches the glad town doth raise,
> And tilts and tourneys are performed at court,
> *Conceited* masques, rich banquets, witty plays.
>> DRAYTON, *The Miseries of Queen Margaret.*

The edge or hem of a garment is distinguished from the rest most commonly by some *conceited* or costly work.—COWELL, *The Interpreter*, s. v. Broderess.

Cicero most pleasantly and *conceitedly.*—HOLLAND, *Suetonius*, p. 21.

CONCUBINE.   Our Dictionaries do not notice that the male paramour no less than the female was sometimes called by this name; on the contrary, their definitions exclude this.

The Lady Anne did falsely and traiterously procure divers of the King's daily and familiar servants to be her adulterers and *concubines.—Indictment of Anne Boleyn.*

CONJURE.   The quotation from Foxe shows that this use of ' to conjure ' as to conspire is not, as one might at first suspect, one of Milton's Latinisms, and as such peculiar to him.

Divers, as well horsemen as footmen, had *conjured* among themselves and conspired against the Englishmen, selling their horses and arms aforehand.—FOXE, *Book of Martyrs*, 1641, vol. i. p. 441.

> Art thou he
> That first broke peace in heaven and faith till then
> Unbroken, and, in proud rebellious arms,
> Drew after him the third part of heaven's sons,
> *Conjured* against the Highest?
>> MILTON, *Paradise Lost*, b. ii.

CONTEMPTIBLE.   ' Adjectives in "able " and "ible," both positive and negative ones, are frequently used by old writers in an active sense ' (S. Walker, *Criticisms on Shakespeare*, vol. i. p. 183 : whom see).

'Contemptible' where we should now use 'contemptuous' is one of these; 'intenible' (*All's well
that ends well*, act i. sc. 3) another; 'discernible'
a third.

Darius wrote to Alexander in a proud and *contemptible* manner.—LORD STERLING, *Darius*, 1603, (in the argument prefixed
to the Play).

If she should make tender of her love, 'tis very possible he'll
scorn it, for the man, as you know all, hath a *contemptible*
spirit.—SHAKESPEARE, *Much Ado about Nothing*, act ii. sc. 3.

> I do not mock, nor lives there such a villain,
> That can do anything *contemptible*
> To you; but I do kneel, because it is
> An action very fit and reverent
> In presence of so pure a creäture.
> > BEAUMONT and FLETCHER, *The Coxcomb*, act v. sc. 2.

CONVINCE. This and 'convict' have been usefully
desynonymized. One is 'convinced' of a sin, but
'convicted' of a crime; the former word moving
always in the sphere of moral or intellectual things,
but the latter often in that of things merely external.

Your Italy contains none so accomplished a courtier to *convince* the honour of my mistress.—SHAKESPEARE, *Cymbeline*,
act i. sc. 4.

> Keep off that great concourse, whose violent hands
> Would ruin this stone-building and drag hence
> This impious judge, piecemeal to tear his limbs,
> Before the law *convince* him.
> > WEBSTER, *Appius and Virginia*, act v. sc. 5.

COPY. A more Latin use of 'copy,' as 'copia' or
abundance, was at one time frequent in English. It
is easy to trace the steps by which the word attained
its present significance. The only way to obtain

' copy ' (in this Latin sense) or abundance of any document, would be by taking ' copies ' (in our present sense) of it. Then, too, it meant often the exemplar, and is so used in the quotations from Shakespeare and Jeremy Taylor.

We cannot follow a better pattern for elocution than God Himself. Therefore He, using divers words in his Holy Writ, and indifferently for one thing in nature, we may use the same liberty in our English versions out of Hebrew or Greek, for that *copy* or store that He hath given us.—*The Translators [of the Bible,* 1611] *to the Reader.*

> Be *copy* now to men of grosser blood,
> And teach them how to war.
>
> Shakespeare, *Henry V*. act iii. sc. 1.

Drayton's heroical epistles are well worth the reading also, for the purpose of our subject, which is to furnish an English historian with choice and *copy* of tongue.—Bolton, *Hypercritica*, p. 235.

The sun, the prince of all the bodies of light, is the principal, the rule and the *copy*, which they in their proportions imitate and transcribe.—J. Taylor, *Exhortation to the Imitation of Christ*.

Coquet. At present all our ' coquets ' are female. But, as is the case with so many other words instanced in this volume, what once belonged to both sexes is now restricted to one.

Cocquet; a beau, a gallant, a general lover; also a wanton girl that speaks fair to several lovers at once.—Phillips, *New World of Words*.

Corpse. Now only used for the body abandoned by the spirit of life, but once for the body of the living equally as of the dead; now only=' cadaver,' but once ' corpus ' as well.

A valiant *corpse*, where force and beauty met.
Surrey, On the Death of Sir T. Wyatt.

But naked, without needful vestiments
To clad his *corpse* with meet habiliments,
He cared not for dint of sword or spear.
Spenser, Fairy Queen, b. vi. c. 4.

Women and maids shall particularly examine themselves about the variety of their apparell, their too much care of their *corps.* —*Richeome's Pilgrim of Loretto, by G. W.*

Your conjuring, cozening, and your dozen of trades
Could not relieve your *corps* with so much linen
Would make you tinder, but to see a fire.
Ben Jonson, The Alchemist, act i. sc. 1.

COUNTERFEIT. Now to imitate with the purpose of passing off the imitation as the original; but no such dishonest intention was formerly implied in the word.

I woll none of the apostles *contrefete* :
I woll have money, wolle chese and whete,
Al were it yeven of the pourest page,
Or of the pourest widewe in a village.
Chaucer, The Pardoner's Tale.

Christ prayseth not the unrighteous stuard, neither setteth him forth to us to *counterfait,* because of his unrighteousness, but because of his wisdom only, in that he with unright so wisely provided for himself.—Tyndale, *The Parable of the Wicked Mammon.*

But for the Greek tong they do note in some of his epistles that he [Brutus] *counterfeited* that brief compendious manner of speech of the Lacedæmonians.—North, *Plutarch's Lives,* p. 818.

COURTESAN. The low Latin 'cortesanus' was once one haunting the court, a courtier, 'aulicus,' though already in Shakespeare we often meet the word in its present use.

By the wolf, no doubt, was meant the Pope, 'but the fox was resembled to the prelates, *courtesans*, priests, and the rest of the spiritualty.—Foxe, *Book of Martyrs*, ed. 1641, vol. i. p. 511.

COURTSHIP. We now assign to this and to ' courtesy ' their own several domains of meanings ; but they were once promiscuously used. See for another example of the same the quotation from Fuller, *s. v.* ' Defalcation.'

As he [Charles I.], to acquit himself, hath not spared his adversaries, to load them with all sorts of blame and accusation, so to him, as in his book alive, there will be used no more *courtship* than he uses.—MILTON, *Iconoclastes*, The Preface.

CUMBER, ⎱ This word, the German 'kümmern,' has
CUMBROUS. ⎰ lost much of the force which it once possessed; it means now little more than passively to burden. It was once actively to annoy, disquiet, or mischief. It was as possessing this force that our Translators rendered ἵνα τί καὶ τὴν γῆν καταργεῖ ; why *cumbereth* it the ground ? (*Luke* xiii. 7.)

The archers in the forefront so wounded the footmen, so galled the horses, and so *combred* the men of arms that the footmen durst not go forward.—HALL, *Henry V.* fol. 17, 6.

We have herde that certayne of oures are departed, and have troubled you and have *combred* [ἀνασκευάζοντες] your myndes, sayenge, Ye must be circumcised and must keep the law.—*Acts* xv. 24. COVERDALE.

But Martha was *cumbered* [περιεσπᾶτο, cf. ver. 41 : μεριμνᾶς καὶ τυρβάζῃ] about much serving.—*Luke* x. 40. Authorized Version.

> A cloud of *cumbrous* gnats do him molest,
> All striving to infix their feeble stings.
>   SPENSER, *Fairy Queen*, i. 1. 23.

CUNNING. The fact that so many words implying knowledge, art, skill, obtain in course of time a secon-

dary meaning of crooked knowledge, art that has degenerated into artifice, skill used only to circumvent,
which meanings partially or altogether put out of
use their primary, is a mournful witness to the way
in which intellectual gifts are too commonly mis-
applied. Thus there was a time when the Latin
'dolus' required the epithet 'malus,' as often as it
signified a treacherous or fraudful device; but it
was soon able to drop this as superfluous, and to
stand by itself. Other words which have gone the
same downward course are the following: τέχνη,
'astutia,' 'calliditas,' 'List,' 'Kunst,' and our
English 'craft' and 'cunning,'—the last, indeed, as
early as Lord Bacon, who says, 'We take *cunning*
for a sinister or crooked wisdom,' had acquired what
is now its only acceptation; but not then, nor till
long after, to the exclusion of its more honourable
use. How honourable that use sometimes was, my
first quotation will testify.

I believe that all these three Persons [in the Godhead] are
even in power and in *cunning* and in might, full of grace and of
all goodness.—Foxe, *Book of Martyrs; Examination of William
Thorpe.*

So the number of them, with their brethren, that were in-
structed in the songs of the Lord, even all that were *cunning*,
was two hundred fourscore and eight.—1 *Chron.* xxv. 7. Authorized Version.

CURATE. Rector, vicar, every one having *cure* of
souls, was a 'curate' once. Thus 'bishops and *curates*'
in the Liturgy.

They [the begging friars] letten *curats* to know Gods law by
holding bookes fro them, and withdrawing of their vantages, by
which they shulden have books and lerne.—WICLIF, *Treatise
against the Friars*, p. 56.

Henry the Second of England commanded all prelates and *curates* to reside upon their dioceses and charges.—J. TAYLOR, *Ductor Dubitantium*, b. iii. c. I.

Curate, a parson or vicar, one that serves a cure, or has the charge of souls in a parish.—PHILLIPS, *New World of Words*.

CUSTOMER. One sitting officially at the receipt of customs, that is, of dues customably paid, and receiving these, and not one repairing customably to a shop to purchase there, was a 'customer' two and three centuries ago.

He healeth the man of the palsye, calleth Levi the *customer*, eateth with open synners, and excuseth his disciples.—*What S. Marke conteyneth.* COVERDALE.

The extreme and horrible covetousness of the farmers, *customers*, and Roman usurers devoured it [Asia].—NORTH, *Plutarch's Lives*, p. 432.

We hardly can abide publicans, *customers*, and toll gatherers, when they keep a ferreting and searching for such things as be hidden.—HOLLAND, *Plutarch's Morals*, p. 138.

DANGER,   ⎫ A feudal term, beset with many diffi-
DANGEROUS. ⎬ culties when we seek to follow it as
it passes to its present use. Ducange has written upon it, and Diez, and Littré (*Hist. de la Langue Franç.* vol. i. p 49), and there is a careful article in Richardson. It is a low Latin word, 'dangerium,' of which the etymology is uncertain, signifying the strict right of the suzerain in regard to the fief of the vassal ; thus, 'fief de *danger*,' a fief held under strict and severe conditions, and therefore in *danger* of being forfeited (juri stricto atque adeo confiscationi obnoxium ; Ducange). There is no difficulty here ; but there is another early use of ' danger ' and ' dangerous ' which is not thus explained, nor yet the

connexion between it and the modern meaning of the words. I refer to that of ' danger ' in the sense of ' coyness,' 'sparingness,' ' niggardliness,' and of ' dangerous ' with the adjectival uses corresponding.

> And if thy voice is faire and clere,
> Thou shalt maken no great *daungere*,
> When to singen they goodly pray ;
> It is thy worship for to obay.
> > CHAUCER, *Romaunt of the Rose*, 2317.

We ourselves also were in times past unwise, disobedient, deceived, in *danger* to lusts [δουλεύοντες ἐπιθυμίαις].—*Tit.* iii. 3. TYNDALE.

> Come not within his *danger* by thy will.
> > SHAKESPEARE, *Venus and Adonis.*

> My wages ben full streyt and eke ful smale ;
> My lord to me is hard and *daungerous.*
> > CHAUCER, *The Friar's Tale.*

> But nathelesse, for his beaute
> So fierce and *dangerous* was he,
> That he nolde graunten her asking,
> For weeping, ne for faire praying.
> > Id. *Romaunt of the Rose*, 1480.

DEADLY. This and ' mortal ' (which see), are sometimes synonymes now ; thus, ' a *deadly* wound ' or ' a *mortal* wound;' but they are not invariably so ; ' deadly ' being always active, while ' mortal ' is far oftenest passive, signifying not that which inflicts death, but that which suffers death ; thus, ' a *mortal* body,' or body subject to death, but not now ' a *deadly* body.' It was otherwise once. ' Deadly ' is the constant word in Wiclif's Bible, wherever in the later Versions 'mortal ' occurs.

Elye was a *deedli* man lyk us, and in preier he preiede that it schulde not reyne on the erthe, and it reynede not three yeeris and sixe monethis.—*Jam.* v. 17. WICLIF.

Many holy prophets that were *deadly* men were martyred violently in the Old Law.—FOXE, *Book of Martyrs ; Examination of William Thorpe.*

DECEIVABLE, ⎫ So far as we use 'deceivable' at
DECEIVABLENESS. ⎭ all now, we use it in the passive sense, as liable to be, or capable of being, deceived. It was active when counted exchangeable with 'deceitful' as at 2 *Pet.* i. 16, where the 'deceivable' of Tyndal appears as the 'deceitful' of Cranmer's Bible. It has fared in like manner with 'discernible' ' contemptible ' and with other words which, active once, are passive now.

> This world is fikel and *desayvable*,
> And fals and unsiker, and unstable.
> RICHARD ROLLE DE HAMPOLE, *Pricke of Conscience*, 1088.

The most uncertain and *deceivable* proof of the people's good will and cities' toward kings and princes are the immeasurable and extreme honours they do unto them.—NORTH, *Plutarch's Lives*, p. 743.

For we folowed not *deceuable* fables, when we openned unto you the power and commynge of our Lorde Jesus Christ.—2 *Pet.* i. 16. Geneva Version.

Whose coming is after the working of Satan with all *deceivableness* of unrighteousness in them that perish.—2 *Thess.* ii. 9, 10. Authorized Version.

DEFALCATION. A word at present of very slovenly and inaccurate use. We read in the newspapers of a 'defalcation' of the revenue, not meaning thereby an active *lopping off* ('defalcatio') of certain taxes with their proceeds, which would be the only correct use, but a passive falling short in its returns from what they previously were. Can it be that some confusion of 'defalcation' with 'default,' or at least a seeing of 'fault' and not 'falx' in its second syllable (there was once a verb 'to defalk'), has led to this ?

My first crude meditations, being always hastily put together, could never please me so well at a second and more leisurable review, as to pass without some additions, *defalcations*, and other alterations, more or less.—SANDERSON, *Sermons*, 1671, Preface.

As for their conjecture that Zorobabel, at the building of this temple purposely abated of those dimensions assigned by Cyrus, as too great for him to compass, in such *defalcation* of measures by Cyrus allowed, he showed little courtship to his master the emperor, and less religion to the Lord his God.—FULLER, *A Pisgah Sight of Palestine*, b. iii. c. 2.

DEFEND, } Now to protect, but once to protect by
DEFENCE. } prohibiting, or fencing round, to forbid, as 'défendre' is still in French.

The sin of maumetrie is the first that is *defended* in the Ten Commandments.—CHAUCER, *The Parson's Tale.*

> When can you say in any manner age
> That ever God *defended* marriage?
> Id., *The Wife of Bath's Tale.*

And oure Lord *defended* hem that thei scholde not tell that avisioun til that He were rysen.—SIR JOHN MANDEVILLE, *Voiage and Travaile*, p. 114.

> O sons, like one of us man is become,
> To know both good and evil, since his taste
> Of that *defended* fruit.
> MILTON, *Paradise Lost*, xi. 84.

Adam afterward ayeins his *defence* freet of that fruit.
> *Piers Ploughman*, 12466.

DEFY, } This means now to dare to the utter-
DEFIANCE. } most hostility, and so, as a consequence

which will often follow upon this, to challenge. But in earlier use 'to defy' is, according to its etymology, to pronounce all bonds of *faith* and fellowship which existed previously between the defier and the defied to be wholly dissolved, so that nothing of treaty or even of the natural faith of man to man shall henceforth hinder extremest hostility between them. But still, when we read of one potentate sending 'defiance' to another, the challenge to conflict did not lie necessarily in the word, however such a message might provoke and would often be the prelude to this: it meant but the releasing of himself from all which hitherto had mutually obliged; and thus it came often to mean simply to disclaim, or renounce.

No man speaking in the Spirit of God *defieth* Jesus [λέγει ἀνάθεμα Ἰησοῦν].—1 *Cor.* xii. 3. TYNDALE.

Despise not an hungry soul, and *defy* not the poor in his necessity.—*Ecclus.* iv. 2. COVERDALE.

> All studies here I solemnly *defy*,
> Save how to gall and pinch this Bolingbroke.
>> SHAKESPEARE, 1 *Henry IV.* act. i. sc. 8.

There is a double people-pleasing. One sordid and servile, made of falsehood and flattery, which I *defy* and detest.— FULLER, *Appeal of Injured Innocence*, p. 38.

Now although I instanced in a question which by good fortune never came to open *defiance*, yet there have been sects formed upon lighter grounds.—J. TAYLOR, *Liberty of Prophesying*, § 3, 5.

DELAY. Like the French 'délayer,' used often in old time where we should now employ 'allay.' Out of an ignorance of this, and assuming it a misprint, some modern editors of our earlier authors have not scrupled to change 'delay' into 'allay.'

The watery showers *delay* the raging wind.

SURREY, *The Faithful Lover.*

Even so fathers ought to *delay* their eager reprehensions and cutting rebukes with kindness and clemency.—HOLLAND, *Plutarch's Morals*, p. 16.

Cup-bearers know well enough and in that regard can discern and distinguish, when they are to use more or less water to the *delaying* of wines.—Id., *Ib.* p. 652.

DELICACY,
DELICATE,
DELICATELY,
DELICIOUS,
DELICIOUSLY.
In the same way as self-indulgence creeps over us by unmarked degrees, so there creeps over the words that designate it a subtle change; they come to contain less and less of rebuke and blame; the thing itself being tolerated, nay allowed, it must needs be that the words which express it should be received into favour too. It has been thus, as I shall have occasion to note, with ' luxury ' ; it has been thus also with this whole group of words. See the quotation from Sir W. Raleigh, *s.v.* ' Feminine.'

Thus much of *delicacy* in general; now more particularly of his first branch, gluttony.—NASH, *Christ's Tears over Jerusalem*, p. 140.

Cephisodorus, the disciple of Isocrates, charged him with *delicacy*, intemperance, and gluttony.—BLOUNT, *Philostratus*, p. 229.

The most *delicate* and voluptuous princes have ever been the heaviest oppressors of the people, riot being a far more lavish spender of the common treasure than war or magnificence.—HABINGTON, *History of King Edward IV.*, p. 196.

She that liveth *delicately* [σπαταλῶσα] is dead while she liveth.— 2 *Tim.* v. 6. Authorised Version (margin).

Yea, soberest men it [idleness] makes *delicious.*—SYLVESTER, *Du Bartas, Second Week, Eden.*

How much she hath glorified herself and lived *deliciously* [ἐστρηνίασε], so much torment and sorrow give her.—*Rev.* xviii. 7. Authorized Version.

DEMERIT. It was plainly a squandering of the wealth of the language, that 'merit' and 'demerit' should mean one and the same thing; however this might be justified by the fact that 'mereor' and 'demereor,' from which they were severally derived, were scarcely discriminated in meaning. It has thus come to pass, according to the desynonymizing processes ever at work in a language, that 'demerit' has ended in being employed only of *ill* desert, while 'merit' is left free to good or ill, having predominantly the sense of the former.

> I fetch my life and being
> From men of royal siege; and my *demerits*
> May speak, unbonneted, to as proud a fortune
> As this that I have reached.
> SHAKESPEARE, *Othello*, act. i. sc. 2.

By our profane and unkind civil wars the world is grown to this pass, that it is reputed a singular *demerit* and gracious act, not to kill a citizen of Rome, but to let him live.—HOLLAND, *Pliny*, vol. i. p. 456.

But the Rhodians, contrariwise, in a proud humour of theirs, reckoned up a beadroll of their *demerits* toward the people of Rome.—Id., *Livy*, p. 1179.

DEMURE, } Used by our earlier writers without
DEMURENESS. } the insinuation, which is now always latent in it, that the external shows of modesty and sobriety rest upon no corresponding realities. On the contrary the 'demure' was the truly modest and virtuous and good. It is one of the many words to which the suspicious nature of man, with the warrants

to a certain extent which these suspicions find, has given a turn for the worse.

These and other suchlike irreligious pranks did this Dionysius play, who notwithstanding fared no worse than the most *demure* and innocent, dying no other death than what usually other mortals do.—H. MORE, *Antidote against Atheism*, b. iii. c. 1.

Which advantages God propounds to all the hearers of the Gospel, without any respect of works or former *demureness* of life, if so be they will but now come in and close with this high and rich dispensation.—Id., *Grand Mystery of Godliness*, b. viii, c. 5.

> She is so nice and so *demure*,
> So sober, courteous, modest, and precise.
> *True History of King Leir*, 1605.

In like manner women also in comely attire; with *demureness* [cum verecundiâ, Vulg.] and sobriety adorning themselves.— 1 *Tim.* ii. 9. Rheims.

> His carriage was full comely and upright,
> His countenance *demure* and temperate.
> SPENSER, *Fairy Queen*, ii. 1, 6

DEPART. Once used as equivalent with 'to separate,' (divido, partior, *Promptorium Parvulorum*)—a fact already forgotten, when, at the last revision of the Prayer-Book in 1662, the Puritan divines objected to the form as it then stood in the Marriage Service, 'till death us *depart*;' in condescension to whose objection the words, as we now have them, 'till death us *do part*,' were introduced.

And he schal *departe* hem atwynne, as a schepherde *departith* scheep fro kidus.— *Matt.* xxv. 32. WICLIF.

And whanne he hadde seid this thing, discenscioun was made betwixe the farisies and the saduceis, and the multitude was *departid.*—*Acts* xxiii. 7. Id.

If my neighbour neede and I geve him not, neyther *depar* liberally with him of that which I have, than withholde I from

F

him unrighteously that which is hys owne.—Tyndale, *Parable of the Wicked Mammon.*

Neither did the apostles put away their wives, after they were called unto the ministry; but they continued with their wives lovingly and faithfully, till death *departed* them.—Becon, *An Humble Supplication unto God* (1554).

Deplored. It is well known that 'deploratus' obtained in later Latin, through a putting of effect for cause, the sense of desperate or past all hope, and was technically applied to the sick man given over by his physicians, 'deploratus a medicis.'

The physicians do make a kind of scruple and religion to stay with the patient after the disease is *deplored*; whereas, in my judgement, they ought both to inquire the skill, and to give the attendances, for the facilitating and assuaging of the pains and agonies of death.—Bacon, *Advancement of Learning*, b. ii.

If a man hath the mind to get the start of other sinners, and desires to be in hell before them, he need do no more but open his sails to the wind of heretical doctrine, and he is like to make a short voyage to hell; for these bring upon their maintainers a swift destruction. Nay, the Spirit of God the more to aggravate their *deplored* state, brings on three most dreadful instances of divine justice that ever were executed upon any sinners.—Gurnall, *The Christian in Complete Armour*, pt. ii. p. 317.

Deprave. As 'pravus' is literally crooked, we may say that 'to deprave' was formerly 'untruly *to present* as crooked,' to defame; while it is now 'wickedly *to make* crooked.' See the quotation from Bacon, *s. v.* 'Disable.'

Their intent was none other than to get him [Cardinal Wolsey] from the king out of the realm; then might they sufficiently adventure, by the help of their chief mistress, to *deprave* him with the king's highness, and so in his absence to bring him in displeasure with the king.—CAVENDISH, *Life of Cardinal Wolsey.*

> That lie, and cog, and flout, *deprave*, and slander.
>> SHAKESPEARE, *Much Ado about Nothing*, act v. sc. 1.

I am *depraved* unjustly; who never deprived the Church of her authority.—FULLER, *Appeal of Injured Innocence*, pt. i. p. 45.

> Unjustly thou *depravest* it with the name
> Of servitude, to serve where God ordains,
> Or nature.
>> MILTON, *Paradise Lost*, b. vi.

DERIVE. Tropical uses of the verb 'to derive' have quite superseded the literal, so that we now 'derive' anything rather than waters from a river.

An infinite deal of labour there is to lade out the water that riseth upon the workmen, for fear it choke up the pits; for to prevent which inconvenience they *derive* it by other drains.—HOLLAND, *Plutarch's Morals.*

Nor may the industry of the citizens of Salisbury be forgotten, who have *derived* the river into every street therein, so that Salisbury is a heap of islets thrown together.—FULLER, *Worthies of England, Wiltshire.*

DESIRE. 'To desire' is only to look *forward* with longing now; the word has lost the sense of regret or looking *back* upon the lost but still loved. This it once possessed in common with 'desiderium' and 'desiderare,' from which more remotely, and 'désirer,' from which more immediately, we derive it.

He [Jehoram] reigned in Jerusalem eight years, and departed without being *desired.*—2 *Chron.* xxi. 20. Authorized Version.

She that hath a wise husband must entice him to an eternal dearness by the veil of modesty and the grave robes of chastity, and she shall be pleasant while she lives, and *desired* when she dies.—J. TAYLOR, *The Marriage Ring*, Sermon 18.

So unremovéd stood these steeds, their heads to earth let fall,
And warm tears gushing from their eyes, with passionate *desire*
Of their kind manager.

CHAPMAN, Homer's Iliad, xvii. 379.

DETEST. For the writers of the seventeenth century
'to detest' still retains often the sense of its original
'detestari,' openly to witness against, and not merely
to entertain an inward abhorrence of, a thing; as in
'attest' and 'protest' the etymological meaning still
survives. It is not easy to adduce passages which
absolutely prove this against one who should be disposed to deny it. There can, however, be no doubt
whatever of the fact. In Dubartas' *Weeks*, 1621,
p. 106, an invective against avarice is called in the
margin '*Detestation* of Avarice, for her execrable and
cruel effects.'

Wherefore God hath *detested* them with his own mouth, and
clean given them over unto their own filthy lusts.—BALE, *The
Image of both Churches*, c. 11.

She cast herself upon him [her dead husband], and with
fearful cries *detested* the governor's inhuman and cruel deceit.—
GRIMESTON, *History of Lewis XI.*, 1614, p. 228.

Satyrs were certain poems, *detesting* and reproving the mis-
demeanours of people and their vices.—HOLLAND, *Explanation of
certain obscure words.*

E'en to vice

They [women] are not constant, but are changing still
One vice but of a minute old, for one
Not half so old as that. I'll write against them,
Detest them, curse them.

SHAKESPEARE, Cymbeline, act. ii. sc. 5.

DIAMOND. This, or 'diamant' as it used to be
spelt, is a popular form of 'adamant.' The Greek
ἀδάμας, originally used of the hardest steel, was,

about the time of Theophrastus, and, so far as we
know, first in his writings, transferred to the diamond, as itself also of a hardness not to be subdued ;
the cutting or polishing of this stone being quite a
modern invention; and the Latin 'adamas' continued
through the Middle Ages to bear this double meaning.
But if ' adamant' meant diamond, then 'diamond,'
by a reactive process frequent in language, would be
employed for adamant as well. So far as I know,
Milton is the last writer who so uses it.

> Have harte as hard as *diamaunt*,
> Stedfast, and nauht pliaunt.
> > CHAUCER, *Romaunt of the Rose.*

This little care and regard did at length melt and break
asunder those strong *diamond* chains with which Dionysius the
Elder made his boast that he left his tyranny chained to his
son.—NORTH, *Plutarch's Lives*, 1656, p. 800.

> But words and looks and sighs she did abhor,
> As rock of *diamond* stedfast evermore.
> > SPENSER, *Fairy Queen*, i. 6, 4.

Zeal, whose substance is ethereal, arming in complete *diamond*,
ascends his fiery chariot drawn with two blazing meteors, figured
like beasts, but of a higher breed than any the zodiack yields,
resembling two of those four, which Ezekiel and St. John saw,
the one visaged like a lion to express power, high authority, and
indignation ; the other of countenance like a man to cast derision
and scorn upon perverse and fraudulent seducers; with these
the invincible warriour Zeal shaking loosely the slack reins
drives over the heads of scarlet prelates, and such as are insolent to maintain traditions, bruising their stiff necks under
his flaming wheels.—MILTON, *Defence of Smectymnuus.*

> On each wing
> Uriel and Raphaël his vaunting foe,
> Though huge and in a rock of *diamond* armed,
> Vanquished, Adramelech and Asmodai.
> > Id., *Paradise Lost*, b. vi.

DIFFIDENCE,⎫ 'Diffidence' expresses now a not
DIFFIDENTLY.⎭ unbecoming distrust of one's own
self, with only a slight intimation, such as 'vere-
cundia' obtained in the silver age of Latin literature,
that perhaps this distrust is carried too far; but it
was once used for distrust of others, and sometimes
for distrust pushed so far as to amount to an entire
withholding of all faith from them, being nearly allied
to despair; as indeed in *The Pilgrim's Progress* Mistress Diffidence is Giant Despair's wife.

Of the impediments which have been in the affections, the
principal whereof hath been despair or *diffidence*, and the strong
apprehension of the difficulty, obscurity, and infiniteness, which
belongeth to the invention of knowledge.—BACON, *Of the Interpretation of Nature*, c. 19.

Every sin smiles in the first address, and carries light in the
face, and honey in the lip; but when we have well drunk, then
comes that which is worse, a whip with ten strings, fears and
terrors of conscience, and shame and displeasure, and a caitiff
disposition, and *diffidence* in the day of death.—J. TAYLOR, *Life
of Christ.*

That affliction grew heavy upon me, and weighed me down
even to a *diffidence* of God's mercy.—DONNE, *Sermons*, 1640,
vol. I. p. 311.

Mediators were not wanting that endeavoured a renewing of
friendship between these two prelates, which the haughtiness,
or perhaps the *diffidence* of Bishop Laud would not accept; a
symptom of policy more than of grace, not to trust a reconciled
enemy.—HACKET, *Life of Archbishop Williams*, pt. ii. p. 86.

It was far the best course to stand *diffidently* against each
other, with their thoughts in battle array.—HOBBES, *Thucydides*,
b. iii. c. 83.

DIGEST. Scholars of the seventeenth century often
employ a word of their own language in the same latitude which its equivalent possessed in the Greek or

the Latin ; as though it entered into all the rights of its equivalent, and corresponded with it on all points, because it corresponded in one. Thus 'coctus' meaning 'digested,' why should not 'digested' mean all which 'coctus' meant? but one of the meanings of 'coctus' is 'ripened ; ' 'digested' therefore might be employed in the same sense.

Repentance is like the sun; it produces rich spices in Arabia, it *digests* the American gold, and melts the snows from the Riphæan mountains.—J. TAYLOR, *Doctrine and Practice of Repentance*, ch. 10, § 8.

Splendid fires, aromatic spices, rich wines, and well-*digested* fruits.—Id. *Discourse of Friendship*.

DISABLE. Our ancestors felt that to injure the character of another was the most effectual way of disabling him ; and out of a sense of this they often used 'to disable' in the sense of to disparage, to speak slightingly of.

Farewell, mounsieur traveller. Look, you lisp, and wear strange suits ; *disable* all the benefits of your own country.— SHAKESPEARE, *As you like it*, act iv. sc. 1.

If affection lead a man to favour the less worthy in desert, let him do it without depraving or *disabling* the better deserver.— BACON, *Essays*, 49.

DISCOURSE. It is very characteristic of the slight acquaintance with our elder literature—the most obvious source for elucidating Shakespeare's text— which was possessed by many of his commentators down to a late day, that the phrase 'discourse of reason,' which he puts into Hamlet's mouth, should have perplexed them so greatly. Gifford, a pitiless animadverter on the real or imaginary mistakes of others, and who tramples upon Warburton for attempting to explain this phrase as though Shakespeare could have ever written it, declares '"discourse *of* reason" is so poor and perplexed a phrase that I should dismiss it at once for what I believe to be his genuine language;' and then proceeds to suggest the obvious but erroneous correction 'discourse *and* reason' (see his *Massinger*, vol. i. p. 148) ; while yet if there be a phrase of continual recurrence among the writers of our Elizabethan age and down to Milton, it is this. I have little doubt that it occurs fifty times in Holland's translation of Plutarch's *Moralia*. What our fathers intended by 'discourse' and 'discourse of reason,' the following passages will abundantly declare.

There is not so great difference and distance between beast and beast, as there is odds in the matter of wisdom, *discourse* of reason, and use of memory between man and man.—HOLLAND, *Plutarch's Morals*, p. 570; cf. pp. 313, 566, 570, 752, 955, 966, 977, 980.

If you mean, by *discourse*, right reason, grounded on Divine Revelation and common notions, written by God in the hearts of all men, and deducing, according to the never-failing rules of logic, consequent deductions from them ; if this be it which you mean by *discourse*, it is very meet and reasonable and necessary that men, as in all their actions, so especially in that of greatest importance, the choice of their way to happiness, should be left unto it.—CHILLINGWORTH, *The Religion of Protestants*, Preface.

As the intuitive knowledge is more perfect than that which insinuates itself into the soul gradually by *discourse*, so more beautiful the prospect of that building which is all visible at one view than what discovers itself to the sight by parcels and degrees.—FULLER, *Worthies of England, Canterbury*.

> Whence the soul
> Reason receives, and reason is her being,
> Discursive or intuitive ; *discourse*
> Is oftest yours, the latter most is ours.
> MILTON, *Paradise Lost*, b.

You, being by nature given to melancholic *discoursing*, do easilier yield to such imaginations.—NORTH, *Plutarch's Lives*, p. 830.

> The other gods, and knights-at-arms, all slept, but only Jove
> Sweet slumber seized not; he *discoursed* how best he might approve
> His vow made for Achilles' grace.
>
> CHAPMAN, *Homer's Iliad*, b. ii.

DISEASE. Our present limitation of 'disease' is a very natural one, seeing that nothing so effectually wars against ease as a sick and suffering condition of body. Still the limitation is modern, and by 'disease' was once meant any *malease*, distress, or discomfort whatever.

Wo to hem that ben with child, and nurishen in tho daies, for a greet *disese* [pressura magna, Vulg.] schal be on the erthe, and wrathe to this peple.—*Luke* xxi. 23. WICLIF.

Thy daughter is dead; why *diseasest* thou the master any further?—*Mark* v. 35. TYNDALE.

This is now the fourteenth day they [the Cardinals] have been in the Conclave, with such pain and *disease* that your grace would marvel that such men as they would suffer it.—*State Papers* (*Letter to Wolsey from his Agent at Rome*), vol. vi. p. 182.

> His double burden did him sore *disease*.
>
> SPENSER, *Fairy Queen*, ii. 2, 12.

DISMAL. Minshew's derivation of 'dismal,' that it is 'dies malus,' the unlucky, ill-omened day, is exactly one of those plausible etymologies to which one learns after a while to give no credit. Yet there can be no doubt that our fathers so understood the word, and that this assumed etymology often over-rules their usage of it.

Why should we then be bold to call them evil, infortunate, and *dismal* days? If God rule our doings continually, why

shall they not prosper on those days as well as on other?—
PILKINGTON, *Exposition on Aggeus*, c. I.

Then began they to reason and debate about the *dismal* days
[tum de diebus *religiosis* agitari cœptum]. And the fifteenth
day before the Kalends of August, so notorious for a twofold
loss and overthrow, they set this unlucky mark upon it, that it
should be reputed unmeet and unconvenient for any business,
as well public as private.—HOLLAND, *Livy*, p. 217.

The particular calendars, wherein their [the Jews'] good or
dismal days are distinguished, according to the diversity of their
ways, we find, Leviticus 26.—JACKSON, *The Eternal Truth of
Scriptures*, b. i. c. 22.

DISOBLIGE. Release from obligation lies at the
root of all uses, present and past, of this word; but it
was formerly more the release from an oath or a duty,
and now rather from the slighter debts of social life,
to which kindness and courtesy on the part of another
would have held us bound or 'obliged;' while the
contraries to these are 'disobliging.'

He did not think that Act of Uniformity could *disoblige* them
[the Non-Conformists] from the exercise of their office.—BATES,
Mr. Richard Baxter's Funeral Sermon.

Many that are imprisoned for debt, think themselves *disobliged* from payment.—J. TAYLOR, *Holy Dying*, c. 5, § 3.

He hath a very great obligation to do that and more; and he
can noways be *disobliged*, but by the care of his natural relations.
—Id., *Measures and Offices of Friendship*.

DITTY. The 'ditty' was once the words of a song
as distinguished from the musical accompaniment.

They fell to challenge and defy one another, whereupon he
commanded the musician Eraton to sing unto the harp, who
began his song on this wise out of the works of Hesiodus—

> Of quarrel and contention
> There were as then more sorts than one;

for which I commended him in that he knew how to apply the *ditty* of his song so well unto the present time.—HOLLAND, *Plutarch's Morals*, p. 786.

So that, although we lay altogether aside the consideration of *ditty* or matter, the very harmony of sounds being framed in due sort, and carried by the ear to the spiritual faculties of the soul, is by a native puissance and efficacy greatly available to bring to a perfect temper whatsoever is there troubled.— HOOKER, *Ecclesiastical Polity*, b. v. c. 38.

DOCUMENT. Now used only of the *material*, and not, as once, of the *moral* proof, evidence, or means of instruction.

They were forthwith stoned to death, as a *document* unto others.—Sir W. RALEIGH, *History of the World*, b. v. c. 2, § 3.

This strange dejection of these three great apostles at so mild and gentle a voice [Mat. xvii. 6], gives us a remarkable *document* or grounded observation of the truth of that saying of St. Paul, Flesh and blood cannot inherit the kingdom of God.— JACKSON, *Of the Primæval State of Man*, b. ii. c. 12.

DOLE. This and 'deal' are one and the same word, and answer to the German 'Theil,' a part or portion. It has now always the subaudition of a *scanty* portion, as 'to dole' is to deal scantily and reluctantly forth ('pittance' has acquired the same); but Sanderson's use of 'dole' is instructive, as show-ing that 'distribution or division' is all which once lay in the word.

There are certain common graces of illumination, and those indeed are given by *dole*, knowledge to one, to another tongues, to another healings; but it is nothing so with the special graces of sanctification. There is no distribution or division here; either all or none.—SANDERSON, *Sermons*, 1671, vol. ii. p. 247.

DRAUGHT. Many 'draughts' we still acknowledge, but not the 'draught' or drawing of a bow.

A large *draught* up to his eare
He drew, and with an arrow ground
Sharpe and new, the queene a wound
He gave.

CHAUCER, *Dreame.*

Then spake another proud one, Would to heaven
I might at will get gold till he hath given
That bow his *draught.*

CHAPMAN, *The Odysseis of Homer,* b. **xxi.** l. 533.

DREADFUL. Now that which *causes* dread, but
once that which *felt* it. See ' Frightful,' ' Hateful.

Forsothe the Lord shall gyve to thee there a *dreedful* herte
and faylinge eyen.—*Deut.* xxviii. 65. WICLIF.

And to a grove faste ther beside
With *dredful* foot than stalketh Palamon.

CHAUCER, *The Knightes Tale.*

All mankind lo ! that *dreadful* is to die,
Thou dost constrain long death to learn by thee.

JASPER HEYWOOD, *Translation of Seneca's Hercules Furens.*

Thou art so set, as thou' hast no cause to be
Jealous, or *dreadful* of disloyalty.

DANIEL, *Panegyric to the King.*

DREARY, ⎫ This word has slightly shifted its
DREARINESS. ⎭ meaning. In our earlier English it was
used exactly as ' traurig,' (the same word, as I need
not say), in German is now, to designate the heavy
at once of countenance and of heart; very much the
σκυθρωπός of the Greeks, though not admitting the
subaudition of anger, which in that word is often
contained.

And the king seide to me, Whi is thi chere *dreri,* sithen I
see thee not sick ?—2 *Esdras* ii. 2. WICLIF.

Bowe down to the pore thin ere withoute *dreryness* [sine tris-
titiâ, Vulg.].—*Ecclus.* iv. 8. WICLIF.

Now es a man light, now es he hevy,
Now es he blithe, now es he *drery*.
RICHARD ROLLE DE HAMPOLE, *Prick of Conscience*, 1454.

DRENCH. As ' to *fell* ' is to make to *fall*, and ' to *lay* ' to make to *lie*, so ' to *drench* ' is to make to *drink*, though with a sense now very short of ' to drown; ' but ' drench' and ' drown,' though desynonymized in our later English, were once perfectly adequate to one another.

He is *drenched* in the flod,
Abouten his hals an anker god.
Havelok the Dane.

They that wolen be maad riche, fallen in to temptacioun, and in to snare of the devil, and in to many unprofitable desiris and noyous, which *drenchen* men in to deth and perdicioun.—1 *Tim.* vi. 9. WICLIF.

Well may men know it was no wight but he
That kept the peple Ebraike fro *drenching*,
With drye feet throughout the see passing.
CHAUCER, *The Man of Lawes Tale.*

DRIFT. A drove of sheep or cattle was once a ' drift; ' so too the act of driving.

Hoc armentum, Anglice, a *dryfte*.—*National Antiquities*, vol. i. p. 279.

By reason of the foulness and deepness of the way divers of the said sheep died in driving; partly for lack of meat and feeding, but especially by mean of the said unreasonable *drift* the said sheep are utterly perished.—*Trevelyan Papers*, p. 130.

And Anton Shiel he loves me not,
For I gat twa *drifts* of his sheep ;
The great Earl of Whitfield he loves me not,
For nae gear fra me he could keep.
Scotch Ballad.

DUKE. One of Shakespeare's commentators charges him with an anachronism, the incongruous transfer of

a modern title to an ancient condition of society, when
he styles Theseus '*Duke* of Athens.' It would be of
very little consequence if the charge was a true one;
but it is not, as his English Bible might have sufficiently taught him; *Gen.* xxxvi. 15–18. 'Duke' has
indeed since Shakespeare's time become that which
this objector supposed it to have been always; but all
were 'dukes' once who were 'duces,' captains and
leaders of their people.

He [St. Peter] techith christen men to be suget to kyngis and
dukis, and to ech man for God.—WICLIF, *Prologe on the first
Pistel of Peter.*

Hannibal, *duke* of Carthage.—Sir T. ELYOT, *The Governor,*
b. i. c. 10.

> These were the *dukes* and princes of avail,
> That came from Greece.
>
> CHAPMAN, *Homer's Iliad,* b. ii.

DUNCE. I have sought elsewhere (*Study of Words,*
14th edit. p. 131) to trace at some length the curious
history of this word. Sufficient here to say that Duns
Scotus, whom Hooker styles 'the wittiest of the
school divines,' has given us this name, which now
ascribes hopeless ignorance, invincible stupidity, to
him on whom it is affixed. The course by which
this came to pass was as follows. When at the Reformation and Revival of Learning the works of the
Schoolmen fell into extreme disfavour, alike with the
Reformers and with the votaries of the new learning,
Duns, a standard-bearer among those, was so often
referred to with scorn and contempt by these, that
his name gradually became that byeword which it
since has been. See the quotation from Stanyhurst,
s. v. 'Trivial.'

Remember ye not how within this thirty years, and far less, and yet dureth unto this day, the old barking curs, *Dunce's* disciples, and like draff called Scotists, the children of darkness, raged in every pulpit against Greek, Latin, and Hebrew?—
TYNDALE, *Works*, 1575, p. 278.

We have set *Dunce* in Bocardo and have utterly banished him Oxford for ever with all his blind glosses. . . . The second time we came to New College after we had declared your injunctions, we found all the great Quadrant Court full of the leaves of *Dunce*, the wind blowing them in every corner.—*Wood's Annals*, A.D. 1535, 62.

What *Dunce* or Sorbonist cannot maintain a paradox?—
G. HARVEY, *Pierce's Supererogation*, p. 159.

As for terms of honesty or civility, they are gibberish unto him, and he a Jewish Rabbin or a Latin *dunce* with him that useth any such form of monstrous terms.—Id. *Ib.* p. 175.

> *Maud.* Is this your tutor?
> *Tutor.*   Yes surely, lady;
> I am the man that brought him in league with logic,
> And read the *Dunces* to him.
>   MIDDLETON, *A Chaste Maid in Cheapside*, act iii. sc. 1.

DUTCH,   ⎫ Till late in the seventeenth century
DUTCHMAN.⎭ 'Dutch' ('deutsch' or 'teutsch,' 'theotiscus') meant generally 'German,' and a 'Dutchman' a native of Germany, while what we now term a Dutchman was then a Hollander. In America this with so many other old usages is retained, and Germans are now often called 'Dutchmen' there.

Though the root of the English language be *Dutch*, yet she may be said to have been inoculated afterwards upon a French stock.—HOWELL, *Lexicon Tetraglotton*, Preface.

Germany is slandered to have sent none to this war [the Crusades] at this first voyage; and that other pilgrims, passing through that country, were mocked by the *Dutch*, and called fools for their pains.—FULLER, *The Holy War*, b. i. c. 13.

At the same time began the *Teutonic* Order, consisting only of *Dutchmen*, well descended.—Id. *Ib.* b. ii. c. 16.

EAGER,⎫ The physical and literal sense of
EAGERNESS.⎭ 'eager,' that is, sharp or acrid (aigre, acris), has quite departed from the word. It occasionally retained this, long after it was employed in the secondary meaning which is its only one at present.

> She was like thing for hunger dead,
> That lad her life only by bread
> Kneden with eisell * strong and *egre*.
> CHAUCER, *Romaunt of the Rose*, 145–147.

Bees have this property by nature to find and suck the mildest and best honey out of the sharpest and most *eager* flowers.—HOLLAND, *Plutarch's Morals*, p. 43.

> Now on the *eager* razor's edge for life or death we stand.
> CHAPMAN, *Homer's Iliad*, b. x.

Asproso, full of sourness or *eagerness*.—FLORIO, *New World of Words*.

EBB. Nothing 'ebbs,' unless it be figuratively, except water now. But 'ebb,' oftenest an adjective, was continually used in our earlier English with a general meaning of shallow. There is still a Lancashire proverb, 'Cross the stream where it is *ebbest*.'

Orpiment, a mineral digged out of the ground in Syria, where it lieth very *ebb*.—HOLLAND, *Pliny*, vol. ii. p. 469.

This you may observe ordinarily in stones, that those parts and sides which lie covered deeper within the ground be more frim and tender, as being preserved by heat, than those outward faces which lie *ebb*, or above the earth. —Id., *Plutarch's Morals*, p. 747.

It is all one whether I be drowned in the *ebber* shore, or in

---

* Vinegar.

the midst of the deep sea.—Bishop HALL, *Meditations and Vows*, cent. ii.

ECSTASY. We still say of madmen that they are *besides themselves*; but 'ecstasy,' or a standing out of oneself, is no longer used as an equivalent to madness.

> This is the very coinage of your brain ;
> This bodiless creation *ecstasy*
> Is very cunning in.
>> SHAKESPEARE, *Hamlet*, act iii. sc. 4.

EDIFY. 'From the Christian Church being called the temple or house of God, this word acquired a metaphorical and spiritual meaning, and is applied in the N. T. and in modern language to mental or spiritual advancement. Old English writers used it in its original sense of *build*.' (*Bible Word Book*).

> I shall overturne this temple, and adoun throwe it,
> And in thre daies after *edifie* it new.
>> *Piers Ploughman*, 11068.

And the Lord God *edifiede* the rib, the which he toke of Adam, into a woman.—*Gen.* ii. 22. WICLIF.

What pleasure and also utility is to a man which intendeth to *edify*, himself to express the figure of the work that he purposeth, according as he hath conceived it in his own fantasy. —ELYOT, *The Governor*, b. i. c. 8.

> A little wide
> There was a holy temple *edified*.
>> SPENSER, *Fairy Queen*, i. 1. 34.

EGREGIOUS. This has always now an ironical sub-audition, which it was very far from having of old.

> *Egregious* viceroys of these eastern parts !
>> MARLOWE, *Tamburlaine the Great*, part i. act. i. sc. 1.

G

It may be denied that bishops were our first reformers, for Wickliffe was before them, and his *egregious* labours are not to be neglected.—MILTON, *Animadversions upon the Remonstrants' Defence.*

ELDER. The German 'eltern' still signifies parents ; as 'elders' did once with us, though now it has quite let this meaning go.

And his disciples axeden hym, Maister, what sinned, this man or the *eldirs* that he schulde be borun blynde ?—*John* ix. 2. WICLIF.

And his *elders* went to Jerusalem every year at the feast of Easter.—*Luke* ii. 41. COVERDALE.

Disobedient to their *elders* [γονεῦσιν ἀπειθεῖς].—*Rom.* i. 30. COVERDALE.

> So, or much like, our rebel *elders* driven
> For aye from Eden, earthly type of heaven,
> Lie languishing near Tigris' grassy side.
> > SYLVESTER, *Dubartas, The Handycrafts.*

ELEMENT. The air, as that among the four elements which is most present everywhere, was frequently 'the element' in our earlier literature.

When Pompey saw the dust in the *element*, and conjectured the flying of his horsemen, what mind he was of then it was hard to say.—NORTH, *Plutarch's Lives*, p. 553.

The face therefore of the *element* you have skill to discern, and the signs of times can you not ?—*Matt.* xvi. 3. Rheims.

> There is no stir or walking in the streets,
> And the complexion of the *element*
> In favour is like the work we have in hand,
> Most bloody, fiery, and most terrible.
> > SHAKESPEARE, *Julius Cæsar*, act i. sc. 3.

> The *element* itself, till seven years' heat,
> Shall not behold her face at ample view.
> > Id., *Twelfth Night*, act. i. sc. 1.

I took it for a faery vision
Of some gay creatures of the *element*,
That in the colours of the rainbow live,
And play in the plighted clouds.

MILTON, *Comus*, 298.

ELEPHANT. I have little doubt that ' elephant ' as
an equivalent for ivory is a Grecism not peculiar to
Chapman, in whose translations from Homer it
several times occurs; but I cannot adduce an example from any other.

I did last afford
The varied ornament, which showed no want
Of silver, gold, and polished *elephant*.

CHAPMAN, *The Odysseis of Homer*, b. xxiii. l. 306.

ELEVATE. There are two intentions with which
anything may be lifted from the place which it occupies; either with that of setting it in a more con-
spicuous position; or else of removing it out of the
way, or, figuratively, of withdrawing all importance
and significance from it. We employ ' to elevate '
now in the former intention; our ancestors for the
most part, especially those whose style was influenced
by their Latin studies, in the latter.

Withal, he forgat not to *elevate* as much as he could the fame
of the foresaid unhappy field fought, saying, That if all had been
true, there would have been messengers coming thick one after
another upon their flight to bring fresh tidings still thereof.—
HOLLAND, *Livy*, p. 1199.

Audience he had with great assent and applause; not more
for *elevating* the fault and trespass of the common people, than
for laying the weight upon those that were the authors culpable.
—Id. *Ib.* p. 1207.

Tully in his oration Pro Flacco, to *elevate* or lessen that conceit which many Romans had of the nation of the Jews, objects
little less unto them than our Saviour in this place doth, to wit

that they were in bondage to the Romans.—JACKSON, *Of the Primeval Estate of Man*, b. x. c. 14.

EMBEZZLE. A man can now only ' embezzle ' another man's property ; he might once ' embezzle ' his own. Thus, while we might now say that the Unjust Steward ' embezzled ' his lord's goods (*Luke* xvi. 1), we could not say that the Prodigal Son ' embezzled ' the portion which he had received from his father, and which had thus become his own (*Luke* xv. 13) ; but the one would have been as free to our early writers as the other. There is a verb, ' to imbecile,' used by Jeremy Taylor and others, which is sometimes confused in meaning with this.

Mr. Hackluit died, leaving a fair estate to an unthrift son, who *embezzled* it.—FULLER, *Worthies of England, Herefordshire.*

The collection of these various readings [is] a testimony even of the faithfulness of these later ages of the Church, and of the high reverence they had of these records, in that they would not so much as *embesell* the various readings of them, but keep them still on foot for the prudent to judge of.—H. MORE, *Grand Mystery of Godliness*, b. vii. c. 11.

If we are ambitious of having a property in somewhat, or affect to call any thing our own, 'tis only by nobly giving that we can accomplish our desire; that will certainly appropriate our goods to our use and benefit; but from basely keeping or vainly *embezzling* them, they become not our possession and enjoyment, but our theft and our bane.—BARROW, *The Duty and Reward of Bounty to the Poor.*

Be not *prodigal* of your time on earth, which is so little in your power. 'Tis so precious a thing that it is to be redeemed; 'tis therefore too precious to be *embezzled* and trifled away.— HOWE, *The Redeemer's Dominion over the Invisible World.*

EMULATION. South in one of his sermons has said excellently well, ' We ought by all means to note the

difference between envy and emulation ; which latter
is a brave and noble thing, and quite of another
nature, as consisting only in a generous imitation of
something excellent ; and that such an imitation as
scorns to fall short of its copy, but strives if possible
to outdo it. The emulator is impatient of a superior,
not by depressing or maligning another, but by per-
fecting himself. So that while that sottish thing
envy sometimes fills the whole soul, as a great fog
does the air ; this on the contrary inspires it with a
new life and vigour, whets and stirs up all the powers
of it to action.' But ' emulation,' though sometimes
used by our early writers in this nobler sense, was by
no means always so; it was often an exact equivalent
to envy.

> So every step,
> Exampled by the first step that is sick
> Of his superior, grows to an envious fever
> Of pale and bloodless *emulation.*
>> SHAKESPEARE, *Troilus and Cressida*, act i. sc. 3.

And the patriarchs through *emulation* [moved with *envy*, E.V.]
sold Joseph into Egypt.—*Acts* vii. 9. Rheims.

ENDEAVOUR. This, connected with ' devoir,' is
used as a reflexive verb in our version of the New
Testament and in the Prayer Book. Signifying now
no more than to try, it signified once to bend all our
energies, not to the attempt at fulfilling, but to the
actual fulfilment of a duty.

This is called in Scripture ' a just man,' that *endeavoureth*
himself to leave all wickedness.—LATIMER, *Sermons*, p. 340.

One thing I do, I forget that which is behind, and *endevour*
myself unto that which is before.—*Phil.* iii. 13. Geneva.

ENGRAVE.   This word has now quite lost the sense of 'to bury,' which it once possessed,   See 'Grave.'

> So both agree their bodies to *engrave*:
> The great earth's womb they open to the sky ; . . .
> They lay therein their corses tenderly.
>> SPENSER, *Fairy Queen*, ii. 1, 60.

> And now with happy wish he closely craved
> For ever to be dead, to be so sweet *ingraved*.
>> *Britain's Ida.*

> Thou death of death, oh! in thy death *engrave* me.
>> PHINEAS FLETCHER, *Poetical Miscellanies.*

ENJOY.   Not, when Wiclif wrote, nor till some time later, distinguished from 'rejoice,' which see.

> And joye and gladinge schal be to thee, and manye schulen *enjoye* in his natyvite.—*Luke* i. 14.   WICLIF.

ENORMOUS,⎫ Now only applied to that which is
ENORMITY. ⎬ irregular *in excess*, in this way tran-
scending the established norm or rule.   But departure from rule or irregularity in *any* direction might
be characterized as 'enormous' once.

> O great corrector of *enormous* times,
> Shaker of o'er-rank states, thou grand decider
> Of dusty and old titles, that heal'st with blood
> The earth when it is sick.
>> BEAUMONT AND FLETCHER, *The Two Noble*
>> *Kinsmen*, act v. sc. 1.

> Wild above rule or art, *enormous* bliss.
>> MILTON, *Paradise Lost*, b. v.

> Pyramids, arches, obelisks, were but the *irregularities* of vain-glory, and wild *enormities* of ancient magnanimity,—Sir T. BROWNE, *Hydriotaphia.*

ENSURE.   None of our Dictionaries, as far as I can observe, have taken notice of an old use of this word,

namely, to betroth, and thus to make *sure* the future
husband and wife to each other. See 'Assure,'
'Sure.'

After his mother Mary was *ensured* to Joseph, before they
were coupled together, it was perceived she was with child.—
Matt. i. 18. Sir JOHN CHEKE.

Albeit that she was by the king's mother and many other put
in good comfort to affirm that she was *ensured* unto the king;
yet when she was solemnly sworn to say the truth, she confessed
that they were never *ensured*.—Sir T. MORE, *History of King
Richard III.*

EPICURE. Now applied only to those who devote
themselves, yet with a certain elegance and refinement, to the pleasures of the table. We may trace
two earlier stages in its meaning. By Lord Bacon
and others, the followers of Epicurus, whom we
should call Epicureans, are often called 'Epicures,'
after the name of the founder of their sect. From
them it was transferred to all who were, like them,
deniers of a divine providence; and this is the
common use of it by our elder divines. But inasmuch as those who have persuaded themselves that
there is nothing above them, will seek their good,
since men must seek it somewhere, in the things
beneath them, in sensual delights, the name has been
transferred, by that true moral instinct which is continually at work in speech, from the philosophical
speculative atheist to the human swine, for whom
the world is but a feeding-trough.

So the *Epicures* say of the Stoics' felicity placed in virtue, that
it is like the felicity of a player, who if he were left of his
auditors and their applause, he would straight be out of heart
and countenance.—BACON, *Colours of Good and Evil*, 3.

Aristotle is altogether an *Epicure*; he holdeth that God careth nothing for human creatures; he allegeth God ruleth the world like as a sleepy maid rocketh a child.—LUTHER, *Table-Talk*, c. 73.

The *Epicure* grants there is a God, but denies his providence. —SYDENHAM, *The Athenian Babbler*, 1627, p. 7.

EQUAL. The ethical sense of 'equal,' as fair, candid, just, has almost, if not altogether, departed from it.

> O my most *equal* hearers, if these deeds
> May pass with suffrance, what one citizen
> But owes the forfeit of his life, yea, fame,
> To him that dares traduce him?
>
> BEN JONSON, *The Fox*, act iv. sc. 2.

Hear now, O house of Israel; is not my way *equal*? are not your ways unequal? *Ezek.* xviii. 25. Authorized Version.

EQUIVOCAL,
EQUIVOCALLY,
EQUIVOCATION.
The calling two or more different *things* by one and the same *name* (æque vocare) is the source of almost all error in human discourse. He who wishes to throw dust in the eyes of an opponent, to hinder his arriving at the real facts of a case, will often have recourse to this artifice, and thus 'to equivocate' and 'equivocation' have attained their present secondary meaning, very different from their original, which was simply the naming of two or more different things by one and the same word.

This visible world is but a picture of the invisible, wherein, as in a portrait, things are not truly, but in *equivocal* shapes, and as they counterfeit some real substance in that invisible fabric. —Sir T. BROWNE, *Religio Medici.*

Which [courage and constancy] he that wanteth is no other than *equivocally* a gentleman, as an image or a carcass is a man. —BARROW, *Sermon on Industry in our several Callings.*

He [the good herald] knows when indeed the names are the same, though altered through variety of writing in various ages; and where the *equivocation* is untruly affected.—FULLER, *The Holy State*, b. ii. c. 22.

All words, being arbitrary signs, are ambiguous; and few disputers have the jealousy and skill which is necessary to discuss *equivocations*; and so take verbal differences for material.— BAXTER, *Catholic Theology*, Preface.

ESSAY. There is no particular modesty now in calling a treatise or dissertation an ' essay;' but from many passages it is plain that there was so once; which indeed is only agreeable to the proper meaning of the word, an ' essay ' being a trial, proof, specimen, taste of a thing, rather than the very and completed thing itself.

To write just treatises requireth leisure in the writer, and leisure in the reader; and therefore are not so fit neither in regard of your highness' princely affairs, nor in regard of my continual service; which is the cause which hath made me choose to write certain brief notes, set down rather significantly than curiously, which I have called *Essays*. The word is late, but the thing is ancient.—BACON, *Intended Dedication of his Essays to Prince Henry*.

> Yet modestly he does his work survey,
> And calls a finished poem an *essay*.
> DRYDEN, *Epistle* 5, *To the Earl of Roscommon*.

EXEMPLARY. A certain vagueness in our use of ' exemplary ' makes it for us little more than a loose synonym for excellent. We plainly often forget that ' exemplary ' is strictly that which serves, or might serve for an exemplar to others, while only through keeping this distinctly before us will passages like the following yield their exact meaning to us.

We are not of opinion, therefore, as some are, that nature in

working hath before her certain *exemplary* draughts or patterns.
—HOOKER, *Ecclesiastical Polity*, b. i. c. 3.

When the English, at the Spanish fleet's approach in eighty-eight [1588] drew their ships out of Plymouth haven, the Lord Admiral Howard himself towed a cable, the least joint of whose *exemplary* hand drew more than twenty men besides.—FULLER, *The Holy State*, b. iv. c. 17.

EXEMPLIFY. The use of 'exemplify' in the sense of the Greek παραδειγματίζειν (*Matt.* i. 19) has now passed away. Observe also in the passage quoted the curious use of 'traduce.'

He is a just and jealous God, not sparing to *exemplify* and traduce his best servants [*i.e.* when they sin], that their blur and penalty might scare all from venturing.—ROGERS, *Matrimonial Honour*, p. 337.

EXPLODE. All our present uses of 'explode,' whether literal or figurative, have reference to bursting, and to bursting with noise; and it is for the most part forgotten that these are all secondary and derived; that 'to explode,' originally an active verb, means to drive off the stage with loud clappings of the hands: and that when one of our early writers speaks of an 'exploded' heresy, or an 'exploded' opinion, his image is not drawn from something which, having burst, has so perished; but he would imply that it has been contemptuously driven off from the world's stage— the fact that 'explosion' in this earlier sense was with a great noise being the connecting link between that sense and our present.

A third sort *explode* this opinion as trespassing on Divine Providence.—FULLER, *The Holy War*, b. iii. c. 18.

A man may with more facility avoid him that circumvents by money than him that deceives with glosing terms, which made

Socrates so much abhor and *explode* them.—BURTON, *Anatomy of Melancholy; Democritus to the Reader.*

> Thus was the applause they meant
> Turned to *exploding* hiss, triumph to shame
> Cast on themselves by their own mouths.
>
> MILTON, *Paradise Lost*, x. 545.

Shall that man pass for a proficient in Christ's school, who would have been *exploded* in the school of Zeno or Epictetus?— SOUTH, *Sermons*, vol. i. p. 431.

EXTERMINATE, ⎱ This now signifies to destroy, to
EXTERMINATION. ⎰ abolish; but our fathers, more true to the etymology, understood by it to drive men out of and beyond their own borders.

Most things do either associate and draw near to themselves the like, and do also drive away, chase, and *exterminate* their contraries.—BACON, *Colours of Good and Evil*, 7.

We believe it to be the general interest of us all, as much as in us lies, with our common aid and succour to relieve our *exterminated* and indigent brethren.—MILTON, *Letter written in Cromwell's name on occasion of the persecutions of the Vaudois.*

The state of the Jews was in that depression, in that conculcation, in that consternation, in that *extermination* in the captivity of Babylon.—DONNE, *Sermons*, 19.

FACETIOUS, ⎱ It is certainly not a little remark-
FACETIOUSNESS. ⎰ able that alike in Greek, Latin, and English, words expressive of witty festive conversation should have degenerated, though not all exactly in the same direction, and gradually acquired a worse signification than that with which they began; I mean εὐτραπελία, 'urbanitas,' and our own 'facetiousness;' this degeneracy of the words warning us how easily the thing itself degenerates; how sure it is to do so, to corrupt and spoil, if it be not seasoned with the only salt which will hinder this.

'Facetiousness' has already acquired the sense of buffoonery, of the making of ignoble mirth for others; there are plain indications that it will ere long acquire the sense of *indecent* buffoonery; while there was a time, as the examples given below will prove, when it could be ascribed in praise to high-bred ladies of the court and to grave prelates and divines.

He [Archbishop Williams] demonstrated that his mind was the lighter, because his friends were about him, and his *facetious* wit was true to him at those seasons, because his heart was true to his company.—HACKET, *Life of Archbishop Williams*, part ii. p. 32.

A grave man, yet without moroseness, as who would willingly contribute his shot of *facetiousness* on any just occasion.—FULLER, *Worthies of England, Oxfordshire.*

The king easily took notice of her [Anne Boleyn]; whether more captivated by the allurements of her beauty, or the *facetiousness* of her behaviour, it is hard to say.—HEYLIN, *History of Queen Mary*, Introduction.

FACT. This and 'act' or 'deed,' have been use-fully desynonymized. An 'act' or 'deed' implies now always a person as the actor or doer; but it is sufficient for a 'fact' that it exists, that it has been done, the author or doer of it falling altogether out of sight.

All the world is witnesse agaynst you, yea, and also your owne *factes* and deedes.—BARNES, *Works*, 1572, p. 251.

> But, when the furious fit was overpast,
> His cruel *facts* he often would repent.
>> SPENSER, *Fairy Queen*, i. iv. 34.

Icetes took but a few of them to serve his turn, as if he had been ashamed of his *fact*, and had used their friendship by stealth.—NORTH, *Plutarch's Lives*, 1656, p. 228.

FAIRY. In whatever latitude we may employ
'fairy' now, it is always restricted to the middle
beings of the *Gothic* mythology; being in no case applied, as it used to be, to the δαίμονες of classical
antiquity.

> Of the *fairy* Manto [daughter of Tiresias] I cannot affirm any
> thing of truth, whether she were a *fairy* or a prophetess.—Sir
> J. HARINGTON, *Orlando Furioso*, b. lxiii.

> So long as these wise *fairies* Μοῖρα and Λάχεσις, that is to
> say Portion and Partition, had the ordering of suppers, dinners,
> and great feasts, a man should never see any illiberal or me-
> chanical disorder.—HOLLAND, *Plutarch's Morals*, p. 679.

FAME. This is now generally applied to the
reputation derived from the report of great actions,
but was constantly used in our Authorized Version
(*Gen.* xlv. 16 ; 1 *Kin.* x. 7 ; *Jer.* vi. 24 ; *Mat.* ix. 26),
and in contemporary writings, as equivalent to report
alone.

> The occasion which Pharaoh took to murder all the Hebrew
> males was from a constant *fame* or prenotion that about this
> time there should a Hebrew male be born that should work
> wonders for the good of his people.—JACKSON, *Christ's Everlast-
> ing Priesthood*, b. x. c. xl.

FAMILY. It is not a good sign that the 'family'
has now ceased to include the servants ; but for a
long while the word retained the largeness of its
classical use, indeed it has only very recently lost it
altogether.

> The same care is to extend to all of our *family*, in their pro-
> portions, as to our children ; for as by S. Paul's reasoning the heir
> differs nothing from a servant while he is in minority, so a ser-
> vant should differ nothing from a child in the substantial part
> of the care.—J. TAYLOR, *Holy Living*, 3, 2.

He [Sir Matthew Hale] kept no greater a *family* than myself.—
BAXTER, *Life*, part 3, § 107.

A just master may have an unconscionable servant; and if he
have a numerous *family* and keep many, it is a rare thing if he
have not some bad.—SANDERSON, *Sermons*, 1671, vol. i. p. 115.

FASTIDIOUS. Persons are 'fastidious' now, as
feeling disgust; things, and indeed persons too, were
'fastidious' once, as occasioning disgust. The
word has shifted from an objective to a subjective
use. 'Fastidiosus' had both uses, but our modern
quite predominated; indeed the other is very rare.

That thing for the which children be oftentimes beaten, is to
them ever after *fastidious.*—Sir T. ELYOT, *The Governor*, b. i.
c. 9.

FEATURE. This, the Italian 'fattura,' is always
the part now of a larger whole, a 'feature' of the
landscape, the 'features' of the face; but there was
no such limitation once; anything *made*, any 'fattura,'
was a 'feature' once. 'Facies' in Latin, according to
Aulus Gellius, xiii. 29, underwent a not very dissimilar
change of meaning. In addition to the examples
which follow, see Spenser, *Fairy Queen*, iv. 2, 44;
iii. 9, 21.

> A body so harmoniously composed,
>   As if nature disclosed
> All her best symmetry in that one *feature.*
>   BEN JONSON, *The Forest*, xi.

We have not yet found them all [the scattered limbs of
Truth], nor ever shall do, till her Master's second coming; He
shall bring together every joint and member, and shall mould
them into an immortal *feature* of loveliness and perfection.—
MILTON, *Areopagitica.*

> So scented the grim *feature*, and upturned
> His nostril wide into the murky air.
> > Id., *Paradise Lost*, x. 278.

But this young *feature* [a commentary on Scripture which Archbishop Williams had planned], like an imperfect embryo, was mortified in the womb by Star-chamber vexations.—HACKET, *Life of Archbishop Williams*, part ii. p. 40.

FEMININE. The distinction between 'feminine' and 'effeminate,' that the first is 'womanly,' the second 'womanish,' the first what becomes a woman, and may under certain limitations without reproach be affirmed of a man, while the second is that which under all circumstances dishonours a man, as 'mannish' would dishonour a woman, is of comparatively modern growth. Neither could it now be used as an antithesis of 'male' as by Milton (*Paradise Lost*, i. 423) it is.

> Till at the last God of veray right
> Displeased was with his condiciouns,
> By cause he [Sardanapalus] was in every mannes sight
> So *femynyne* in his affectiouns.
> > LYDGATE, *Poem against Idleness.*

But Ninias being esteemed no man of war at all, but altogether *feminine*, and subject to ease and delicacy, there is no probability in that opinion.—Sir W. RALEIGH, *History of the World*, b. ii. c. 1, § 1.

Commodus, the wanton and *feminine* son of wise Antoninus, gave a check to the great name of his father.—J. TAYLOR, *Apples of Sodom.*

FIRMAMENT. We now use 'firmament' only for that portion of the sky on all sides visible above the horizon, having gotten this application of the word from the Vulgate (*Gen.* i. 6), or at any rate from the

Church Latin ('*firmamentum* cæleste,' Tertullian, *De Bapt.* 3), as that had derived it from the Septuagint. This by στερέωμα had sought to express the firmness and stability of the sky-tent, which phenomenally (and Scripture for the most part speaks phenomenally), is drawn over the earth; and to reproduce the force of the original Hebrew word,—in which, however, there is rather the notion of expansion than of firmness (see H. More, *Defence of Cabbala,* p. 60). But besides this use of 'firmament,' totally strange to the classical 'firmamentum,' being derived to us from the ecclesiastical employment of the word, there is also an occasional use of it by the scholarly writers of the seventeenth century in the original classical sense, as that which makes strong or confirms.

I thought it good to make a strong head or bank to rule and guide the course of the waters; by setting down this position or *firmament*, namely, that all knowledge is to be limited by religion, and to be referred to use and action.—BACON, *Of the Interpretation of Nature.*

Religion is the ligature of all communities, and the *firmament* of laws.—J. TAYLOR, *Ductor Dubitantium,* iii. 3, 8.

FLICKER.   This, sometimes written 'flacker,' and 'flutter' are thoroughly desynonymized now; a flame 'flickers,' a bird 'flutters;' but it was not so once.

But being made a swan,
With snowy feathers in the air to *flicker* he began.
GOLDING, *Ovid's Metamorphosis,* b. vii.

And the Cherubins *flackered* with their wings, and lift themselves up from the earth.—*Ezek.* x. 19. COVERDALE.

FLIRT.   Much graver charges were implied once in this name than are at the present, as will be sufficiently clear from the quotations which follow.

For why may not the mother be naught, a peevish, drunken *flurt*, a waspish choleric slut, a crazed piece, a fool, as soon as the nurse ?—BURTON, *Anatomy of Melancholy*, part. i. sect. 2.

Gadrouillette, *f.* A minx, giggle, *flirt*, callet, gixie ; (a feigned word, applicable to any such cattell).—COTGRAVE, *A French and English Dictionary*, 1660.

FONDLING. 'Fond' retains to this day, at least in poetry, not seldom the sense of foolish ; but a 'fondling' is no longer a fool.

An epicure hath some reason to allege, an extortioner is a man of wisdom, and acteth prudently in comparison to him ; but this *fondling* [the profane swearer] offendeth heaven and abandoneth happiness he knoweth not why or for what.—BARROW, *Sermon* 15.

We have many such *fondlings*, that are their wives' packhorses and slaves.—BURTON, *Anatomy of Melancholy*, part iii. sect. 3.

FORGETFUL. Exactly the converse of what has happened to 'dreadful' and 'frightful' (which see) has befallen 'forgetful.'

It may be the *forgetful* wine begot
Some sudden blow, and thereupon this challenge.
WEBSTER, *A Cure for a Cuckold*, act iii. sc. 1.

If the sleepy drench
Of that *forgetful* lake benumb not still.
MILTON, *Paradise Lost*, b. ii. l. 73.

FORLORN,
FORLORN HOPE. } There are two points of difference between the past use of 'forlorn hope' and the present. The first, that it was seldom used,—I can recall no single example,—in that which is now its only application, namely, of those who, being the first to mount the breach, thus set their lives upon a desperate hazard ; but always of the

H

skirmishers and others thrown out in front of an army
about to engage. Here indeed the central notion of
the word may be said to have been the same as it is
now. These first come to hand-strokes with the
enemy; they bear the brunt of their onset; and there
may therefore seem less likelihood that they will escape
than those who come after. This is quite true, and
it comes remarkably out in my first quotation from
Holland; just as in a retreat they are the 'forlorn
hope' (*Swedish Intelligencer*, vol. i. p. 163), who
bring up the rear. But in passages innumerable this
of the greater hazard to which the 'forlorn hope' are
exposed, has quite disappeared, and the 'forlorn,' for
'hope' is often omitted, are simply that part of the
army which, being posted in the front, is first engaged. There can be no doubt that the phrase is an
importation from Germany, and that 'hope' is a corruption of 'Haufe,' heap, or crew. I find it first in
Gascoigne's *Fruits of War*, st. 74.

'The fearful are in the *forlorn* [see *Rev.* xxi. 8] of those
that march for hell.'—GURNALL, *The Christian in Complete
Armour*, c. 1.

'They [the Enniskillen horse] offered with spirit to make
always the *forlorn* of the army.'—DRYDEN (Scott's edition),
vol. vii. p. 303.

These [the Roman Velites] were loose troops, answerable in a
manner to those which we call now by a French name *Enfans
Perdues*, but when we use our own terms, *The Forlorn Hope.*—
Sir W. RALEIGH, *History of the World*, b. v. c. 3, § 8.

Before the main battle of the Carthaginians he sets the auxi-
liaries and aid-soldiers, a confused rabble and medley of all sorts
of nations, who, as the *forlorn hope*, bearing the furious heat of
the first brunt, might, if they did no other good, yet, with receiving many a wound in their bodies dull and turn the edge of
the enemy's sword.—HOLLAND, *Livy*, p. 765.

Upon them the light-armed *forlorn hope* [qui primi agminis erant] of archers and darters of the Roman host, which went before the battle to skirmish, charged forcibly with their shot.—Id., *Ib.* p. 641 ; cf. pp. 1149, 1150, 1195.

Christ's descent into hell was not ad prædicandum, to preach; useless, where his auditory was all the *forlorn hope.*—FULLER, *Worthies of England, Hampshire.*

FORMAL, ⎫
FORMALLY, ⎬ It has been observed already, *s. v.*
FORMALITY. ⎭ 'Common Sense,' that a vast number of our words have descended to us from abstruse sciences and speculations, we accepting them often in a total unconsciousness of the quarter from which they come. Another proof of this assertion is here; only, as it was metaphysics there, it is logic here which has given us the word. It is curious to trace the steps by which 'formality,' which meant in the language of the schools the essentiality, the innermost heart of a thing, that which gave it its form and shape, the 'forma formans,' should now mean something not merely so different, but so opposite.

> Be patient; for I will not let him stir,
> Till I have used the approved means I have,
> With wholesome syrups, drugs, and holy prayers
> To make of him a *formal* man again.
>   SHAKESPEARE, *Comedy of Errors*, act v. sc. 1.

Next day we behold our bride a *formal* wife.—FULLER, *Of the Clothes and Ornaments of the Jews*, § 6.

There are many graces required of us, whose material and *formal* part is repentance.—J. TAYLOR, *Doctrine and Practice of Repentance*, i. 3, 47.

It is not only as impious and irreligious a thing, but as senseless and as absurd a thing to deny that the Son of God hath redeemed the world, as to deny that God hath created the world; and he is as *formally* and as gloriously a martyr that dies for this article, The Son of God is come, as he that dies for this, There is a God.—DONNE, *Sermons*, 1640, p. 69.

According to the rule of the casuists, the *formality* of pro-digality is inordinateness of our laying out, or misbestowing on what we should not.—WHITLOCK, *Zootomia*, p. 497.

When the school makes pertinacy or obstinacy to be the *formality* of heresy, they say not true at all, unless it be meant the obstinacy of the will and choice ; and if they do, they speak impertinently and inartificially, this being but one of the causes that make error become heresy ; the adequate and perfect *for-mality* of heresy is whatsoever makes the error voluntary and vicious.—J. TAYLOR, *Liberty of Prophesying*, § 2, 10.

Strong and importunate persuasions have not the nature and *formality* of force ; but they have oftentimes the effect of it ; and he that solicits earnestly, sometimes determines as certainly as if he did force.—SOUTH, *Sermons*, 1744, vol. viii. p. 288.

FRANCE,   ⎫ We consider now, and consider
FRENCHMAN. ⎭ rightly, that there was properly no
' France ' before there were Franks ; and, speaking of the land or people before the Frankish occupation, we use Gaul, Gauls, and Gaulish ; just as we should not now speak of Cæsar's ' journey into *England*.' Our fathers had not these scruples (North, *Plutarch's Lives*).   See the quotation from Milton, *s. v.* ' Civil.'

When Cæsar saw his army prone to war,
And fates so bent, lest sloth and long delay
Might cross him, he withdrew his troops from *France*,
And in all quarters musters men for Rome.
                    MARLOWE, *First Book of Lucan*.

A *Frenchman* together with a *Frenchwoman*, likewise a Gre-cian man and woman, were let down alive in the beast-market into a vault under the ground, stoned all about.—HOLLAND, *Livy*, p. 467.

FRET.   This, the A.S. 'fretan,' the German 'fres-sen,' to eat, is with us restricted now, though once it

was otherwise, to the eating of the heart through care,
according to an image which we all can only too well
understand; and which has given the Pythagorean
' Cor ne edito,' the French 'devoré de chagrins.'

> Adam afterward ayeins his defence
> *Freet* of that fruyt.
>
> *Piers Ploughman*, 12469.

> He [Hercules] slew the cruel tirant Busirus,
> And made his hors to *fret* his flesh and bon.
>
> CHAUCER, *The Monk's Tale.*

> Thou makest his beauty to consume away, like as it were a
> moth *fretting* a garment.—*Ps.* xxxix. 12. Prayer Book Version.

FRIGHTFUL. Now always active, that which inspires fright; but formerly as often passive, that
which is, or is liable to be, frightened. See ' Dreadful,' ' Hateful.'

> The wild and *frightful* hĕrds,
> Not hearing other noise, but this of chattering birds,
> Feed fairly on the lawns.
>
> DRAYTON, *Polyolbion*, song 13.

FRIPPERY. Now such trumpery, such odds and
ends of cheap finery, as one might expect to meet at
an old-clothes shop; but in our early dramatists and
others of their time, the shop itself where old clothes
were by the ' fripper ' or broker scoured, ' interpo-
lated,' and presented anew for sale (officina vestium
tritarum, Skinner); nor had 'frippery' then the contemptuous subaudition of worthlessness in the objects
offered for sale which its present use would imply.
See Littré, *Dictionnaire*, s. v. *Friperie.*

> *Trinculo.* O worthy Stephano, look what a wardrobe here is for
> thee.
> *Caliban.* Let it alone, thou fool, it is but trash.
> *Trinculo.* O, ho, monster! we know what belongs to a *frippery.*
>
> SHAKESPEARE, *The Tempest*, act. iv. sc. 1.

Enter Luke, with shoes, garters, fans, and roses.
Gold. Here he comes, sweating all over,
    He shows like a walking *frippery*.
        MASSINGER, *The City Madam*, act i. sc. 1.

Hast thou foresworn all thy friends in the Old Jewry? or dost thou think us all Jews that inhabit there? Yet, if thou dost, come over, and but see our *frippery*. Change an old shirt for a whole smock with us.—BEN JONSON, *Every Man in his Humour*, act i. sc. 1.

FULSOME,   ⎫ I have seen it questioned whether
FULSOMENESS. ⎬ in the first syllable of 'fulsome' we
are to find 'foul' or 'full.' There should be no question on the matter; seeing that 'fulsome' is properly no more than 'full,' and then secondly that which by its fulness and overfulness produces first satiety, and then loathing and disgust. This meaning of 'fulsome' is still retained in our only present application of the word, namely to compliments and flattery, which by their grossness produce this effect on him who is their object; but the word had once many more applications than this. See the quotation from Pope, *s. v.* 'Bacchanal.'

His lean, pale, hoar, and withered corpse, grew *fulsome*, fair, and fresh.
        GOLDING, *Ovid's Metamorphosis*, b. vii.

The next is Doctrine, in whose lips there dwells
A spring of honey, sweeter than its name,
Honey which never *fulsome* is, yet *fills*
The widest souls.
        BEAUMONT, *Psyche*, b. xix. st. 210.

Making her soul to loathe dainty meat, or putting a surfeit and *fulsomeness* into all which she enjoys.—ROGERS, *Naaman the Syrian*, p. 32.

Chaste and modest as he [Persius] is esteemed, it cannot be denied but that in some places he is broad and *fulsome*. No decency is considered; no *fulsomeness* omitted.—DRYDEN, *Dedication of Translations from Juvenal.*

GARB. One of many words, all whose meaning has run to the surface. A man's dress was once only a portion, and a very insignificant portion, of his 'garb,' which included his whole outward presentment to other men ; now it is all.

> First, for your *garb*, it must be grave and serious,
> Very reserved and locked; not tell a secret
> On any terms, not to your father.
> > BEN JONSON, *The Fox*, act iv. sc. 1.

The greatest spirits, and those of the best and noblest breeding, are ever the most respective and obsequious in their *garb*, and the most observant and grateful in their language to all.—FELTHAM, *Resolves*, lxxv.

> Have thy observing eyes
> E'er marked the spider's *garb*, how close she lies
> Within her curious web, and by and by
> How quick she hastes to her entangled fly ?
> > QUARLES, *History of Samson*, sect. 19.

A σεμνοπρέπεια in his person, a grave and a smiling *garb* compounded together to bring strangers into a liking of their welcome.—HACKET, *Life of Archbishop Williams*, part ii. p. 32.

> Horace's wit and Virgil's state
> He did not steal but emulate,
> And when he would like them appear,
> Their *garb*, but not their clothes, did wear.
> > DENHAM, *On the Death of Cowley.*

GARBLE. Writings only are 'garbled' now ; and 'garbled' extracts are extracts dishonestly made, so shifted, mutilated, or otherwise dealt with, that, while they are presented as fair specimens, they convey a false impression. It is not difficult to trace the downward progress of the word. It is derived from the

low Latin ' garba,' a wheatsheaf, and ' garbellare,' to
sift or cleanse corn from any dust or rubbish which
may have become mingled with it. It was then applied to any separation of the good from the bad,
retaining that, rejecting this, and used most commonly of spices ; then generally to picking and
choosing, but without any intention to select the
better and to dismiss the worse : and lastly, as at
present, to picking and choosing with the distinct
purpose of selecting that which should convey the
worse impression, and dismissing that which should
have conveyed a truer and a better. It is a very
favourite word in its earlier uses with Fuller.

Garbling of bow-staves (anno 1 R. 3, cap. 11) is the sorting
or culling out of the good from the bad.—Cowell, *The Interpreter*, s. v.

There was a fair hospital, built to the honour of St. Anthony
in Bennet's Fink, in this city ; the protectors and proctors
whereof claimed a privilege to themselves, to *garble* the live pigs
in the markets of the city ; and such as they found starved or
otherwise unwholesome for man's sustenance they would slit in
the ear, tie a bell about their necks, and turn them loose about
the city.—Fuller, *Worthies of England, London.*

> *Garbling* men's manners you did well divide,
> To take the Spaniard's wisdom, not their pride ;
> With French activity you stored your mind,
> Leaving to them their fickleness behind ;
> And soon did learn, your temperance was such,
> A sober industry even from the Dutch.
> > Id., *Worthies of England. A Panegyric
> > on Charles II.*

To *garble*, to cleanse from dross and dirt, as grocers do their
spices, to pick or cull out.—Phillips, *New World of Words.*

GARLAND. At present we know no other ' garlands ' but of flowers; but ' garland ' was at one time

a technical name for the royal crown or diadem, and not a poetical one, as might at first sight appear; as witness these words of Matthew of Paris in his *Life of Henry III.* : Rex veste dèauratâ, et coronulâ aureâ, quæ vulgariter *garlanda* dicitur, redimitus.

In the adoption and obtaining of the *garland*, I being seduced and provoked by sinister counsel did commit a naughty and abominable act.—GRAFTON, *Chronicle of King Richard III.*

In whose [Edward the Fourth's] time, and by whose occasion, what about the getting of the *garland*, keeping it, losing and winning again, it hath cost more English blood than hath twice the winning of France.—Sir T. MORE, *History of King Richard III.* p. 107.

What in me was purchased,
Falls unto thee in a more fairer sort;
So thou the *garland* wear'st successively.
SHAKESPEARE, 2 *Henry IV.* act iv. sc. 4.

GAZETTE. An Italian word designating a small piece of tin money current at Venice; to this the name 'gazzetta' a diminutive of 'gaza,' the proper name of the treasure of Persian kings, was probably given in a certain irony, as being a very small treasure indeed. Being the price at which the flying sheets of news, first published there, were sold, it gave to them their name; and they also were called 'gazettes,' (see Mahn, *Etymol. Untersuch.* p. 91). We see the word in this its secondary sense, but not as yet thoroughly at home in English, for it still retains an Italian termination, in Ben Jonson's *Volpone* (act v. sc. 2), of which the scene is laid at Venice. Curiously enough the same play gives also an example, quoted below, of 'gazette' in its earlier use.

If you will have a stool, it will cost you a *gazet*, which is almost a penny.—CORYAT, *Crudities*, vol. ii. p. 15.

> What monstrous and most painful circumstance
> Is here to get some three or four *gazettes*,
> Some threepence in the whole.
> BEN JONSON, *Volpone*, act ii. sc. 1.

GELDING. Restrained at present to *horses* which have ceased to be entire ; but until 'eunuch,' which is of somewhat late adoption, had been introduced into the language, serving the needs which that serves now.

Thanne Joseph was lad in Egepte, and bought him Potiphar, the *gelding* of Pharao.—*Gen.* xxxix. 1. WICLIF.

And whanne thei weren come up of the water, the spirit of the Lord ravyschid Filip, and the *geldynge* saw hym no more.— *Acts* viii. 39. Id.

Lysimachus was very angry, and thought great scorn that Demetrius should reckon him a *gelding.*—NORTH, *Plutarch's Lives*, p. 741.

GENEROSITY. We still use 'generous' occasionally in the sense of highly or nobly born ; but 'generosity' has quite lost this its earlier sense, and acquired a purely ethical meaning.

Nobility began in thine ancestors and ended in thee ; and the *generosity* that they gained by virtue, thou hast blotted by vice. —LYLY, *Euphues and his England.*

Their eyes are commonly black and small, noses little, nails almost as long as their fingers, but serving to distinguish their *generosity.*—HARRIS, *Voyages*, vol. i. p. 465.

GESTATION. Now a technical word applied only to the period during which the females of animals carry their young; but acknowledging no such limitation once.

Gestation in a chariot or wagon hath in it a shaking of the body, but some vehement, and some more soft.—Sir T. ELYOT, *Castle of Health*, b. ii. c. 34.

Gestation, an exercise of the body, by being carried in coach, litter, upon horseback, or in a vessel on the water.—HOLLAND, *Pliny, Explanation of the Words of Art.*

GHOST. It is only in the very highest use of all that ' Ghost ' and ' Spirit ' are now synonymous and exchangeable. They once were so through the entire range of their several uses.

> And in this manere was man maad,
> And thus God gaf hym a *goost*.
> > *Piers Ploughman*, 5240.

> As well in *gost* as body, chast was she.
> > CHAUCER, *The Doctoure's Tale.*

He sawe that the heavens opened, and the *goost* as a dove commynge downe upon Him.—*Mark* i. 10. COVERDALE.

GIRL. A diminutive of a root ' gir ' (gir+l), a little child, and this of either sex. In Old English a ' knave girle ' occurs in the sense of boy. It fared in earliest English not otherwise with 'wench.' This, in its diminutive form ' wenchel,' is applied in *The Ormulum*, 3356, to the newly born Babe in the manger.

Thorugh wyn and thorugh wommen ther was Loth acombred,
And there gat in glotonie *gerles* that were cherles.
> *Piers Ploughman*, 525.

> In danger hadde he at his owen gise
> The yonge *girles* of the diocese,
> And knew hir counseil and was of hir rede.
> > CHAUCER, *Canterbury Tales, The Prologue.*

GIST. This, the French 'gîte,' from the old 'gésir,' meant formerly, as the French word means still, the

place where one lodges for the night. A scroll containing the route and resting-places of a royal party
during a progress was sometimes so called. It must
be owned, however, that it is difficult to trace the
point of contact and connexion between 'gist' in this
sense, and 'gist' as we use it now.

After he had sent Popilius before in spial, and perceived that
the avenues were open in all parts, he marched forward himself,
and by the second *gist* came to Dium [secundis castris pervenit
ad Dium].—HOLLAND, *Livy*, p. 1174.

The guides who were to conduct them on their way had commandment so to cast their *gists* and journeys that by three of
the clock in the morning of the third day they might assail Pythoum.—Id., *Ib.* p. 1193.

GLORY,　) 'Glory' is never employed now in the
GLORIOUS. ∫ sense of '*vain*-glory,' nor 'glorious' in
that of '*vain*-glorious,' as once they often were.

In military commanders and soldiers *vain-glory* is an essential
point; for as iron sharpens iron, so by *glory* one courage sharpeneth another.—BACON, *Essays*, 54.

So commonly actions begun in *glory* shut up in shame.—
Bishop HALL, *Contemplations, On Babel*.

Some took this for a *glorious* brag; others thought he [Alcibiades] was like enough to have done it.—NORTH, *Plutarch's
Lives*, p. 183.

Likewise *glorious* followers, who make themselves as trumpets
of the commendation of those they follow, are full of inconvenience; for they taint business through want of secrecy, and they
export honour from a man and make him a return in envy.—
BACON, *Essays*, 48.

He [Anselm] little dreamt then that the weeding-hook of
Reformation would after two ages pluck up his *glorious* poppy
[prelacy] from insulting over the good corn [presbytery].—
MILTON, *Reason of Church Government*, b. i. c. 5.

GOOD-NATURE,⎫ As metaphysics have yielded us
GOOD-NATURED. ⎭ 'common sense,' and logic 'formal,'
and 'formality,' so we owe to theology 'good-nature.'
By it out elder divines understood far more than we
understand by it now ; even all which it is possible
for a man to have, without having the grace of God,
The contrast between grace and nature was of course
unknown to the Greeks; but, this being kept in
mind, we may say that the 'good-nature' of our old
theology was as nearly as possible expressed by the
εὐφυΐα of Aristotle (*Eth. Nic.* iii. 7 ; compare the
'heureusement né' of the French); the genial pre-
paredness for the reception of every high teaching.
In the paper of *The Spectator*, quoted below, which
treats exclusively of 'good-nature,' the word is passing,
but has by no means passed, into its modern meaning.
See 'Ill-nature.'

Good-nature, being the relics and remains of that shipwreck
which Adam made, is the proper and immediate disposition to
holiness. When *good-nature* is heightened by the grace of God,
that which was natural becomes now spiritual.—J. TAYLOR,
Sermon preached at the Funeral of Sir George Dalstone.

Good-nature! alas, where is it? Since Adam fell, there was
never any such thing in rerum naturâ; if there be any good
thing in any man, it is all from grace. We may talk of this and
that, of *good-natured* men, and I know not what; but the very
truth is, set grace aside (I mean all grace, both renewing grace
and restraining grace), there is no more *good-nature* in any man
than there was in Cain and in Judas. That thing which we use
to call *good-nature* is indeed but a subordinate means or instru-
ment, whereby God restraineth some men more than others, from
their birth and special constitution, from sundry outrageous ex-
orbitances, and so is a branch of this restraining grace whereof
we now speak.—SANDERSON, *Sermons*, 1671, vol. i. p. 279.

If any good did appear in the conversation of some men who

followed that religion [the Pagan], it is not to be imputed to the influence of that, but to some better cause; to the relics of *good-nature*, to the glimmerings of natural light, or (perhaps also) to secret whispers and impressions of divine grace on some men's minds vouchsafed in pity to them.—BARROW, *Sermon* 14 *on the Apostles' Creed.*

They [infidels] explode all natural difference of good and evil; deriding benignity, mercy, pity, gratitude, ingenuity; that is, all instances of *good-nature*, as childish and silly dispositions.— Id., *Sermon* 6 *on the Apostles' Creed.*

Xenophon, in the Life of his imaginary Prince, is always celebrating the philanthropy or *good-nature* of his hero, which he tells us he brought into the world with him.—*Spectator*, no. 169.

GOSPELLER.   Now seldom used save in ritual language, and there designating the priest or deacon who in the divine service reads the Gospel of the day; but employed once as equivalent to ' Evangelist,' and subsequently applied to adherents of the Reformed faith; both which meanings have since departed from it.

Marke, the *gospeller*, was the goostli sone of Petre in baptysm. —WICLIF, *The Prologe of Marke.*

The persecution was carried on against the *gospellers* with much fierceness by those of the Roman persuasion.—STRYPE, *Memorials of Archbishop Cranmer*, b. iii. c. 16.

GOSSIP. It would be interesting to collect instances in which the humbler classes of society have retained the correct use of a word, which has been let go by those of higher education. ' Gossip ' is one, being still used by our peasantry in its first and etymological sense, namely as a sponsor in baptism—one *sib* or akin in *God*, according to the doctrine of the medieval Church, that sponsors contracted a spiritual affinity with the child for whom they stood. 'Gossips,' in this primary sense, would often be familiar with one another—and thus the word was applied to all familiars and intimates. At a later day it came to signify such idle talk, the 'commérage' (which word has exactly the same history), as too often would find place in the intercourse of such.

They had mothers as we had; and those mothers had *gossips* (if their children were christened), as we are.—BEN JONSON, *The Staple of News, The Induction.*

Thus fareth the golden mean, through the misconstruction of the extremes. Well-tempered zeal is lukewarmness; devotion is hypocrisy; charity, ostentation; constancy, obstinacy; gravity, pride; humility, abjection of spirit; and so go through the whole parish of virtues, where misprision and envy are *gossips*, be sure the child shall be nicknamed.—WHITLOCK, *Zootomia*, p. 3.

Should a great lady that was invited to be a *gossip*, in her place send her kitchen-maid, 'twould be ill-taken.—SELDEN, *Table-Talk, Prayer.*

GRAVE. The German 'graben,' and once used in the senses which 'graben' still retains. See 'Engrave.'

> They set markes hir meetings should be
> There King Ninus was *graven*, under a tree.
> > CHAUCER, *Legend of Tisbe of Babilon.*

I wil laye sege to the rounde aboute, and *grave* up dykes against the.—*Isai.* xxix. 3. COVERDALE.

He hath *graven* and digged up a pit, and is fallen himself into the destruction that he made for other.—*Ps.* vii. 16. Prayer Book Version.

GROPE. Now to feel *for*, and uncertainly, as does a blind man or one in the dark; but once simply to feel, to gripe or grasp.

Handis thei hav, and thei shal not *grope* [et non *palpabunt*, Vulg.]—*Ps.* cxiii. 7. WICLIF.

I have touched and tasted the Lord, and *groped* Him with hands, and yet unbelief hath made all unsavoury.—ROGERS, *Naaman the Syrian*, p. 231.

GRUDGE. Now to repine at the good which others already have, or which we may be required to impart to them ; but it formerly implied *open* utterances of discontent and displeasure against others, and did the work which 'to murmur' does now. Traces of this still survive in our English Bible.

And the farisies and scribis *grucchiden* ; seiynge for this resceyveth synful men and eteth with hem.—*Luke* xv. 2. WICLIF.

After backbiting cometh *grutching* or murmurance, and sometime it springeth of impatience ayenst God, and sometime ayenst man. -CHAUCER, *The Persones Tale.*

Yea without *grudging* Christ suffered the cruel Jews to crown Him with most sharp thorns, and to strike Him with a reed.— FOXE, *Book of Martyrs ; Examination of William Thorpe.*

Use hospitality one to another without *grudging* [ἄνευ γογγυσμῶν].—1 *Pet.* iv. 9. Authorized Version.

GUARD. Is ' guard,' in the sense of welt or border to a garment, nothing more than a *special* application of ' guard,' as it is familiar to us all ? or is it altogether a different word with its own etymology, and only by accident offering the same letters in the same sequence ? I have assumed, though not with perfect confidence, the former ; for indeed otherwise the word would have no right to a place here.

Antipater wears in outward show his apparel with a plain white welt or *guard*, but he is within all purple, I warrant you, and as red as scarlet.—HOLLAND, *Plutarch's Morals*, p. 412.

Then were the fathers of those children glad men to see their sons apparelled like Romans, in fair long gowns, *garded* with purple.—NORTH, *Plutarch's Lives*, p. 492.

> Give him a livery
> More *guarded* than his fellows.
> SHAKESPEARE, *The Merchant of Venice*, act ii. sc. 2.

HAG. One of the many words applied formerly to both sexes, but now restrained only to one. See ' Harlot,' ' Hoyden,' ' Witch.'

> And that old *hag* [Silenus] that with a staff his staggering limbs doth stay,
> Scarce able on his ass to sit for reeling every way.
> GOLDING, *Ovid's Metamorphosis*, b. iv.

HANDSOME, } Now referred exclusively to come-
HANDSOMENESS. } liness, either literal or figurative. It is of course closely connected with ' handy,' indeed differs from it only in termination, and in all early uses means having prompt and dexterous use of the hands, and then generally able, adroit. In Cotgrave's *Dictionary*, ' habile,' ' adroit,' ' maniable,' take precedence of ' beau,' ' belle,' as its French equivalents. See ' Unhandsome.'

Few of them [the Germans] use swords or great lances ; but carry javelins with a narrow and short iron, but so sharp and *handsome*, that, as occasion serveth, with the same weapon they can fight both at hand and afar off.—GREENWEY, *Tacitus*, vol. i. p. 259.

A light footman's shield he takes unto him, and a Spanish blade by his side, more *handsome* to fight short and close [ad propiorem *habili* pugnam].—HOLLAND, *Livy*, p. 255.

Philopœmen sought to put down all exercise, which made men's bodies unmeet to take pains, and to become soldiers to fight in defence of their country, that otherwise would have been

I

very able and *handsome* for the same.—NORTH, *Plutarch's Lives*,
p. 306.

> Both twain of them made haste,
> And girding close for *handsomeness* their garments to their
> waist,
> Bestirred their cunning hands apace.
>
> GOLDING, *Ovid's Metamorphosis*, b. vi.

HARBINGER. This word belongs at present to our
poetical diction, and to that only; its original significance being nearly or quite forgotten; as is evident from the inaccurate ways in which it has come
to be used; as though a ‘harbinger’ were merely
one who announced the coming, and not always one
who prepared a place and lodging, a ‘harbour,’
for another. He did indeed announce the near
approach, but only as an accidental consequence of
his office. Our Lord, if we may reverently say it,
assumed to Himself precisely the office of a ‘harbinger,’ when He said, ‘I go to prepare a place for
you’ (*John* xiv. 2).

There was a *harbinger* who had lodged a gentleman in a very
ill room; who expostulated with him somewhat rudely; but the
harbinger carelessly said, ‘You will take pleasure in it when you
are out of it.’—BACON, *Apophthegms*.

> I'll be myself the *harbinger*, and make joyful
> The hearing of my wife with your approach.
>
> SHAKESPEARE, *Macbeth*, act i. sc. 4.

The fame of Frederick's valour and maiden fortune, never as
yet spotted with ill success, like a *harbinger* hastening before,
had provided victory to entertain him at his arrival.—FULLER,
The Holy War, b. iii. c. 31.

> A winged *harbinger* from bright heaven flown
> Bespeaks a lodging-room
> For the mighty King of love,
> The spotless structure of a virgin womb.
>
> J. TAYLOR, *On the Annunciation*.

HARDY, ⎱ When used of *persons*, 'hardy' means
HARDILY. ⎰ always now enduring, indifferent to
fatigue, hunger, thirst, heat, cold, and the like. But
it had once a far more prevailing sense of bold, which
now only remains to it in connexion with *things*, as
we should still speak of a 'hardy,' meaning thereby
a bold, assertion ; though never now of a 'hardy,' if
we intended a bold or daring person. Lord Bacon's
Charles the *Hardy* is Charles le *Téméraire*, or Charles
the *Bold*, as we always style him now.

> Hap helpeth *hardy* man alway, quoth he.
> CHAUCER, *The Legend of Good Women.*

> It is not to be forgotten what Commineus observeth of his
> first master, duke Charles the *Hardy*, namely, that he would
> communicate his secrets with none.—BACON, *Essays*, 27.

> *Hardily* [audacter, Vulg.] he entride in to Pilat, and axide
> the body of Jhesu.—*Mark* xv. 43. WICLIF.

HARLOT. I have no desire to entangle myself in
the question of this word's etymology (see Donkin,
Etymological Dictionary, s. v. Arlotto ; and *Piers
Ploughman*, Wright's edition, Glossary s. v.) ;
it is sufficient to observe that it was used of
both sexes alike ; and though for the most part a
word of slight and contempt (in the *Promptorium
Parvulorum*, which see, 'scurrus' is the Latin equivalent of it), implied nothing of that special *form*
of sin to which it now exclusively refers.

> Salle never *harlotte* have happe, thorowe helpe of my Lord
> To kille a crownde kynge, with crysome enoynttede.
> *Morte Arthure*, 2446.

He was unhardy, that *harlot,* and hidde hym in Inferno.
Piers Ploughman, 11581.

A sturdy *harlot* went hem ay behind,
That was his hostes man, and bare a sakke,
An what men gave him, laid it on his bakke.
CHAUCER, *The Sompnoure's Tale.*

No man but he and thou and such other false *harlots* praiseth any such preaching.—FOXE, *Book of Martyrs; Examination of William Thorpe.*

About this time [A.D. 1264] a redress of certain sects was intended, among which one by name specially occurreth, and called the assembly of *harlots,** a kind of people of a lewd disposition and uncivil.—Id., *Ib.* vol. i. p. 435.

HARNESS. In French the difference between the 'harness' of a man and of a horse is expressed by a slight difference in the spelling, 'harnois' in one case, 'harnais' in the other. In English we only retain it now in the second of these uses.

But when a stronger than he cometh upon him and overcometh him, he taketh from him his *harness* wherein he trusted, and divideth his goods.—*Luke* xi. 22. TYNDALE.

When Abram herde that his brother was taken, he *harnessed* his bonde-servauntes, and followed after them untill Dan.— *Gen.* xiv. COVERDALE.

Those that sleep in Jesus shall God bring with Him, and *harness* them with the bright armour of life and immortality.— H. MORE, *Grand Mystery of Godliness,* b. iv. c. 18.

And all about the courtly stable
Bright-*harnessed* angels sit in order serviceable.
MILTON, *On the Nativity.*

HARVEST. It is remarkable that while spring, ummer, winter, have all their Anglo-Saxon names,

---

* 'Qui se *harlotos* appellant' are the important words in Henry the Third's letter to the Sheriff of Oxfordshire, requiring their dispersion.

we designate the other quarter of the year by its
Latin title 'autumn,' 'hearfest' (= the German
'Herbst'), having been appropriated to the in-
gathering of the *fruits* of this season, not to the season itself.   In this indeed we are truer to the proper
meaning of 'harvest' than the Germans, who have
transferred the word from the former to the latter;
for it is closely related with the Greek καρπός and
the Latin 'carpo.'   Occasionally, however, as in the
passages which follow, 'harvest' assumes with us
also the signification of autumn.

These been *harvest* trees [arbores autumnales, Vulg.] with
outen fruyt, twies deede, drawun up bi the roote.—*Jude* 12.
WICLIF.

There stood the Springtime with a crown of fresh and fragrant
    flowers ;
There waited Summer naked stark, all save a wheaten hat ;
And *Harvest* smeared with treading grapes late at the pressing
    fat ;
And lastly quaking for the cold stood Winter all forlorn.
                    GOLDING, *Ovid's Metamorphosis*, b. ii.

HASSOCK.   Already in Phillips's *New World of
Words*, 1706, the 'hassock' was what it is now, 'a
kind of straw cushion used to kneel upon in churches;'
and some of us may remember to have seen in country churches 'hassocks' of solid tufts of coarse black
grass which had so grown and matted together that
they served this purpose sufficiently well.   But this
is only the secondary and transferred use of the word.
It was once the name by which this coarse grass
growing in these rank tufts was itself called ; and this
name, as Forby tells us, in Norfolk it still bears.
See the *Promptorium Parvulorum*, s. v. 'Hassok.'

Land so full of *hassocks* as to be impossible to find the deer among them.—HUTCHINSON, *Drainage of Land.*

These *hassocks,* in bogs, were formerly taken up with a part of the soil, matted together with roots, shaped, trimmed, and dressed, a sufficient part of their shaggy and tufted surface being left to make kneeling much easier than on the pavement of the church or the bare-boarded floor of a pew.—FORBY, *East Anglia.*

HATEFUL. This has undergone exactly the same limitation of meaning as 'Dreadful' and 'Frightful,' which see.

Little office
The *hateful* Commons will perform for us,
Except like curs to tear us all to pieces.

SHAKESPEARE, *Richard II.,* act. ii. sc. 2.

HEAR. Our scholars of the seventeenth century occasionally use the Latin idiom, 'to hear well,' or 'to hear ill,' *i.e.* concerning oneself (bene audire, male audire), instead of, to be praised, or to be b'amed.

[Fabius] was well aware, that not only within his own camp. but also now at Rome, he *heard ill* for his temporizing and slow proceedings.—HOLLAND, *Livy,* p. 441.

What more national corruption, for which England *hears ill* abroad, than household gluttony? — MILTON, *Areopagitica,* p. 431.

The abbot made his mind known to the Lord Keeper, that he would gladly be present in the Abbey of Westminster on our Christmas-day in the morning, to behold and hear how that great feast was solemnized in our congregations, which *heard* very *ill* beyond the seas for profaneness.—HACKET, *Life of Archbishop Williams,* part i. p. 210.

HIDE. This word is at present only contemptuously applied to the skin of man, being reserved almost exclusively for that of beasts; but it had once the same extent of meaning as by the German 'haut' is still retained, which is 'cutis' and 'pellis' both.

> The ladye fayre of hew and *hyde*
> Shee sate downe by the bedside.
>> *Eger and Grine*, 263.

> Her kerchers were all of silk,
> Her hayre as white as any milke,
> Lovesome of hue and *hyde*.
>> *Ballad of John de Reeve*, 226.

HOBBY. The 'hobby' being the ambling nag ridden for pleasure, and then the child's toy in imitation of the same, had in these senses nearly passed out of use, when the word revived, by a very natural transfer, in the sense which it now has, of a favourite pursuit which carries a man easily and pleasantly forward.

They have likewise excellent good horses (we term the *hobbies*), which have not the same pace that other horses in their course, but a soft and round amble, setting one leg before another very finely.—HOLLAND, *Camden's Ireland*, p. 63.

King Agesilaus, having a great sort of little children, was one day disposed to solace himself among them in a gallery where they played, and took a little *hobby*-horse of wood, and bestrid it.—PUTTENHAM, *Art of English Poesy*, b. iii. c. 24.

> A *hobby*-horse, or some such pretty toy,
> A rattle would befit you better, boy.
>> RANDOLPH, *Poems*, p. 19.

HOMELY. The etymology of 'homely' which Milton puts into the mouth of Comus,

> 'It is for *homely* features to keep *home*;
> They had their name hence,'

witnesses that in his time it had the same meaning
which it has in ours. At an earlier day, however, it
much more nearly corresponded to the German
' heimlich,' that is, secret, inward, familiar, as those
may be presumed to be that share in a common *home.*
' Homeliness' is more than once the word by which
Wiclif translates ' mansuetudo ' : thus, 2 *Cor.* x. 1 ;
Jam. i. 21.

And the enemyes of a man ben thei that ben *homeli* with him.
—*Matt* x. 36. WICLIF; cf. *Judg.* xix. 4, and often.

> God grante thee thine *homly* fo to espie;
> For in this world n'is werse pestilence
> Than *homly* fo, all day in thy presence.
> CHAUCER, The Merchantes Tale.

Such peple be able and worthi to be admytted into the
homeli reding of Holi Writt.—PECOCK, *Repressor*, c. 3.

With all these men I was right *homely*, and communed with
them long time and oft.—FOXE, *Book of Martyrs ; Examination
of William Thorpe.*

HOYDEN. Now and for a long time since a
clownish ill-bred *girl* ; what is vulgarly called in
America a ' gal-boy,' yet I cannot doubt that Skinner
is right when he finds in it only another form of
' heathen.' Remote as the words appear at starting,
it will not be hard to bring them close together. In
the first place, it is only by a superinduced meaning
that ' heathen ' has its present sense of non-christian ;
it is properly, as Grimm has abundantly shown, as
indeed *Piers Ploughman* had told us long ago, a
dweller on the heath ; then any living a wild
savage life ; thus we have in Wiclif (*Acts* xxviii. 1),
' And *hethen* men [barbari, Vulg.] dide unto us not
litil curtesie ; ' and only afterwards was the word

applied to those who resisted to the last the human-
izing influences of the Christian faith. This 'heathen' is in Dutch 'heyden;' while less than two
hundred years ago 'hoyden' was by no means confined, as it now is, to the female sex, the clownish ill-
bred girl, but was oftener applied to men.

Shall I argue of conversation with this *hoyden*, to go and
practise at his opportunities in the larder?—MILTON, *Colas-
terion.*

Falourdin, *m.* A bucke, lowt, lurden, a lubberly sloven, heavy
sot, lumpish *hoydon.*—COTGRAVE, *A French and English Dictionary.*

Badault, *m.* A fool, dolt, sot, fop, ass, coxcomb, gaping *hoydon.*
— Id., *Ib.*

A rude *hoidon* ; Grue, badault, falourdin, becjaune ; Balordo,
babionetto, rustico ; Bouaron.—HOWELL, *Lexicon Tetraglotton.*

HUMOUR, ⎫ The four ' humours ' in man, accord-
HUMOUROUS, ⎬ ing to the old physicians, were
HUMOURIST, ⎭ blood, choler, phlegm, and melancholy. So long as these were duly tempered, all
would be well. But so soon as any of them unduly
preponderated, the man became 'humourous,' one
'humour' or another bearing too great a sway in
him. As such, his conduct would not be according
to the received rule of other men, but have something peculiar, whimsical, self-willed in it. In this
the self-asserting character of the ' humourous ' man
lay the point of contact, the middle term, between
the modern use of ' humour ' and the ancient. It was
his ' humour ' which would lead a man to take an
original view and aspect of things, a 'humourous'
aspect, first in the old sense, which in some of our
provincial dialects still lives on, and then in that

which we now employ. The classical passage in English literature on 'humour' and its history is the Prologue, or 'Stage,' as it is called, to Ben Jonson's *Every Man out of his Humour* ; it is, however, too long to cite ; an earlier occurs in Gower's *Confessio Amantis*, lib. 7, in init. See 'Temper.' 'Humourous' has been sometimes used in quite another sense, as simply equivalent to moist ; so in the passage from Chapman's *Homer*, quoted below.

In which [kingdom of heaven] neither such high-flown enthusiasts, nor any dry churlish reasoners and disputers, shall have either part or portion, till they lay down those gigantic *humours*, and become (as our Saviour Christ, who is that unerring Truth, has prescribed), like little children.—H. MORE, *Grand Mystery of Godliness*, b. viii. c. 15.

> Yet such is now the duke's condition,
> That he misconstrues all that you have done ;
> The duke is *humourous*.
> SHAKESPEARE, *As You Like it*, act i. sc. 2.

The people thereof [Ephraim] were active, valiant ambitious of honour ; but withal hasty, *humourous*, hard to be pleased ; forward enough to fight with their foes, and too forward to fall out with their friends.—FULLER, *A Pisgah Sight of Palestine*, b. ii. c. 9.

Or it may be (what is little better than that), instead of the living righteousness of Christ, he will magnify himself in some *humourous* pieces of holiness of his own.—H. MORE, *Grand Mystery of Godliness*, b. viii. c. 14.

Upon his sight of the first signs and experiments of the plagues which did accompany them, he [Pharaoh] demeaned himself like a proud phantastic *humorist*.—JACKSON, *Christ's Everlasting Priesthood*, b. x c. 40.

The seamen are a nation by themselves, a *humourous* and fantastic people.—CLARENDON, *History of the Rebellion*, b. ii. in init.

Wretched men, that shake off the true comely habit of religion, to bespeak them a new-fashioned suit of profession at an *humourist's* shop!—ADAMS, *The Devil's Banquet*, p. 52.

> This eased her heart and dried her *humourous* eye.
> CHAPMAN, *Homer's Odysseis*, b. iv. l. 120.

HUNGER. It was long before this and 'famine' were desynonymized, and indeed the great famine year is still spoken of in Ireland as 'the year of the hunger.' Still in the main they are distinguished, 'famine' expressing an outward fact, the dearth of food, and 'hunger' the inward sense and experience of this fact.

And aftir that he hadde endid alle thinges, a strong *hunger* was made in that cuntre.—*Luke* xv. 14. WICLIF.

> Pestilences and *hungers* shall be
> And erthedyns in many contré.
> RICHARD ROLLE DE HAMPOLE, *Pricke of Conscience*, 4035.

Oon of hem roos up, Agabus bi name, and signyfied bi the spirit a greet *hungre* to comynge in alle the world, which *hungre* was made undir Claudius.—*Acts* xi. 28. WICLIF.

Behold the tyme commeth that I shal sende an *hunger* in to the earth ; not the *hunger* of bread, nor the thyrst of water.—*Amos* viii. 11. COVERDALE.

HUSBAND. This, the Anglo-Saxon 'hus-bonda,' the old French 'mesnagier,' is much more nearly the Latin 'paterfamilias' than 'vir.' As the house, above all that of him who owns and tills the soil, stands by a wise and watchful economy, it is easy to see how 'husband' came to signify one who knows how prudently to spare and save.

All good *husbands* agree in this, That every work should have the due and convenient season.—HOLLAND, *Pliny*, vol. i. p. 556.

They are too good *husbands*, and too thrifty of God's grace, too sparing of the Holy Ghost, that restrain God's general pro-positions, Venite omnes, Let all come, so particularly as to say that when God says *all*, he means some.—DONNE, *Sermon* 33.

> Thou dost thyself wise and industrious deem ;
> A mighty *husband* thou wouldst seem ;
> Fond man, like a bought slave thou all the while
> Dost but for others sweat and toil.
> COWLEY, *The Shortness of Life and Uncertainty of Riches.*

After we come once to view the seam or vein where the hidden treasure lies, we account all we possess besides as dross ; for whose further assurance we alienate all our interest in the world, with as great willingness as good *husbands* do base tenements or hard-rented leases, to compass some goodly royalty offered them more than half for nothing.—JACKSON, *The Eternal Truth of the Scriptures*, b. iv. c. 8.

IDIOT,   ⎫ A word with a very interesting and in-
IDIOTICAL.⎭ structive history, which, however, is only fully intelligible by a reference to the Greek. The ἰδιώτης or 'idiot' is first the private man as distinguished from the man sustaining a public office ; then, inasmuch as public life was considered an absolutely necessary condition of man's highest education, the untaught or mentally undeveloped, as distinguished from the educated ; and only after it had run through these courses did 'idiot' come to signify what ἰδιώτης never did, the man whose mental powers are not merely unexercised but deficient, as distinguished from him in full possession of them. This is the only employment to which we now put the word ; but examples of its earlier and more Greek uses are frequent in Jeremy Taylor and others.

And here, again, their allegation out of Gregory the First and Damascene, That images be the laymen's books, and that pictures are the Scripture of *idiots* and simple persons, is worthy to be considered.—*Homilies ; Against Perils of Idolatry.*

It is clear, by Bellarmine's confession, that S. Austin affirmed that the plain places of Scripture are sufficient to all laics, and all *idiots* or private persons.—J. TAYLOR, *A Dissuasive from Popery*, part ii. b. i. § 1.

Christ was received of *idiots*, of the vulgar people, and of the simpler sort, while He was rejected, despised, and persecuted even to death by the high priests, lawyers, scribes, doctors, and rabbies.—BLOUNT, *Philostratus*, p. 237.

It [Scripture] speaks commonly according to vulgar apprehension, as when it tells of 'the ends of the heaven;' which now almost every *idiot* knows hath no ends at all.—JOHN SMITH, *Select Discourses*, vi., *On Prophecy.*

Truth is content, when it comes into the world, to wear our mantles, to learn our language; it speaks to the most *idiotical* sort of men in the most *idiotical* way. The reason of this plain and *idiotical* style of Scripture it may be worth our farther taking notice of.—Id. *ibid.*

ILL-NATURE, ⎫ This is now rather one special evil
ILL-NATURED. ⎭ quality, as κακία is often in Greek; it was once the complex of all, or more properly the natural substratum on which they all were superinduced. See 'Good-nature,' and, in addition to the passage from South, quoted below, a very instructive discussion on both words in his *Sermons*, 1737, vol. vi. pp. 104–111.

I may truly say of the mind of an ungrateful person, that it is kindness-proof. It is impenetrable, unconquerable; unconquerable by that which conquers all things else, even by love itself. And the reason is manifest; for you may remember that I told you that ingratitude sprang from a principle of *ill-nature*; which being a thing founded in such a certain constitution of blood and spirit, as being born with a man into the world, and upon that account called *nature*, shall prevent all remedies that can be applied by education.—SOUTH, *Sermons*, 1737, vol. i. p. 429.

King Henry the Eighth was an *ill-natured* prince to execute so many whom he had so highly favoured.—Sir T. OVERBURY, *Crumbs fallen from King James' Table*

He is the worst of men, whom kindness cannot soften, nor endearments oblige; whom gratitude cannot tie faster than the bands of life and death.—He is an *ill-natured* sinner.—J. TAYLOR, *The Miracles of the Divine Mercy*, serm. 27.

IMP. Employed in nobler senses formerly than now. ' To imp ' is properly to engraft, and an ' imp ' a graft, scion, or young shoot; and, even as we now speak of the ' scions ' of a noble house, so there was in earlier English the same natural transfer of ' imps ' from plants to persons.

> I was some tyme a frere, and the conventes gardyner
> For to graffen *impes.*
>> *Piers Ploughman*, 2744.

> Of feble trees there comen wretched *impes.*
>> CHAUCER, *The Monkes Prologue.*

The sudden taking away of those most goodly and virtuous young *imps*, the Duke of Suffolk and his brother, by the sweating sickness, was it not also a manifest token of God's heavy displeasure towards us ?—BECON, *A Comfortable Epistle.*

The king returned into England with victory and triumph; the king preferred there eighty noble *imps* to the order of knighthood.—STOW, *Annals*, 1592, p. 385.

IMPOTENT,} The inner connexion between weak-
IMPOTENCE.} ness and violence is finely declared in Latin in the fact that ' impotens ' and ' impotentia ' imply both; so once did ' impotent' and 'impotence' in English (see Spenser's *Fairy Queen*, ii. 11, 23) though they now retain only the meaning of weak.

> An *impotent* lover
> Of women for a flash; but his fires quenched,
> Hating as deadly.
>> MASSINGER, *The Unnatural Combat*, act iii. sc. 2.

The Lady Davey, ever *impotent* in her passions, was even distracted with anger, that she was crossed in her will.—HACKET, *Life of Archbishop Williams*, part i. p. 194.

The truth is, that in this battle and whole business the Britons never more plainly manifested themselves to be right barbarous; such confusion, such *impotence*, as seemed likest not to a war, but to the wild hurry of a distracted woman, with as mad a crew at her heels.—MILTON, *History of England*, b. ii.

If a great personage undertakes an action passionately and upon great interest, let him manage it indiscreetly, let the whole design be unjust, let it be acted with all the malice and *impotency* in the world, he shall have enough to flatter him, but not enough to reprove him.—J. TAYLOR, *Holy Living*, c. 2, § 6.

IMPROVE. So long as the verb 'to improve' was directly connected in men's thoughts with the Latin 'improbare,' it was inevitable that it should have a meaning very different from that which now attaches to it; and so we find it used as equivalent to the Greek ἐλέγχειν, the Latin 'reprobare,' to disapprove of, to disallow.

If tho thre [opinions] be sufficiently *improved*, that is to saie, if it be sufficiently schewen that the thre be nought and untrewe and badde, alle the othere untrewe opiniouns bilded upon hem muste needis therebi take her fal.—PECOCK, *Repressor*, part i. c. i.

For love of the world the olde pharesies blasphemed the Holy Ghost, and persecuted the manifest truth which they could not *improve*.—TYNDALE, *Exposition on the First Epistle of S. John*.

If ye cannot *improve* it [my doctrine] by God's word, and yet of an hate and malicious mind that you bear to the truth, labour to resist it and condemn it that it should not spread, I ensure you your sin is irremissible and even against the Holy Ghost.—FRITH, *Works*, 1572, p. 3.

Be instant in season and out of season; *improve* [ἔλεγξον], rebuke, exhort with all longsuffering and doctrine.—2 *Tim.* iv. 2. Geneva Version.

INCENSE.   Now to kindle *anger* only ; but once
to kindle or inflame any passion, good or bad, in the
breast.   Anger, as the strongest passion, finally appropriated the word, just as in Greek it made θυμός
and ὀργή its own.

He [Asdrubal] it was, that when his men were weary and
drew back, *incensed* [accendit] them again, one while by fair
words and entreaty, another while by sharp checks and rebukes.
—HOLLAND, *Livy*, p. 665.

Prince Edward struck his breast and swore, that though all
his friends forsook him, yet he would enter Ptolemais, though
only with Fowin, his horsekeeper. By which speech he *incensed*
the English to go on with him.—FULLER, *The Holy War*, b. iv.
c. 28.

INCIVILITY.   See ' Civil.'

By this means infinite numbers of souls may be brought from
their idolatry, bloody sacrifices, ignorance, and *incivility*, to the
worshipping of the true God.—Sir W. RALEIGH, *Of the Voyage
for Guiana.*

INCREDULOUS,⎫ In Low Latin, and in ages of a
INCREDULITY. ⎭ blind unintelligent faith, ' credu-
litas ' came to be regarded as equivalent to ' fides,'
and ' credulity ' to ' faith.'   The two latter, with
their negatives, 'incredulity' and 'unbelief,' have been
usefully desynonymized in our later English ; but
the quotations which follow will show that this was
not always the case.

For we also were sometime unwise, *incredulous*, erring, serving
divers lusts and voluptuousnesses.—*Tit.* iii. 3.   Rhemish Version.

And we see that they could not enter in because of *incredulity*.
—*Heb.* iii. 19.   The same.

But let us take heed ; as God hates a lie, so He hates *incre-*

dulity, an obstinate, a foolish, and pertinacious understanding.—
J. TAYLOR, *Sermon at the Funeral of the Lord Primate.*

INDIFFERENT, It is a striking testimony of the
INDIFFERENCE, low general average which we
INDIFFERENTLY. assume common to most things,
that a thing which does not *differ* from others, is
thereby qualified as poor ; a sentence of depreciation
is pronounced upon it when it is declared to be ' indifferent.' When in Greek διαφέρειν means ' præ-
stare,' and τὰ διαφέροντα ' præstantiora,' we have exactly the same feeling embodying itself at the other
end. But this use of these words is modern. ' Indifferent' was impartial once, not *making* differences
where none really were.

God receiveth the learned and unlearned, and casteth away
none, but is *indifferent* unto all.—*Homilies ; Exhortation to the
Reading of Holy Scripture.*

If overseer of the poor, he [the good parishioner] is careful the
rates be made *indifferent*, whose inequality oftentimes is more
burdensome than the sum.—FULLER, *The Holy State*, b. ii. c. 11.

> Come Sleep, O Sleep, the certain knot of peace,
> The baiting place of wit, the balm of woe,
> The poor man's wealth, the prisoner's release,
> The *indifferent* judge between the high and low.
> > Sir P. SIDNEY, *Astrophel and Stella*, 39.

Requesting that they might speak before the senate, and be
heard with *indifference.*—HOLLAND, *Livy*, p. 1214.

That they may truly and *indifferently* administer justice.—*Book
of Common Prayer.*

INDIVIDUAL. Properly not capable of division ;
indivisible, as is an atom ; then undivided, insepara-
ble, and so used in the quotations which follow. We,
using ' individual ' as = person, have in fact re-
curred to the earlier meaning.

Then long eternity shall greet our bliss
With an *individual* kiss,
And joy shall overtake us like a flood.

MILTON, *On Time.*

Anacreon,
My *individual* companion.

HOLIDAY, *Marriages of the Arts*, act ii. sc. 6.

INDOLENCE. 'Indolentia' was a word first invented by Cicero, when he was obliged to find some
equivalent for the ἀπάθεια of certain Greek schools.
That it was not counted one of his happiest coinages
we may conclude from the seldom use of it by any
other authors but himself, as also from the fact that
Seneca, a little later proposing 'impatientia' as the
Latin equivalent for ἀπάθεια, implied that none such
had hitherto been found. The word has taken
firmer root in English than it ever did in Latin. At
the same time, meaning as it does now a disposition
or temper of languid non-exertion, it has lost the
accuracy of use which it had in the philosophical
schools, where it signified a state of freedom from
passion and pain ; which signification it retained
among our own writers of the Caroline period, and
even later. To this day, indeed, surgeons call pain-
less swellings '*indolent* tumours.'

Now, to begin with fortitude, they say it is the mean between
cowardice and rash audacity, of which twain the one is a defect,
the other an excess of the ireful passion ; liberality between
niggardise and prodigality, clemency and mildness between
senseless *indolence* and cruelty.—HOLLAND, *Plutarch's Morals*,
p. 69.

Now though Christ were far from both, yet He came nearer to
an excess of passion than to an *indolency*, to a senselessness, to a
privation of natural affections. Inordinateness of affections may

sometimes make some men like some beasts ; but *indolency,* absence, emptiness, privation of affections, makes any man, at all times, like stones, like dirt.—DONNE, *Sermons,* 1640, p. 156.

The submission here spoken of in the text is not a stupid *indolence,* or insensibility under such calamities as God shall be pleased to bring upon us.—SOUTH, *Sermons,* 1744, vol. x. p. 97.

INGENIOUS, INGENUOUS, INGENIOUSLY, INGENUITY, INGENUOUSNESS. } We are now pretty well agreed in our use of these words ; but there was a time when the uttermost confusion reigned amongst them. Thus, in the first and second quotations which follow, ' ingenious ' is used where we should now use, and where oftentimes the writers of that time would have used, ' ingenuous,' and the converse in the third ; while in like manner ' ingenuity ' in each of the succeeding three quotations stands for our present ' ingenuousness,' and ' ingenuousness ' in the last for ' ingenuity.' In respect of ' ingenious ' and ' ingenuous,' the arrangement at which we have now arrived regarding their several meanings, namely that the first indicates *mental,* the second *moral* qualities is good ; ' ingenious ' being from ' ingenium ' and ' ingenuous ' from ' ingenuus.' But ' ingenuity,' being from ' ingenuous,' should have kept the meaning, which it has now quite let go, of innate nobleness of disposition ; while ' ingeniousness,' against which there can be no objection to which ' ingenousness ' is not equally exposed, might have expressed what ' ingenuity ' does now.

Now as an *ingenious* debtor desires his freedom at his creditor's hands, that thereby he may be capable of paying his debt, as well as to escape the misery which himself should endure by his imprisonment; so an *ingenious* soul (and such is every saint) deprecates hell, as well with an eye to God's glory as to his own ease and happiness.—GURNALL, *The Christian Armour*, part ii. c. 54, § 2.

> Here let us breathe and haply institute
> A course of learning and *ingenious* studies.
> > SHAKESPEARE, *Taming of the Shrew*, act i. sc. 1.

An *ingenious* person will rather wear a plain garment of his own than a rich livery, the mark of servitude.—BATES, *Spiritual Perfection*, Preface.

> Thou art true and honest; *ingeniously* I speak;
> No blame belongs to thee.
> > SHAKESPEARE, *Timon of Athens*, act ii. sc. 2.

Since heaven is so glorious a state, and so certainly designed for us, if we please, let us spend all that we have, all our passions and affections, all our study and industry, all our desires and stratagems, all our witty and *ingenuous* faculties, towards the arriving thither.—J. TAYLOR, *Holy Dying*, c. 2, § 4.

Christian simplicity teaches openness and *ingenuity* in contracts and matters of buying and selling.—Id., *Sermon* 24, part ii.

When a man makes use of the name of any simple idea, which he perceives is not understood, or is in danger to be mistaken, he is obliged by the laws of *ingenuity* and the end of speech, to declare his meaning, and make known what idea he makes it stand for.—LOCKE, *An Essay concerning Human Understanding*, b. iii. c. 11, § 14.

It [gratitude] is such a debt as is left to every man's *ingenuity* (in respect to any legal coaction) whether he will pay it or no.—SOUTH, *Sermons*, vol. i. p. 410.

By his *ingenuousness* he [the good handicrafts-man] leaves his art better than he found it.—FULLER, *The Holy State*, b. ii. c. 19.

INSOLENT, The 'insolent' is properly no more
INSOLENCE. than the unusual. This, as the violation of the fixed law and order of society, is com-

monly offensive, even as it indicates a mind willing
to offend ; and thus ' insolent' has acquired its present meaning. But for the poet, the fact that he is
forsaking the beaten track, that he can say,

> ' peragro loca, *nullius ante*
> *Trita solo,*'

in this way to be ' insolent' or original, as we should
now say, may be his highest praise. The epithet
' furious' joined to 'insolence' in the second quotation is to be explained of that 'fine madness' which
Spenser as a Platonist esteemed a necessary condition of the poet.

For ditty and amorous ode I find Sir Walter Raleigh's vein
most lofty, *insolent*, and passionate.—PUTTENHAM, *Art of English
Poesy*, b. i. c. 3.

> Her great excellence
> Lifts me above the measure of my might,
> That being filled with furious *insolence*
> I feel myself like one yrapt in spright.
> SPENSER, *Colin Clout's come Home again.*

INSTITUTE, } These all had once in English mean_
INSTITUTER, } ings coextensive with those of the
INSTITUTION. } Latin words which they represent.
We now inform, instruct (the images are nearly the
same), but we do not ' institute,' children any more.

> A painful schoolmaster, that hath in hand
> To *institute* the flower of all a land,
> Gives longest lessons unto those, where Heaven
> The ablest wits and aptest wills hath given.
> SYLVESTER, *Du Bartas ; Seventh Day of the
> First Week.*

Neither did he this for want of better instructions, having
had the learnedest and wisest man reputed of all Britain, the
instituter of his youth.—MILTON, *History of England*, b. iii.

A Short Catechism for the *institution* of young persons in the Christian Religion.— *Title of a Treatise by Jeremy Taylor.*

INTEND, ⎫ The inveterate habit of procrastina-
INTENTION. ⎰ tion has brought us to say now that we ' intend ' a thing, when we mean hereafter to do it. Our fathers with a more accurate use of the word 'intended' that which they were at that moment actually and earnestly engaged in doing. The same habit of procrastination has made ' by-and bye ' mean not straightway, but at a comparatively remote period ; and ' presently ' not at this present, but in a little while. ' Intention ' too, or ' intension,' for Jeremy Taylor in the same work spells the word both ways, was once something not future but present.

So often as he [Augustus] was at them [the games], he did nothing else but *intend* the same.—HOLLAND, *Suetonius,* p. 60.

He [Lord Bacon] saw plainly that natural philosophy hath been *intended* by few persons, and in them hath occupied the least part of their time.—BACON, *Filum Labyrinthi,* 6.

It is so plain that every man profiteth in that he most *intendeth,* that it needeth not to be stood upon.—Id., *Essays,* 29.

> I suffer for their guilt now, and my soul,
> Like one that looks on ill-affected eyes,
> Is hurt with mere *intention* on their follies.
> > BEN JONSON, *Cynthia's Revels.*

> But did you not
> Observe with what *intention* the duke
> Set eyes on Domitilla ?
> > SHIRLEY, *The Royal Master,* act ii. sc. 1.

According as we neglect meditation, so are our prayers imperfect ; meditation being the soul of prayer, and the *intention* of our spirit.—J. TAYLOR, *Life of Christ,* part i. § 5.

The second accessory [to effectual prayer] is *intension* of spirit or fervency.—Id., *Ib*. part ii. § 12.

JACOBIN. The great French Revolution has stamped itself too deeply and terribly upon the mind of Europe for 'Jacobin' ever again to have any other meaning than that which the famous Club, assembling in the hall of the Jacobin convent, has given it; but it needs hardly to say that a 'Jacobin' was once a Dominican friar, though this name did not extend beyond France.

> Now am I young and stout and bold,
> Now am I Robert, now Robin,
> Now frere Minour, now *Jacobin*.
> > CHAUCER, *Romaunt of the Rose*, 6339.

> Agent for England, send thy mistress word,
> What this detested *Jacobin* hath done.
> > MARLOWE, *The Massacre at Paris*, act iii. sc. 4.

A certain *Jacobin* offered himself to the fire to prove that Savonarola had true revelations, and was no heretic.—J. TAYLOR, *The Liberty of Prophesying*, The Epistle Dedicatory.

JOLLY. For a long time after its adoption into the English language, 'jolly' kept the meaning of beautiful, which it brought with it from the French, and which 'joli' in French still retains.

> Then sete thei thre to solas hem at the windowe,
> Even over the *joly* place that to that paleis longed.
> > *William of Palerne*, 5478.

> I know myself to be
> A *jolly* fellow: for even now I did behold and see
> Mine image in the water sheer, and sure methought I took
> Delight to see my goodly shape and favour in the brook.
> > GOLDING, *Ovid's Metamorphosis*, b. 13.

When all the glorious realm of pure delight,
Illustrious Paradise, waited on the feet
Of *jolly* Eve.

BEAUMONT, *Psyche*, iv. 4.

KINDLY. Nothing ethical was connoted in ' kindly'
once ; it was simply the adjective of ' kind.' But it is
God's ordinance that ' kind ' should be ' kindly,' in
our modern sense of the word as well; and thus the
word has attained this meaning. See ' Unkind.'

This Joon in the Gospel witnesseth that the *kyndeli* sone cf
God is maad man.—WICLIF, *Prologe of John.*

Forasmuch as his mind gave him, that, his nephews living,
men would not reckon that he could have right to the realm, he
thought therefore without delay to rid them, as though the kill-
ing of his kinsmen could amend his cause, and make him a
kindly king.—Sir T. MORE, *History of King Richard III.*

The royal eagle is called in Greek Gnesios, as one would say,
true and *kindly*, as descended from the gentle and right aery of
eagles.—HOLLAND, *Pliny*, vol. i. p. 272.

Whatsoever as the Son of God He may do, it is *kindly* for Him
as the Son of Man to save the sons of men.—ANDREWS, *Sermons*,
vol. iv. p. 253.

Where are they? Gone to their own place, to Judas their
brother; and, as is most *kindly*, the sons, to the father, of wickedness, there to be plagued with him for ever.—Id., *Of the Conspiracy of the Gowries*, serm. 4.

What greater tyranny and usurpation over poor souls would
he have than is now exercised, since the perjured prelates, the
kindly brood of the Man of sin, have defiled and burdened our
poor Church ?—*Jus Populi Vindicatum*, 1665.

KINGDOM. This and ' reign,' which see, have been
conveniently desynonymized, this concrete, and that
abstract; thus the ' kingdom ' of Great Britain, the
' reign ' of Queen Victoria.

In the four and twenti yer of his *kynedom*
Renulf wende out of this worlde, and to the joye of hevene com.
Life of St. Kenelm, 1858, part ii. p. 50.

KNAVE. How many serving-lads must have been unfaithful and dishonest before ' knave,' which meant at first no more than boy, acquired the meaning which it has now ! Note the same history in the German ' Bube,' ' Dirne,' ' Schalk,' and see ' Varlet.'

If it is a *knave* child, sle ye him; if it is a womman, kepe ye.
—*Exodus* i. 16. WICLIF.

> The time is come; a *knave* childe she bare.
> CHAUCER, *The Man of Lawes Tale.*

> O murderous slumber,
> Lay'st thou thy leaden mace upon my boy,
> That plays thee music ? gentle *knave*, good night.
> SHAKESPEARE, *Julius Cæsar*, act iv. sc. 3.

KNUCKLE. The German ' Knöchel' is any joint whatsoever; nor was our 'knuckle' limited formerly, as now it well nigh exclusively is, at least in regard of the human body, to certain smaller joints of the hand.

Thou, Nilus, wert assigned to stay her pains and travels past,
To which as soon as Io came with much ado, at last,
With weary *knuckles* on thy brim she kneeled sadly down.
GOLDING, *Ovid's Metamorphosis*, b. i.

But when
> ' his scornful muse could ne'er abide
> With tragic shoes her *ancles* for to hide,'

the pace of the verse told me that her maukin *knuckles* were never shapen to that royal buskin.—MILTON, *Apology for Smectymnuus*, p. 186.

LACE. That which now commonly bears this name has it on the score of its curiously woven

threads; but ' lace,' probably identical with the Latin
' laqueus,' though it has not reached *us* through the
Latin, being the same word, only differently spelt, as
' latch,' is commonly used by our earlier writers in
the more proper sense of a noose.

> And in my mind I measure pace by pace,
> To seek the place where I myself had lost,
> That day that I was tangled in the *lace*
> In seeming slack, that knitteth ever most.
>
> SURREY, *The Restless State of a Lover.*

Yet if the polype can get and entangle him [the lobster] once
within his long *laces*, he dies for it.—HOLLAND, *Plutarch's
Morals,* p. 973.

LANDSCAPE. The second syllable in ' land*scape* '
or ' land*skip* ' is only a solitary example of an earlier
form of the same termination which we meet in
' friend*ship*,' ' lord*ship*,' ' fellow*ship*,' and the like.
As these mean the manner or fashion of a friend, of a
lord, and so on, so ' landscape ' the manner or fashion
of the land ; and in our earlier English this rather as
the pictured or otherwise counterfeited model, than
in its very self. As this imitation would be necessarily in small, the word acquired the secondary
meaning of a compendium or multum in parvo ; cf.
Skinner, *Etymologicon,* s. v. *Landskip* : Tabula cho-
rographica, primario autem terra, provincia, seu
topographica σκιαγραφία ; Phillips, *New World of
Words,* s. v.; and Earle, *Philology of the English
Tongue,* p. 275, who suggests that the word has
been borrowed by us from the Dutch painters, which
would at once account for the termination in ' schap '
or ' shape.'

The sins of other women show in *landskip*, far off and full of shadow ; hers [a harlot's] *in statue*, near hand and bigger in the life.—Sir THOMAS OVERBURY, *Characters*.

London, as you know, is our Ἑλλάδος Ἑλλάς, our England of England, and our *landskip* and representation of the whole island.—HACKET, *Life of Archbishop Williams*, part ii. p. 59.

The detestable traitor, that prodigy of nature, that opprobrium of mankind, that *landscape* of iniquity, that sink of sin, and that compendium of baseness, who now calls himself our Protector.—*Address sent by the Anabaptists to the King*, 1658, in CLARENDON's *History of the Great Rebellion*, b. xv.

LATCH. Few things now are ' latched ' or caught except a door or casement ; but the word, the same as ' lace,' was once of much wider use.

Those that remained threw darts at our men, and *latching* our darts, sent them again at us.—GOLDING, *Cæsar*, p. 60.

Peahens are wont to lay by night, and that from an high place where they perch ; and then, unless there be good heed taken that the eggs be *latched* in some soft bed underneath, they are soon broken.—HOLLAND, *Pliny*, vol. i. p. 301.

LECTURE. Where words like ' lecture' and ' reading ' exist side by side, it is very usual for one after a while to be appropriated to the doing of the thing, the other to the thing which is done. So it has been here ; but they were once synonymous.

After the *lecture* of the law and of the prophets, the rulers of the synagogue sent unto them, saying, Good brethren, if ye have any sermon to exhort the people, say on.—*Acts* xiii. 15. COVERDALE.

That may be gathered out of Plutarch's writings, out of those especially where he speaketh of the *lecture* of the poets.—NORTH, *Plutarch's Lives*, p. 982.

In my *lecture* I often perceive how my authors commend examples for magnanimity and force, that rather proceed from a thick skin and hardness of the bones.—FLORIO, *Montaigne's Essays*, p. 72.

LEGACY. This now owns no relation except with 'legatum,' which meant in juristic Latin a portion of the inheritance by testamentary disposition withdrawn from the heir, and bestowed upon some other; but formerly with 'legatus' and 'legatio,' ambassador and embassage.

They were then preaching bishops, and more often seen in pulpits than in princes' palaces; more often occupied in his *legacy*, who said, Go ye into the whole world and preach the gospel to all men, than in embassages and affairs of princes.— *Homilies, Against Peril of Idolatry.*

Otherwise, while he is yet far off, sending a *legacy*, he asketh those things that belong to peace.—*Luke* xiv. 32. Rheims.

And his citizens hated him, and they sent a *legacie* after him, saying, We will not have this man to reign over us.—*Luke* xix. 14. Ibid.

LEVY. Troops are now raised, or 'levied,' indifferently : but a siege is only raised, and not 'levied,' as it too once might have been.

Euphranor having *levied* the siege from this one city, forthwith led his army to Demetrias.—HOLLAND, *Livy*, p. 1178.

'LEWD,
LEWDLY,
LEWDNESS.} There are three distinct stages in the meaning of the word 'lewd;' of these it has entirely overlived two, and survives only in the third, namely in that of wanton or lascivious. Without discussing here its etymology or its exact relation to 'lay,' it is sufficient to observe, that, as 'lay,' it was often used in the sense of ignorant, or rather unlearned. Next, according to the

proud saying of the Pharisees, 'This people who knoweth not the law are cursed' (*John* vii. 49), and on the assumption, which would have its truth, that those untaught in the doctrines, would be unexercised in the practices, of Christianity, it came to signify vicious, though without designating one vice more than others. While in its present and third stage, it has, like so many other words, retired from this general designation of all vices, to express one of the more frequent, alone.

Archa Dei in the olde law Levytes it kepte ;
Had never *lewed* men leve to leggen honde on that cheste.
Piers Ploughman, 7668.

For as moche as the curatis ben often so *lewed*, that thei understonden not bookis of Latyn for to teche the peple, it is spedful not only to the *lewed* peple, but also to the *lewed* curatis, to have bookis in Englisch of needful loore to the *lewed* peple.—*Wycliffe Mss.*, p. 5.

Of sondry doutes thus they jangle and trete,
As *lewed* people demen comunly
Of thinges that ben made more subtilly
Than they can in hir *lewdnesse* comprehend.
CHAUCER, *The Squieres Tale.*

Neither was it Christ's intention that there should be any thing in it [the Lord's Prayer] dark or far from our capacity, specially since it belongeth equally to all, and is as necessary for the *lewd* as the learned.—*A Short Catechism*, 1553.

This is servitude,
To serve the unwise, or him who hath rebelled
Against his worthier, as these now serve thee,
Thyself not free, but to thyself enthralled,
Yet *lewdly* darest our ministering upbraid.
MILTON, *Paradise Lost*, b. vi.

If it were a matter of wrong or wicked *lewdness* [ῥᾳδιούργημα], O ye Jews, reason would that I should bear with you.—*Acts* xviii. 14. Authorized Version.

LIBERAL. Often used by Shakespeare and his co-temporaries as free of tongue, licentious or wanton in speech.

> There with fantastic garlands did she come,
> Of crow-flowers, nettles, daisies, and long purples,
> That *liberal* shepherds give a grosser name,
> But our cold maids do dead-men's-fingers call them.
>> SHAKESPEARE, *Hamlet*, act iv. sc. 7.

Desdemona [of *Iago*]. Is he not a most profane and *libera* counsellor?—Id., *Othello*, act ii. sc. 1.

> But that we know thee, Wyatt, to be true,
> Thy overboldness should be paid with death;
> But cease, for fear your *liberal* tongue offend.
>> WEBSTER, *The Famous History of Sir Thomas Wyatt.*

LIBERTINE. A striking evidence of the extreme likelihood that he who has no restraints on his belief will ere long have none upon his life, is given by this word 'libertine.' Applied at first to certain heretical sects, and intended to mark the licentious *liberty* of their creed, 'libertine' soon let go altogether its relation to what a man believed, and acquired the sense which it now has, a 'libertine' being one who has released himself from all moral restraints, and especially in his relations with the other sex.

That the Scriptures do not contain in them all things necessary to salvation, is the fountain of many great and capital errors ; I instance in the whole doctrine of the *libertines*, familists, quakers, and other enthusiasts, which issue from this corrupted fountain. —J. TAYLOR, *A Dissuasive from Popery*, part ii. b. 1, § 2.

It is not to be denied that the said *libertine* doctrines do more contradict the doctrine of the Gospel, even Christianity itself, than the doctrines of the Papists about the same subjects do.— BAXTER, *Catholic Theology*, part iii. p. 289.

It is too probable that our modern *libertines*, deists, and atheists, took occasion from the scandalous contentions of Chris tians about many things, to disbelieve all.—*A Discourse of Logomachies*, 1711.

LITIGIOUS. This word has changed from an objective to a subjective sense. Things were 'litigious' once, which offered matter for going to law; persons are 'litigious' now, who are prone to going to law. Both meanings are to be found in the Latin 'litigiosus,' though predominantly that which we have now made the sole meaning.

Dolopia he hath subdued by force of arms, and could not abide to hear that the determination of certain provinces, which were debatable and *litigious*, should be referred to the award of the people of Rome.—HOLLAND, *Livy*, p. 1111.

Of the articles gainsaid by a great outcry, three and no more did seem to be *litigious*.—HACKET, *Life of Archbishop Williams*, part i. p. 140.

> No fences parted fields, nor marks nor bounds
> Distinguished acres of *litigious* grounds.
> DRYDEN, *Virgil's Georgics*, b. i. 193, 4.

LIVELY. This was once nearly, if not altogether, equipollent with 'living.' We have here the explanation of a circumstance which many probably have noted and regretted in the Authorized Version of the New Testament, namely that while λίθον ζῶντα at 1 *Pet.* ii. 4 is 'a *living* stone,' λίθοι ζῶντες, which follows immediately, ver. 5, is only '*lively* stones,' 'living' being thus brought down to 'lively' with no correspondent reduction in the original to warrant it. But when our Version was made, there was scarcely any distinction between the forces of the words. Still it would certainly have been better to adhere to one word or the other.

Was it well done to suffer him, imprisoned in chains, lying in a dark dungeon, to draw his *lively* breath at the pleasure of the hangman?—HOLLAND, *Livy*, p. 228.

> Had I but seen thy picture in this plight,
> It would have madded me ; what shall I do
> Now I behold thy *lively* body so ?
> > SHAKESPEARE, *Titus Andronicus*, act iii. sc. 1.

> That his dear father might interment have,
> See, the young man entered a *lively* grave.
> > MASSINGER, *The Fatal Dowry*, act ii. sc. 1.

LIVERY. It need hardly be observed that the explanation of 'livery' which Spenser offers (see below) is perfectly correct; but we do not any longer recognize the second of those uses of the word there mentioned by him. It is no longer applied to the ration, or stated portion of food, delivered at stated periods (the σιτομέτριον of *Luke* xii. 42), either to the members of a household, to soldiers, or to others.

> To bed they busked them anon,
> Their *liveryes* were served them up soone,
> With a merry cheer.
> > *Ballad of John de Reeve*, 155.

What *livery* is, we by common use in England know well enough, namely, that is, allowance of horse-meat, as to keep horses at *livery*, the which word, I guess, is derived of livering or delivering forth their nightly food. So in great houses the *livery* is said to be served up for all night. And *livery* is also the upper weed which a servant-man weareth, so called, as I suppose, for that it was delivered and taken from him at pleasure.— SPENSER, *View of the State of Ireland*.

The emperor's officers every night went through the town from house to house, whereat any English gentleman did repast or lodge, and served their *liveries* for all night ; first the officers brought into the house a cast of fine manchet, and of silver two great pots, with white wine, and sugar, to the weight of a pound, &c.—CAVENDISH, *Life of Cardinal Wolsey*.

LOITER, ⎫ Whatever may be the derivation of ' to
LOITERER. ⎭ loiter ' it is certain that it formerly
implied a great deal more and worse than it implies
now. The 'loiterer' then was very much what the
tramp is now.

God bad that no such strong lubbers should *loyter* and goe a
begging, and be chargeable to the congregation.—TYNDALE,
Works, p. 217.

He that giveth any alms to an idle beggar robbeth the truly
poor; as S. Ambrose sometimes complaineth that the maintenance of the poor is made the spoil of the *loiterer.*—SANDERSON,
Sermons, 1671, vol. i. p. 198.

If he be but once so taken idly roguing, he [the Provost
Martial] may punish him more lightly, as with stocks or such
like; but if he be found again so *loitering* he may scourge him
with whips or rods; after which if he be again taken, let him
have the bitterness of martial law.—SPENSER, *View of the State
of Ireland.*

LOVER. This word has undergone two restric-
tions, of which formerly it knew nothing. A natural
delicacy, and an unwillingness to confound under a
common name things essentially different, has caused
'lover' no longer to be equivalent with friend, but
always to imply a relation resting on the difference
of sex; while further, and within these narrower
limits, the 'lover' is always the man, not as once
the man or the woman indifferently. We might
still indeed speak of 'a pair of lovers,' but then datur
denominatio a potiori.

If ye love them that love you, what thank have ye therefore?
for sinners also love their *lovers.*—*Luke* vi. 32. COVERDALE.

For Hiram was ever a *lover* of David.—1 *Kin.* v. 1. Authorized Version.

> This Posthumus,
> Most like a noble lord in love, and one
> That had a royal *lover*, took his hint.
> > SHAKESPEARE, *Cymbeline*, act v. sc. 5.

> If I freely may discover
> What would please me in a *lover*,
> I would have *her* fair and witty,
> Savouring more of court than city.
> > BEN JONSON, *The Poetaster*.

LUCID INTERVAL. We limit this at present to the brief and transient season when a mind, ordinarily clouded and obscured by insanity, recovers for a while its clearness. It had no such limitation formerly, but was of very wide use, as the four passages quoted below, in each of which its application is different, will show.*

East of Edom lay the land of Uz, where Job dwelt, so renowned for his patience, when the devil heaped afflictions upon him, allowing him no *lucid intervals.*—FULLER, *A Pisgah Sight of Palestine*, b. iv. c. 2.

---

* One would willingly know a little more of this phrase 'lucid interval,' which had evidently about the time of the first of my quotations recently come into the language, but from what quarter, whether from the writings of physicians or naturalists, or from what other source, I am unable to say. Of its recent introduction I find evidence in the following passage:—' The saints have their *turbida intervalla*, their ebbing and flowing, their full and their wane ; but yet all their cloudings do but obscure their graces, not extinguish them. All the goodness of other men that seem to live, are but *lucida intervalla*, they are good but by fits.' (PRESTON, *Description of Spiritual Death and Life*, 1636, p. 73.) No one would have used this Latin phrase in a sermon had ' lucid interval' been already familiar in English, or had ' lucidum intervallum ' not already somewhere existed. The word ' interval,' it may be here remarked, was only coming into use at the beginning of the seventeenth century. Holland in his *Pliny* uses, but using explains it ; while Chillingworth still regards it as Latin, and writes ' intervalla.'

Some beams of wit on other souls may fall,
Strike through, and make a *lucid interval*:
But Shadwell's genuine night admits no ray,
His rising fogs prevail upon the day.

DRYDEN, Mac-Flecknoe.

Such is the nature of man, that it requires *lucid intervals*; and the vigour of the mind would flag and decay, should it always jog on at the rate of a common enjoyment, without being sometimes quickened and exalted with the vicissitude of some more refined pleasures.—SOUTH, *Sermons*, 1744, vol. viii. p. 403.

Thus he [Lord Lyttelton] continued, giving his dying benediction to all around him. On Monday morning a *lucid interval* gave some small hopes; but these vanished in the evening.— *Narrative of the Physician, inserted in Johnson's Life of Lord Lyttelton.*

LUMBER. As the Lombards were the bankers, so also they were the pawnbrokers of the middle ages; indeed, as they would often advance money upon pledges, the two businesses were very closely joined, would often run in, to one another. The 'lumber' room was originally the Lombard room, or room where the Lombard banker and broker stowed away his pledges; 'lumber' then, as in the passage from Butler, the pawns and pledges themselves. As these would naturally often accumulate here till they became out of date and unserviceable, the steps are easy to be traced by which the word came to possess its present meaning.

Lumber, potius *lumbar*, as to put one's clothes to *lumbar, i.e.* pignori dare, oppignorare.—SKINNER, *Etymologicon.*

And by an action falsely laid of trover
The *lumber* for their proper goods recover.

BUTLER, Upon Critics.

They put up all the little plate they had in the *lumber*, which is pawning it, till the ships came.—Lady MURRAY, *Lives of George Baillie and of Lady Grisell Baillie.*

LURCH. 'To lurch' is seldom used now except of a ship, which 'lurches' when it makes something of a headlong dip in the sea; the fact that by so doing it, partially at least, hides itself, and so 'lurks,' for 'lurk' and 'lurch' are identical, explains this employment of the word. But 'to lurch,' generally as an active verb, was of much more frequent use in early English; and soon superinduced on the sense of lying concealed that of lying in wait with the view of intercepting and seizing a prey. After a while this superadded notion of intercepting and seizing some booty quite thrust out that of lying concealed; as in all three of the quotations which follow.

It is not an auspicate beginning of a feast, nor agreeable to amity and good fellowship, to snatch or *lurch* one from another, to have many hands in a dish at once, striving a vie who should be more nimble with his fingers.—HOLLAND, *Plutarch's Morals*, p. 679.

I speak not of many more [discommodities of a residence] ; too far off from great cities, which may hinder business ; or too near them, which *lurcheth* all provisions, and maketh every thing dear.—BACON, *Essays*, 45.

At the beginning of this war [the Crusades] the Pope's temporal power in Italy was very slender ; but soon after he grew within short time without all measure, and did *lurch* a castle here, gain a city there from the emperor, while he was employed in Palestine.—FULLER, *The Holy War*, b. i. c. 11.

LUST. Used at this present only in an ill sense, not as ἐπιθυμία, but as ἐπιθυμία κακή (*Col.* iii. 5), and this mainly in one particular direction. 'Lust' had formerly no such limitations, nor has it now in German. The same holds good of the verb.

Of prikyng and of huntyng for the hare
Was al his *lust*, for no cost wolde he spare.
CHAUCER, *Canterbury Tales*, 192.

Through faith a man is purged of his sins, and obtaineth *lust* unto the law of God.—TYNDALE, *Prologue upon the Epistle to the Romans*.

It was not because of the multitude of you above all nations that the Lord had *lust* unto you and chose you.—*Deut.* vii. 7. COVERDALE.

Thou mayest kill and eat flesh in all thy gates, whatsoever thy soul *lusteth* after.—*Deut.* xii. 15. Authorized Version.

LUXURY, } 'Luxuria' in classical Latin was very
LUXURIOUS. } much what our 'luxury' is now. The meaning which in our earlier English was its only one, namely indulgence in sins of the flesh, is derived from the use of 'luxuria' in the medieval ethics, where it never means anything else but this. The weakening of the influence of the scholastic theology, joined to a more familiar acquaintance with classical Latinity, has probably caused its return to the classical meaning. In the definition given by Phillips (see below), we note the process of transition from its old meaning to its new, the old still remaining, but the new superinduced upon it.

O foule lust of *luxurie*, to thin ende
Not only that thou taintest mannes mind,
But veraily thou wolt his body shende.
CHAUCER, *The Man of Lawes Tale*.

Luxury and lust fasten a rust and foulness on the mind, that it cannot see sin in its odious deformity, nor virtue in its unattainable beauty.—BATES, *Spiritual Perfection*, c. 1.

Luxury, all superfluity and excess in carnal pleasures, sumptuous fare or building; sensuality, riotousness, profuseness.—PHILLIPS, *New World of Words*.

> She knows the heat of a *luxurious* bed.
> Shakespeare, *Much Ado about Nothing*, act iv. sc. 1.

Again, that many of their Popes be such as I have said, naughty, wicked, *luxurious* men, they openly confess.—Jackson, *The Eternal Truth of Scriptures*, b. ii. c. 14.

Magnificent,) Frequently used by our elder
Magnificence.) writers where we should employ munificent or generous. Yet there lay in the word something more than in these; something of the μεγαλοπρεπεία of Aristotle; a certain grandeur presiding over and ordering this large distribution of wealth. Behind both uses an earlier and a nobler than either may be traced, as is evident from my first quotation.

Then cometh *magnificence*, that is to say when a man doth and performeth gret werkes of goodnesse.—Chaucer, *The Persones Tale*.

Every amorous person becometh liberal and *magnificent*, although he had been aforetime a pinching snudge; in such sort as men take more pleasure to give away and bestow upon those whom they love, than they do to take and receive of others.— Holland, *Plutarch's Morals*, p. 1147.

> Am I close-handed,
> Because I scatter not among you that
> I must not call my own? know, you court-leeches,
> A prince is never so *magnificent*
> As when he's sparing to enrich a few
> With the injuries of many.
> Massinger, *The Emperor of the East*, act ii. sc. 1.

Bounty and *magnificence* are virtues very regal; but a prodigal king is nearer a tyrant than a parsimonious.—Bacon, *Essays, Of a King*.

Maid. A word which, in its highest sense as= virgin, might once be applied to either sex, to Sir

Galahad as freely as to the *Pucelle*, but which is now restricted to one. Compare παρθένος in Greek.

To him [John the Apostle] God hangyng in the cross bitook his modir, that a *mayde* schulde kepe a mayde.—WICLIF, *Prolog of John.*

> I wot wel that the Apostle was a *maid* ;
> But natheless, though that he wrote and said
> He wold that every wight were swiche as he,
> All n'is but conseil to virginitee.
>
> <div align="right">CHAUCER, <i>Wife of Bath's Tale.</i></div>

Sir Galahad is a *maid* and sinned never; and that is the cause he shall achieve where he goeth that ye nor none such shall not attain.—Sir T. MALORY, *Morte D'Arthur*, b. xiii. c. 16.

MAKE, } The very early use of 'maker,' as equiva-
MAKER. } lent to poet, and 'to make' as applied to the exercise of the poet's art, is evidence that the words are of genuine home-growth, and not mere imitations of the Greek ποιητής and ποιεῖν, which Sir Philip Sydney, as will be seen below, suggests as possible. The words, like the French 'trouvère' and 'troubadour,' the O.H.D. 'scof,' and the A.S. 'scop,' mark men's sense that invention, and in a certain sense, creation, is the essential character of the poet The quotation from Chaucer will sufficiently prove how entirely mistaken Sir John Harrington was, when he affirmed (*Apology for Poetry*, p. 2) that Puttenham in his *Art of English Poesy*, 1589, was the first who gave 'make' and 'maker' this meaning. Sir Walter Scott somewhere claims them as Scotticisms; but exclusively such they certainly are not.

> And eke to me it is a great penaunce,
> Sith rime in English hath such scarcite,

> To follow word by word the curiosite
> Of Graunson, flour of hem that *make* in Fraunce.
> > CHAUCER, *Complaint of Mars and Venus.*

> The God of shepherds, Tityrus, is dead,
> Who taught me, homely as I can, to *make.*
> > SPENSER, *The Shepherd's Calendar, June.*

The old famous poet Chaucer, for his excellency and wonderful skill in *making*, his scholar Lidgate (a worthy scholar of so excellent a master) calleth the lode-star of our language.—E. K., *Epistle Dedicatory to Spenser's Shepherd's Calendar.*

There cannot be in a *maker* a fouler fault than to falsify his accent to serve his cadence, or by untrue orthography to wrench his words to help his rhyme.—PUTTENHAM, *Art of English Poesy*, b. ii. c. 8.

The Greeks named the poet ποιητής, which name, as the most excellent, hath gone through other languages. It cometh of this word ποιεῖν, to make; wherein I know not whether by luck or wisdom we Englishmen have met well with the Greeks in calling him a *maker.*—Sir P. SIDNEY, *Defence of Poetry.*

MANURE. This is the same word as 'manœuvre,' to work with the hand; and thus, to till or cultivate the earth; this tillage being in earlier periods of society the great and predominant labour of the hands. We restrain the word now to one particular branch of this cultivation, but our ancestors made it to embrace the whole.

The *manuring* hand of the tiller shall root up all that burdens the soil.—MILTON, *Reason of Church Government.*

It [Japan] is mountainous and craggy, full of rocks and stony places, so that the third part of this empire is not inhabited or *manured.*—*Memorials of Japan* (Hackluyt Society), p. 3.

A rare and excellent wit untaught doth bring forth many good and evil things together; as a fat soil, that lieth *unmanured*, bringeth forth both herbs and weeds.—NORTH, *Plutarch's Lives*, p. 185.

Every man's hand itching to throw a cudgel at him, who, like a nut-tree, must be *manured* by beating, or else would never bear fruit.—Fuller, *The Holy War*, b. ii. c. 11.

MEAN, } This word was originally used in the
MEANNESS. } sense of 'common,' 'lowly,' without
the notion of moral baseness which now attaches to it.

Thys man is *meane* of stature, yonge enough, well wittyd, well manerd.—*Paston Letters*, vol. v. p. 124.

And the *mean* man boweth down, and the great man humbleth himself.—Isai. ii. 9. Authorized Version.

> But, for his *meanness* and disparagement,
> My sire, who me too dearly well did love,
> Unto my choice by no means would assent.
> Spenser, *Fairy Queen*, iv. 7, 16.

MEASLES. This has only been by later use restrained to one kind of *spotted* sickness; but 'meazel'
(it is spelt in innumerable ways) was once leprosy,
or more often the leper himself, and the disease,
'meselry.'

Forsothe he was a stronge man and riche, but *mesell.*— 4 *Kin.* v. 1. Wiclif.

In this same year the *mysseles* thorow oute Cristendom were slaundered that thei had mad covenaunt with Sarasenes for to poison all Christen men.—Capgrave, *Chronicle of England*, p. 186.

He [Pope Deodatus] kissed a *mysel*, and sodeynly the *mysel* was whole.—Id., *Ib.* p. 95.

MECHANIC, } This now simply expresses a fact,
MECHANICAL. } and is altogether untinged with passion or sentiment; but in its early history it ran
exactly parallel to the Greek βάναυσος, which, expressing first the sitting by the stove, as one plying

a handicraft might do, came afterwards, in obedience to certain constant tendencies of language, to imply the man ethically illiberal. See the quotation from Holland, *s. v.* 'Fairy.'

Base and *mechanical* niggardise they [flatterers] account temperate frugality.—HOLLAND, *Plutarch's Morals*, p. 93.

Base dunghill villain and *mechanical*.
                    SHAKESPEARE, 2 *Henry VI.*, act i. sc. 3.

It was never a good world, since employment was counted *mechanic*, and idleness gentility.—WHITLOCK, *Zootomia*, p. 30.

MEDDLE. This had once no such offensive meaning of mixing oneself up in other people's business as now it has. On the contrary, Barrow in one of his sermons draws expressly the distinction between 'meddling' and being meddlesome, and only condemns the latter.

In the drynke that she *meddlid* to you, mynge ye double to her.—*Apoc.* xviii. 6. WICLIF.

How is it that thou, being a Jew, askest drink of me, which am a Samaritan? For the Jews *meddle* not [οὐ συγχρῶνται] with the Samaritans.—*John* iv. 9. CRANMER.

We beseech you, brethren, that ye study to be quiet, and to *meddle* with your own business.—1 *Thess.* iv. 10, 11. TYNDALE.

Tho he, that had well y-conned his lere,
Thus *medled* his talk with many a tear.
                    SPENSER, *The Shepherd's Calendar, May.*

MEDITERRANEAN. Only seas are 'mediterranean' now, and for us only one Sea; but there is no reason why cities and countries should not be characterized as 'mediterranean' as well; and they were so once. We have preferred, however, to employ 'inland.'

Their buildings are for the most part of tymber, for the *mediterranean* countreys have almost no stone.—*The Kyngdome of Japonia*, p. 6.

An old man, full of days, and living still in your *mediterranean* city, Coventry.—HENRY HOLLAND, *Preface to Holland's Cyropædia*.

It [Arabia] hath store of cities as well *mediterranean* as maritime.—HOLLAND, *Ammianus*.

MEDLEY. It is plain from the frequent use of the French 'mêlée' in the description of battles that we feel the want of a corresponding English word. There have been attempts, though hardly successful ones, to naturalize 'mêlée,' and as ' volée ' has become in English 'volley,' that so 'mêlée' should become 'melley.' Perhaps, as Tennyson has sanctioned these, employing 'mellay' in his *Princess*, they may now succeed. But there would have been no need of this, nor yet of borrowing a foreign word, if 'medley' had been allowed to keep this more passionate use, which once it possessed.

The consul for his part forslowed not to come to hand-fight. The *medley* continued above three hours, and the hope of victory hung in equal balance.—HOLLAND, *Livy*, p. 1119.

Now began the conflict for the winning and defending of that old castle, which proved a *medley* of twelve hours long.—*Swedish Intelligencer*, vol. ii. p. 41.

MELANCHOLY. This has now ceased, nearly or altogether, to designate a particular form of moody madness, the German 'Tiefsinn,' which was ascribed by the old physicians to a predominance of *black bile* mingling with the blood. It was not, it is true, always restrained to this peculiar form of mental unsoundness; thus Burton's 'Anatomy of *Melan-*

choly' has not to do with this one form of madness, but with all. This, however, was its prevailing use, and here is to be found the link of connexion between its present use, as a deep pensiveness or sadness, and its past.

That property of *melancholy*, whereby men become to be delirious in some one point, their judgment standing untouched in others.—H. MORE, *A Brief Discourse of Enthusiasm*, sect. xiv.

Luther's conference with the devil might be, for ought I know, nothing but a *melancholy* dream.—CHILLINGWORTH, *The Religion of Protestants*, Preface.

Though I am persuaded that none but the devil and this *melancholy* miscreant were in the plot [the Duke of Buckingham's murder], yet in foro Dei many were guilty of this blood, that rejoiced it was spilt.—HACKET, *Life of Archbishop Williams*, part ii. p. 80.

Some *melancholy* men have believed that elephants and birds and other creatures have a language whereby they discourse with one another.—REYNOLDS, *Passions and Faculties of the Soul*, c. 39.

MERE, ⎫ There is a good note on these words, and
MERELY. ⎭ on the changes of meaning which they
have undergone, in Craik's *English of Shakespeare*, p. 80. He there says: 'Merely (from the Latin merus and mere) means purely, only. It separates that which it designates and qualifies from everything else. But in so doing the chief or most emphatic reference may be made either to that which is included, or to that which is excluded. In modern English it is always to the latter. In Shakespeare's day the other reference was more common, that namely to what was included.'

With them all the people of Mounster went out, and many other of them which were *mere* English, thenceforth joined themselves with the Irish against the king, and termed themselves very Irish.—SPENSER, *View of the State of Ireland.*

Our wine is here mingled with water and with myrrh; there [in heaven] it is *mere* and unmixed.—J. TAYLOR, *The Worthy Communicant.*

The great winding-sheets, that bury all things in oblivion, are two, deluges and earthquakes. As for conflagrations and great droughts, they do not *merely* dispeople and * destroy. Phaethon's car went but a day; and the three years' drought, in the time of Elias, was but particular, and left people alive.—BACON, *Essays,* 58.

> Fye on't; O fye! 'tis an unweeded garden,
> That grows to seed; things rank and gross in nature
> Possess it *merely.*
>
> SHAKESPEARE, *Hamlet,* act i. sc 2.

MESS. This used continually to be applied to a quaternion, or group of *four* persons or things. Probably in the distribution of food to large numbers, it was found most convenient to arrange them in *fours,* and hence this application of the word. A 'mess' at the Inns of Court still consists of four. A phrase-book published in London in 1617 bears this title, 'Janua Linguarum *Quadrilinguis,* or A Messe of Tongues, Latine, English, French, and Spanish.'

There lacks a fourth thing to make up the *mess.*—LATIMER, *Sermon* 5.

> Where are your *mess*† of sons to back you now?
> SHAKESPEARE, 3 *Henry VI.,* act i. sc. 4.

Amongst whom [converted Jews] we meet with a *mess* of most

---

* A recent editor of Bacon, I need hardly say not the *most* recent, has made a hopeless confusion by changing this 'and' into 'but,' evidently from not understanding the old use of 'merely.'

† Edward, George, Richard, and Edmund.

eminent men ; Nicolaus Lyra, that grand commentator on the
Bible ; Hieronymus de Sanctâ Fide, turned Christian about anno
1412 ; Ludovicus Carettus, living in Paris anno 1553 ; and the
neversufficiently to be praised Emmanuel Tremellius.—FULLER,
A Pisgah Sight of Palestine, part ii. b. 5.

METAL. The Latin 'metallum' signified a mine
before it signified the metal which was found in the
mine ; and Jeremy Taylor uses 'metal' in this sense
of mine. This may be a latinism peculiar to him, as
he has of such not a few ; in which case it would
scarcely have a right to a place in this little volume,
which does not propose to note the peculiarities of
single writers, but the general course of the language.
I, however, insert it, counting it more probable that
my limited reading hinders me from furnishing an
example of this use from some other author, than
that such does not somewhere exist.

It was impossible to live without our king, but as slaves live,
that is, such who are civilly dead, and persons condemned to
metals.—J. TAYLOR, *Ductor Dubitantium, Epistle Dedicatory.*

METHODIST. This term is restricted at present to
the followers of John Wesley ; but it was once applied to those who followed a certain 'method' in
philosophical speculation, or in the ethical treatment
of themselves or others.

The finest *methodists,* according to Aristotle's golden rule of
artificial bounds, condemn geometrical precepts in arithmetic, or
arithmetical precepts in geometry, as irregular and abusive.—
G. HARVEY, *Pierce's Supererogation,* p. 117.

For physick, search into the writings of Hippocrates, Galen
and the *methodists.*—SANDERSON, *Sermons,* vol. ii. p. 135.

All of us have some or other tender parts of our souls, which
we cannot endure should be ungently touched ; every man must

be his own *methodist* to find them out.—JACKSON, *Justifying Faith,* b. iv. c. 5.

MILITIA. By this name, as the contests between Charles I. and his Parliament have made us all to know, the entire military force of the nation, and not a part of it only, was designated in the seventeenth century. It is true indeed that this force did much more nearly resemble our militia than our standing army, but it was never used for that to the exclusion of this.

It was a small thing to contend with the Parliament about the sole power of the *militia*, when we see him doing little less than laying hands on the weapons of God Himself, which are his judgements, to wield and manage them by the sway and bent of his own frail cogitations.—MILTON, *Iconoclastes,* c. 26.

The king's captains and soldiers fight his battles, and yet he is *summus imperator*, and the power of the *militia* is his.— J. TAYLOR, *Ductor Dubitantium,* iii. 3, 7.

Ye are of his flock and his *militia*; ye are now to fight his battles, and therefore to put on his armour.—Id., *On Preparation for Confirmation,* § 7.

MINION. Once no more than darling or dearling (mignon). It is quite a superaddition of later times that the 'minion' is an unworthy object, on whom an excessive fondness is bestowed.

> Map now an Adam in thy memory,
> By God's own hand made with great majesty;
> No idiot fool, not drunk with vain opinion,
> But God's disciple, and his dearest *minion*.
> >   SYLVESTER, *Du Bartas' Weeks, The Imposture.*

> Whoso to marry a *minion* wife
>   Hath had good chance and hap,
> Must love her and cherish her all his life,
>   And dandle her in his lap.
> >   *Old Song.*

MINUTE. 'Minutes' are now 'minúte' portions of *time*; they might once be 'minúte' portions of anything.

But whanne a pore widewe was come, sche cast two *mynutis*, that is a ferthing.—*Mark* xii. 42. WICLIF.

Let us, with the poor widow of the Gospel, at least give two *minutes*.—BECON, *The Nosegay*, Preface.

An enquiry into the *minutes* of conscience is commonly the work of persons that live holily.—J. TAYLOR, *Doctrine and Practice of Repentance*, Preface.

And now, after such a sublimity of malice, I will not instance in the sacrilegious ruin of the neighbouring temples, which needs must have perished in the flame. These are but *minutes*, in respect of the ruin prepared for the living temples.—Id., *Sermon on the Gunpowder Treason.*

MISCREANT. A settled conviction that to believe wrongly is the way to live wrongly has caused that in all languages words, which originally did but indicate the first, have gradually acquired a meaning of the second. There is no more illustrious example of this than 'miscreant,' which now charges him to whom it is applied not with religious error, but with extreme moral depravity; while yet, according to its etymology, it did but mean at the first misbeliever, and as such would have been as freely applied to the morally most blameless of these as to the vilest and the worst. In the quotation from Shakespeare York means to charge the Maid of Orleans, as a dealer in unlawful charms, with apostasy from the Christian faith, according to the low and unworthy estimate of her character, above which even Shakespeare himself has not risen.

We are not therefore ashamed of the Gospel of our Lord Jesus

Christ, because *miscreants* in scorn have upbraided us that the highest of our wisdom is, Believe.—HOOKER, *Ecclesiastical Polity*, b. v.

One sort you say be those that believe not in Christ, but deny Christ and his Scripture; as be the Turks, paynims, and such other *miscreants.*—FRITH, *Works*, 1572, p. 62.

> Curse, *miscreant*, when thou comest to the stake.
> SHAKESPEARE, 1 *Henry VI.*, act v. sc. 2.

The consort and the principal servants of Soliman had been honourably restored without ransom; and the emperor's generosity to the *miscreant* was interpreted as treason to the Christian cause.—GIBBON, *Decline and Fall of the Roman Empire*, c. 58.

MISER,
MISERY,
MISERABLE.
We may notice a curious shifting of parts in 'miser,' 'misery,' 'miserable.' There was a time when the 'miser' was the wretched man, he is now the covetous; at the same time 'misery,' which is now wretchedness, and 'miserable,' which is now wretched, were severally covetousness and covetous. They have in fact exactly reversed their uses. Men still express by some words of this group, although not by the same, by 'miser' (and 'miserly'), not as once by 'misery' and 'miserable,' their deep moral conviction that the avaricious man is his own tormentor, and bears his punishment involved in his sin. A passage, too long to quote, in Gascoigne's *Fruits of War*, st. 72–74, is very instructive on the different uses of the word 'miser' even in his time, and on the manner in which it was even then hovering between the two meanings.

Because thou sayest, That I am rich and enriched and lack nothing; and knowest not that thou art a *miser* [et nescis quia

M

tu es *miser*, Vulg.] and miserable and poor and blind and naked.
—*Rev.* iii. 17. Rhemish Version.

Vouchsafe to stay your steed for humble *miser's* sake.
Spenser, *Fairy Queen*, ii. 1, 8.

He [Perseus] returned again to his old humour which was
born and bred with him, and that was avarice and *misery.*—
North, *Plutarch's Lives*, p. 215.

But Brutus, scorning his [Octavius Cæsar's] *misery* and niggardliness, gave unto every band a number of wethers to sacrifice, and fifty silver drachmas to every soldier.—Id., *Ib.* p. 830.

If *avarice* be thy vice, yet make it not thy punishment ;
miserable men commiserate not themselves ; bowelless unto
themselves, and merciless unto their own bowels.—Sir T. Browne,
Letter to a Friend.

The liberal-hearted man is by the opinion of the prodigal,
miserable; and by the judgment of the *miserable*, lavish.—
Hooker, *Ecclesiastical Polity*, b. v. c. 65.

Miss. Now to be conscious of the loss of, and
nearly answering to the Latin ' desiderare,' but once
to do without, to dispense with.

But as 'tis,
We cannot *miss* him ; he does make our fire,
Fetch in our wood, and serves in offices
That profit us.
Shakespeare, *Tempest*, act i. sc. 2.

I will have honest valiant souls about me :
I cannot *miss* thee.
Beaumont and Fletcher, *The Mad Lover*, act ii.

Model. 'Module,' or 'modulus,' a diminutive of
'modus ;' but this diminutive sense which once went
constantly with the word, and which will alone explain the quotations which follow, when it lies in the
word now, lies in it only by accident.

O England, *model* to thy inward greatness,
Like little body with a mighty heart.
Shakespeare, *Henry V.*, act ii. Chorus.

And nothing can we call our own but death,
And that small *model* of the barren earth
Which serves as paste and cover to our bones.

Id., Richard II., act iii. sc. 2.

If Solomon's Temple were compared to some structures and fanes of heathen gods, it would appear as St. Gregory's to St. Paul's (the babe by the mother's side), or rather this David's *model* would be like David himself standing by Goliath, so gigantic were some pagan fabrics in comparison thereof.—FULLER, *A Pisgah Sight of Palestine*, b. iii. c. 3.

MOOD. It is hardly necessary to observe that there are two 'moods' in the English language, the one the Latin 'modus,' and existing in the two forms of 'mood' (grammatical) and 'mode;' the other the Anglo-Saxon 'mod,' the German 'muth.' It is this last with which we are dealing here. It would seem as if its homonym had influenced it so far as to take out in great part the force from it, though not from 'moody;' but it had not always so done.

And on hire bare knees adown they fall,
And wolde have kist his feet there as he stood,
Till at the last aslaked was his *mood*.

CHAUCER, The Knightes Tale.

And as a lion skulking all in night
Far off in pastures, and come home all dight
In jaws and breastlocks with an oxe's blood
New feasted on him, his looks full of *mood*,
So looked Ulysses.

CHAPMAN, Homer's Odysseis, b. xxii. l. 518.

Then Phœbus gathered up his steeds that yet for fear did run,
Like flaighted fiends, and in his *mood* without respect begun
To beat his whipstock on their pates, and lash them on their sides.

GOLDING, Ovid's Metamorphosis, b. ii.

MOROSE. It is very curious that while the classical 'mōrosus' expressed one given overmuch to his

M 2

own manners, habits, ways (mores), very nearly the Greek αὐθέκαστος, the medieval 'mŏrosus' was commonly connected with 'mora,' a delay; and in treatises of Christian ethics was the technical word to express the sin of *delaying* upon impure, wanton, or, as in the quotation from South, malignant thoughts, instead of rejecting them on the instant. See, for instance, Gerson, *Opp.*, vol. i. p. 377, for evidence constantly recurring of its connexion for him with 'mora.' So long as the scholastic theology exerted more or less influence on our own, 'morose' was often employed in this sense; which, however, it has since entirely foregone. I owe the third quotation given below to Todd, who is so entirely unaware of this history of 'morose,' that he explains it there as ungovernable!

Here are forbidden all wanton words, and all *morose* delighting in venereous thoughts, all rolling and tossing such things in our minds.—J. TAYLOR, *Doctrine and Practice of Repentance*, c. 4, § 1.

All *morose* thoughts, that is, *delaying*, dwelling, or insisting on such thoughts, fancying of such unclean matters with delectation. —HAMMOND, *Practical Catechism*, b. ii. § 6.

In this [the seventh] commandment are forbidden all that feed this sin [adultery], or are incentives to it, as luxurious diet, inflaming wines, an idle life, *morose* thoughts, that dwell in the fancy with delight.—NICHOLSON, *Exposition of the Catechism*, 1662, p. 123.

For we must know that it is the *morose* dwelling of the thoughts upon an injury, a long and sullen meditation upon a wrong, that incorporates and rivets it into the mind.—SOUTH, *Sermons*, vol. x. p. 278.

MORTAL. We speak still of a 'mortal' sin or a 'mortal' wound, but the active sense has nearly departed from the word, as the passive has altogether departed from ' deadly,' which see.

> Were there a serpent seen with forkèd tongue
> That slily glided towards your majesty,
> It were but necessary you were waked,
> Lest, being suffered in that harmful slumber,
> The *mortal* worm might make the sleep eternal.
>> SHAKESPEARE, 2 *Henry VI.*, act iii. sc. 2.

> Come, thou *mortal* wretch,
> With thy sharp teeth this knot intrinsicate
> Of life at once untie.
>> Id., *Antony and Cleopatra*, act v. sc. 2.

MOUNTEBANK. Now *any* antic fool ; but once restrained to the quack-doctor who at fairs and such places of resort having *mounted* on a *bank* or *bench*, from thence proclaimed the virtue of his drugs; being described by Whitlock (*Zootomia*, p. 436) as ' a fellow above the vulgar more by three planks and two empty hogsheads than by any true skill.' See the quotation from Jackson, *s. v.* ' Authentic.'

Such is the weakness and easy credulity of men, that a *mountebank* or cunning woman is preferred before an able physician.—WHITLOCK, *Zootomia*, p. 437.

Giving no cause of complaint to any but such as are unwilling to be healed of their shameful and dangerous diseases, who love ignorant and flattering *mountebanks* more than the most learned and faithful physicians of souls.—GAUDEN, *Hieraspistes*, p. 427.

> Above the reach of antidotes, the power
> Of the famed Pontic *mountebank* to cure.
>> OLDHAM, *Third Satire upon the Jesuits.*

MUTTON. It is a refinement in the English language, one wanting in some other languages which count themselves as refined or more, that it has in so

many cases one word to express the living animal,
and another its flesh prepared for food; ox and beef,
calf and veal, deer and venison, sheep and mutton.
In this last instance the refinement is of somewhat
late introduction. At one time they were syno-
nyms.

Peucestas, having feasted them in the kingdom of Persia, and
given every soldier a *mutton* to sacrifice, thought he had won
great favour and credit among them.—NORTH, *Plutarch's Lives*,
p. 505.

A starved *mutton's* carcass would better fit their palates.—
BEN JONSON, *The Sad Shepherd*, act i. sc. 2.

NAMELY. Now only designates; but, like the
German 'namentlich,' once designated as first and
chief, as deserving above all others to be named.

For there are many disobedient, and talkers of vanity, and
deceivers of minds, *namely* [μάλιστα] they of the circumcision.—
Tit. i. 10. TYNDALE.

For in the darkness occasioned by the opposition of the earth
just in the mids between the sun and the moon, there was
nothing for him [Nicias] to fear, and *namely* at such a time,
when there was cause for him to have stood upon his feet, and
served valiantly in the field.—HOLLAND, *Plutarch's Morals*,
p. 265.

NATURALIST. At present the student of natural
history; but in the sixteenth and seventeenth centuries
the name was often given to the deist, as one who
denied any but a religion *of nature.* 'Natural religion men' such were sometimes called. See the
quotation from Rogers, *s. v.* 'Civil.'

But that he [the atheist] might not be shy of me, I have con-
formed myself as near his own garb as I might, without par-

taking of his folly or wickedness; and have appeared in the plain shape of a mere *naturalist* myself, that I might, if it were possible, win him off from downright atheism.—H. MORE, *Antidote against Atheism*, Preface, p. 7.

This is the invention of Satan, that whereas all will not be profane, nor *naturalists*, nor epicures, but will be religious, lo, he hath a bait for every fish, and can insinuate himself as well into religion itself as into lusts and pleasures.—ROGERS, *Naaman the Syrian*, p. 115.

Heathen *naturalists* hold better consort with the primitive Church concerning the nature of sin original than the Socinians. —JACKSON, *Of Christ's Everlasting Priesthood*, b. x. c. 8, § 4.

NEEDFUL. This was once often equivalent to 'needy.' The words, however, have in more recent times been discriminated in use, and 'needy' is active, and 'needful' passive.

These ferthinges shal be gaderid at everi moneth ende, and delid forth to the *needful* man in honor of Christ and his moder. —*English Gilds*, p. 38.

Grieve not the heart of him that is helpless, and withdraw not the gift from the *needful.—Ecclus.* iv. 2. COVERDALE.

For Thou art the poor man's help, and strength for the *needful* in his necessity.—Isai. xxv. 3. Id.

Great variety of clothes have been permitted to princes and nobility, and they usually give those clothes as rewards to servants and other persons *needful* enough.—J. TAYLOR, *Holy Living*, iv. 8, 13.

NEPHEW. Restrained at this present to the son of a brother or a sister; but formerly of much laxer use, a grandson, or even a remoter lineal descendant. In East Anglia it is still so used in the popular language (see Nall, *Dialects of the East Coast*, s. v.). 'Nephew' in fact has undergone exactly the same change of meaning that 'nepos' in Latin under-

went; which in the Augustan age meaning grandson, in the post-Augustan acquired the signification
of ' nephew ' in our present acceptation of that word.
See ' Niece.'

The warts, black moles, spots and freckles of fathers, not
appearing at all upon their own children's skin, begin afterwards
to put forth and show themselves in their *nephews*, to wit, the
children of their sons and daughters.—HOLLAND, *Plutarch's
Morals*, p. 555.

With what intent they [the apocryphal books] were first
published, those words of the *nephew* of Jesus do plainly enough
signify : After that my *grandfather* Jesus had given himself to
the reading of the law and the prophets, he purposed also to
write something pertaining to learning and wisdom.—HOOKER,
Ecclesiastical Polity, b. v. c. 20.

If any widow have children or *nephews* [ἔκγονα], let them
learn first to show piety at home, and to requite their parents.—
1 *Tim.* v. 4.   Authorized Version.

NICE.   The use of ' nice ' in the sense of fastidious,
difficult to please, still survives, indeed this is now,
as in times past, the ruling notion of the word ; only
this ' niceness ' is taken now much oftener in good
part than in ill ; nor, even when taken in an ill sense,
would the word be used exactly as in the passage
which follows.

A. W. [Anthony Wood] was with him several times, ate and
drank with him, and had several discourses with him concerning
arms and armory, which he understood well ; but he found him
nice and supercilious.—ANTHONY WOOD, *Athenæ Oxonienses*,
1848, vol. i. p. 161.

NIECE.   This word has undergone the same change
and limitation of meaning as ' nephew,' with indeed
the further limitation that it is now applied to the

female sex alone, to the *daughter* of a brother or a
sister, being once used, as 'neptis' was at the first,
for children's children, male and female alike. See
'Nephew.'

Laban answeride to hym: My dowytres and sones, and the
flockis, and alle that thou beholdist, ben myne, and what may I
do to my sones and to my *neces?*—*Gen.* xxi. 43 (cf. *Exod.*
xxxiv. 7). WICLIF.

The Emperor Augustus, among other singularities that he had
by himself during his life, saw, ere he died, the nephew of his
niece, that is to say, his progeny to the fourth degree of lineal
descent.—HOLLAND, *Pliny*, vol. i. p. 162.

Within the compass of which very same time he [Julius
Cæsar] lost by death first his mother, then his daughter Julia,
and not long after his *niece* by the said daughter.—Id., *Suetonius*,
p. 11.

NOISOME, } At present offensive and moving dis-
NOISOMENESS. } gust; but once noxious and actually
hurtful; thus a skunk would be 'noisome' now; a
tiger was 'noisome' then. In all passages of the
Authorized Translation of the Bible where the word
occurs, as at *Ezek.* xiv. 15, 21, it is used not in the
present meaning, but the past.

They that will be rich fall into temptations and snares, and
into many foolish and *noisome* [βλαβεράς] lusts, which drown
men in perdition and destruction.—1 *Tim.* vi. 9. Geneva.

He [the superstitious person] is persuaded that they be gods
indeed, but such as be *noisome*, hurtful, and doing mischief unto
men.—HOLLAND, *Plutarch's Morals*, p. 260.

They [the prelates] are so far from hindering dissension, that
they have made unprofitable, and even *noisome*, the chiefest
remedy we have to keep Christendom at one, which is, by
Councils.—MILTON, *Reason of Church Government*, b. i. c. 6.

Sad in his time was the condition of the Israelites, oppressed
by the Midianites, who swarmed like grasshoppers for number,

and *noisomeness*, devouring all which the other had sown.—
FULLER, *A Pisgah Sight of Palestine,* part i. b. ii. c. 8.

NOVEL,   } 'Novels' once were simply news, 'nou-
NOVELIST. } velles;' and the 'novelist' not a writer
of new tales, but an innovator, a bringer in of new
fashions into the Church or State.

> She brynges in her bille som *novels* new;
> Behold! it is of an olif tree
> A branch, thynkes me.
>
> *Townley Mysteries.*

But, see and say what you will, *novelists* had rather be talked
of, that they began a fashion and set a copy for others, than to
keep within the imitation of the most excellent precedents.—
HACKET, *Life of Archbishop Williams,* part ii. p. 36.

Every *novelist* with a whirligig in his brain must broach new
opinions, and those made canons, nay sanctions, as sure as if a
General Council had confirmed them.—ADAMS, *The Devil's
Banquet,* 1614, p. 52.

I can hardly believe my eyes while I read such a petit *novelist*
charging the whole Church as fools and heretics for not subscrib-
ing to a silly heretical notion, solely of his own invention.—
SOUTH, *Animadversions on Dr. Sherlock's Book,* p. 3.

NURSERY. We have but one use of 'nursery' at
this present, namely as the place of nursing; but it
was once applied as well to the person nursed, or the
act of nursing.

A jolly dame, no doubt; as appears by the well battling of the
plump boy, her *nursery.*—FULLER, *A Pisgah Sight of Palestine,*
part i. b. ii. c. 8.

If *nursery* exceeds her [a mother's] strength, and yet her
conscience will scarce permit her to lay aside and free herself
from so natural, so religious a work, yet tell her, God loves
mercy better than sacrifice.—ROGERS, *Matrimonial Honour,*
p. 247.

I loved her most, and thought to set my rest
On her kind *nursery*.
SHAKESPEARE, *King Lear*, act i. sc. 1.

OBELISK. The ' obelus ' is properly a sharp-pointed
spear or spit; with a sign resembling this, spurious
or doubtful passages were marked in the books of
antiquity, which sign bore therefore this name of
' obelus,' or sometimes of its diminutive ' obeliscus.'
It is in this sense that we find ' obelisk ' employed
by the writers in the seventeenth century; while for
us at the present a small pillar tapering towards the
summit is the only ' obelisk ' that we know.

The Lord Keeper, the most circumspect of any man alive to
provide for uniformity, and to countenance it, was scratched with
their *obelisk*, that he favoured Puritans, and that sundry of them
had protection through his connivency or clemency.—HACKET,
Life of Archbishop Williams, part i. p. 95.

I have set my mark upon them [*i.e.* affected pedantic words];
and if any of them may have chanced to escape the *obelisk*, there
can arise no other inconvenience from it but an occasion to exercise the choice and judgment of the reader.—PHILLIPS, *New
World of Words*, Preface.

OBNOXIOUS. This, in its present lax and slovenly
use a vague unserviceable synonym for offensive, is
properly applied to one who on the ground of a
mischief or wrong committed by him is justly liable
to punishment (*ob noxam* pœnæ obligatus); and is
used in this sense by South (see below). But there
often falls out of the word the sense of a wrong
committed; and that of liability to punishment,
whether just or unjust, only remains; it does so
very markedly in the quotation from Donne. But
we punish, or wish to punish, those whom we dislike,

and thus 'obnoxious' has obtained its present sense of offensive.

They envy Christ, but they turn upon the man, who was more *obnoxious* to them, and they tell him that it was not lawful for him to carry his bed that day [*John* v. 10].—Donne, *Sermon* 20.

Examine thyself in the particulars of thy relations; especially where thou governest and takest accounts of others, and art not so *obnoxious* to them as they to thee.—J. Taylor, *The Worthy Communicant*, c. vi. sect. 2.

What shall we then say of the power of God Himself to dispose of men? little, finite, *obnoxious* things of his own making? —South, *Sermons*, 1744, vol. viii. p. 315.

He [Satan] is in a chain, and that chain is in God's hand; and consequently, notwithstanding his utmost spite, he cannot be more malicious than he is *obnoxious*.—Id., *Ib.* vol. vi. p. 287.

Obsequious,   } There lies ever in 'obsequious'
Obsequiousness. } at the present the sense of an observance which is overdone, of an unmanly readiness to fall in with the will of another; there lay nothing of this in the Latin 'obsequium,' nor yet in our English word as employed two centuries ago. See the quotation from Feltham, *s. v.* 'Garb.'

Besides many other fishes in divers places, which are very obeisant and *obsequious*, when they be called by their names.— Holland, *Plutarch's Morals*, p. 970.

I ever set this down, that the only course to be held with the Queen was by *obsequiousness* and observance.—Lord Bacon, *Defence of Himself*.

His corrections are so far from compelling men to come to heaven, as that they put many men farther out of their way, and work an obduration rather than an *obsequiousness*.—Donne, *Sermon* 45.

In her relation to the king she was the best pattern of conjugal love and *obsequiousness*. —Bates, *Sermon upon the Death of the Queen*.

OCCUPY, } He now 'occupies,' who has in present
OCCUPIER. } possession; but the word involved once
the further signification of using, employing, laying
out that which was thus possessed; and by an 'occupier' was meant a trader or retail dealer.

He [Eumenes] made as though he had occasion to *occupy*
money, and so borrowed a great sum of them.—NORTH, *Plutarch's
Lives*, p. 505.

If they bind me fast with new ropes that never were *occupied*,
then shall I be weak, and be as another man.—*Judges* xvi. 11.
Authorized Version.

Mercury, the master of merchants and *occupiers* [ἀγοραίων].—
HOLLAND, *Plutarch's Morals*, p. 692.

OFFAL. This, bearing its derivation on its front,
namely that it is that which, as refuse and of little
or no worth, is suffered or caused to *fall off*, we
restrict at the present to the refuse of the butcher's
stall; but it was once employed in a much wider
acceptation, an acceptation which here and there
still survives. Thus, as one writes to me, 'in all
her Majesty's dockyards there is a monthly sale by
auction of "offal wood," being literally that which
falls off from the log under the saw, axe, or adze.'

> Glean not in barren soil these *offal* ears,
> Sith reap thou may'st whole harvests of delight.
> SOUTHWELL, *Lewd Love is Loss.*

Of gold the very smallest filings are precious, and our Blessed
Saviour, when there was no want of provision, yet gave it in
charge to his disciples, the *off-fall* should not be lost.—SANDER-
SON, *Preface to the Clavi Trabales.*

Poor Lazarus lies howling at his gates for a few crumbs; he
only seeks chippings, *offals*; let him roar and howl, famish and
eat his own flesh; he respects him not.—BURTON, *Anatomy of
Melancholy*, part iii. sect. 1.

OFFICIOUS, ⎫ Again and again we light on
OFFICIOUSNESS.⎭ words used once in a good, but
now in an unfavourable, sense. An 'officious' person
is now a busy uninvited meddler in matters which
do not belong to him; so late as Burke's time he
might be one prompt and forward in due *offices* of
kindness. The more honourable use of 'officious'
now only survives in the distinction familiar to
diplomacy between an 'official' and 'officious' com-
munication.

> With granted leave *officious* I return.
> MILTON, *Paradise Regained*, b. ii.

Officious, ready to do good offices, serviceable, friendly, very
courteous and obliging.—PHILLIPS, *New World of Words.*

They [the nobility of France] were tolerably well bred, very
officious, humane, and hospitable.—BURKE, *Reflections on the
Revolution in France*, p. 251.

Which familiar and affectionate *officiousness* and sumptuous
cost, together with that sinister fame that woman was noted with
[*Luke* vii. 37], could not but give much scandal to the Pharisees
there present.—H. MORE, *Grand Mystery of Godliness*, b. viii.
c. 13.

ORIENT. This had once a beautiful use, as clear,
bright, shining, which has now wholly departed from
it. Thus, the 'orient' pearl of our earlier poets is
not 'oriental,' but pellucid, white, shining. Doubtless it acquired this meaning originally from the
greater clearness and lightness of the east, as the
quarter whence the day breaks.

Those shells that keep in the main sea, and lie deeper than
that the sunbeams can pierce unto them, keep the finest and
most delicate pearls. And yet they, as *orient* as they be, wax
yellow with age.—HOLLAND, *Pliny*, vol. i. p. 255.

He, who out of that dark chaos made the glorious heavens, and garnished them with so many *orient* stars, can move upon thy dark soul and enlighten it, though now it be as void of knowledge as the evening of the first day was of light.—GURNALL, *Christian Armour*, ii. 22, 1.

> Her wings and train of feathers, mixed fine
> Of *orient* azure and incarnadine.
>
> SYLVESTER, *Dubartas, Fifth Day.*

Κόκκος βαφική, a shrub, whose red berries or grains gave an *orient* tincture to cloth.—FULLER, *A Pisgah Sight of Palestine*, b. iv. c. 6.

ORTOLAN. This, the name now of a delicate bird haunting *gardens*, was once the name of the gardener ('hortolanus,' 'ortolano') himself.

Though to an old tree it must needs be somewhat dangerous to be oft removed, yet for my part I yield myself entirely to the will and pleasure of the most notable *ortolan.*—*State Papers*, 1536, vol. vi. p. 534.

OSTLER. Not formerly the servant of the inn having care of the horses, but the innkeeper or host, the 'hosteller' himself.

And another dai he broughte forth tweie pens, and gaf to the *ostler* [stabulario, Vulg.].—*Luke* x. 35. WICLIF.

> The *innkeeper* was old, fourscore almost;
> Indeed an emblem, rather than an host;
> In whom we read how God and Time decree
> To honour thrifty *ostlers*, such as he.
>
> CORBET, *Iter Boreale.*

OUGHT. Of the two perfects of the verb 'to owe' (see Morris, *English Accidence*, p. 189), namely 'ought' and 'owed,' the former has come now to be used of a moral owing or obligation only, never of a material; but it was not always so. Among the many tacit alterations which our Authorized Version has at various times undergone, the substitution in many places of 'owed' for 'ought' is one.

> But the Elfin knight which *ought* that warlike wage,
> Disdained to lose the meed he won in fray.
>
> SPENSER, Fairy Queen, i. 4, 39.

There was a certain creditor, which had two debtors. The one *ought* five hundred pence, and the other fifty.—*Luke*, vii. 41. Authorized Version.

Also we forgive the oversights and faults committed against us, and the crown-tax that ye *ought* us.—1 *Macc.* xiii. 39. Geneva Version.

PAINFUL, PAINFULNESS, PAINFULLY. } 'Painful' is now feeling pain, or inflicting it; it was once taking pains. Many things would not be so 'painful' in the present sense of the word, if they had been more 'painful' in the earlier, as perhaps some sermons.

Within fourteen generations, the royal blood of the kings of Judah ran in the veins of plain Joseph, a *painful* carpenter.—FULLER, *Holy War*, b. v. c. 29.

I think we have some as *painful* magistrates as ever was in England.—LATIMER, *Sermons*, p. 142.

Painfulness by feeble means shall be able to gain that which in the plenty of more forcible instruments is through sloth and negligence lost.—HOOKER, *Ecclesiastical Polity*, b. v. § 22.

O the holiness of their living, and *painfulness* of their preaching!—FULLER, *Holy State*, b. ii. c. 6.

Whoever would be truly thankful, let him live in some honest vocation, and therein bestow himself faithfully and *painfully*.—SANDERSON, *Sermons*, vol. i. p. 251.

PALESTINE. This is now a name for the entire Holy Land; but in the Authorized Version 'Pales-

tine' or 'Palestina' as it is written three times out
of the four on which it occurs, is used in a far more
restricted sense, namely, as equivalent to Philistia,
that narrow strip of coast possessed by the Philistines.
This a close examination of the several passages (see
the *Dictionary of the Bible* s. v., p. 660) will make
abundantly clear. And it is also invariably so employed by Milton; thus see besides the passage quoted
below *Samson Agonistes*, 144, and *On the Nativity*, 199.

Rejoice not thou, whole *Palestina*, because the rod of him that
smote thee is broken.—*Isai.* xiv. 29. Authorized Version.

> Dagon his name, sea-monster, upward man
> And downward fish: yet had his temple high
> Reared in Azotus, dreaded through the coast
> Of *Palestine*, in Gath and Ascalon,
> And Accaron, and Gaza's frontier bounds.
> > MILTON, *Paradise Lost*, i. 462.

PALLIATE, ⎫ 'To palliate' is at this day to extenu-
PALLIATION. ⎭ ate a fault through the setting out of
whatever will best serve to diminish the estimate of
its gravity; and does not imply any endeavour wholly
to deny it; nay, implies rather a certain recognition
and admission of the fault itself. Truer to its etymology once, it expressed the *cloking* of it, the attempt, successful or otherwise, entirely to conceal
and cover it. Eve 'palliates' her fault in the modern
sense of the word (*Gen.* iii. 13), Gehazi in the earlier
(2 *Kin.* v. 25).

> You cannot *palliate* mischief, but it will
> Through all the fairest coverings of deceit
> Be always seen.
> > DANIEL, *The Tragedy of Philotas*, act iv. sc. 2.

You see the Devil could fetch up nothing of Samuel at the
request of Saul, but a shadow and a resemblance, his countenance

and his mantle, which yet was not enough to cover the cheat, or to *palliate* the illusion.—SOUTH, *Sermon on Easter Day.*

The generality of Christians make the external frame of religion but a *palliation* for sin.—H. MORE, *Grand Mystery of Godliness*, p. ix.

PANTOMIME. Now the mimic show itself, but at the first introduction of the word (Bacon's constant use of 'pantomimus' and 'pantomimi,' and Ben Jonson's as well, testify that it was new in their time), the player who presented the show.

I would our *pantomimes* also and stage-players would examine themselves and their callings by this rule.—SANDERSON, *Sermon on 1 Cor.* vii. 24.

The hypocrite cometh forth in a disguise, and acteth his part, and because men applaud him, thinketh God is of their mind, as the *pantomime* in Seneca, who observing the people well pleased with his dancing, did every day go up unto the Capitol and dance before Jupiter, and was persuaded that he was also delighted in him.—FARINDON, *Sermon* 10.

> Not that I think those *pantomimes*,
> Who vary actions with the times,
> Are less ingenious in their art
> Than those who dully act one part.
>> BUTLER, *Hudibras*, pt. 3, can. 2.

PATHETIC, PATHETICAL, PATHETICALLY. The 'pathetic' is now only *one* kind of the passionate, that which, feeling *pity*, is itself capable of stirring it; but 'pathetic' or 'pathetical' and 'passionate' were once of an equal reach. When in a language like ours two words, derived from two different languages, as in this case from the Greek and from the Latin, exist side by side, being at the same time identical in signification, the desynonymizing process which we may note here, continually comes into play.

He [Hiel, cf. *Josh.* vi. 26 and 1 *Kings* xvi. 34] mistook Joshua's curse rather for a *pathetical* expression than prophetical prediction.—FULLER, *A Pisgah Sight of Palestine*, b. ii. c. 12.

> Whatever word enhanceth Joseph's praise,
> Her echo doubles it, and doth supply
> Some more *pathetic* and transcendant phrase
> To raise his merit.
>
> BEAUMONT, *Psyche*, c. i. st. 148.

For Truth, I know not how, hath this unhappiness fatal to her, ere she can come to the trial and inspection of the understanding; being to pass through many little wards and limits of the several affections and desires, she cannot shift it, but must put on such colours and attire as those *pathetical* handmaids of the soul please to lead her in to their queen.—MILTON, *Reason of Church Government*, b. ii. c. 3.

But the principal point whereon our apostle pitcheth for evincing the priesthood of Christ to be far more excellent than the Levitical priesthood was, was reserved to the last, and *pathetically* though briefly avouched, ver. 20 [*Heb.* vii. 20].— JACKSON, *Of the Divine Essence and Attributes*, b. ix. § 2.

PATTERN. One is at first tempted to accuse our Translators of an inaccuracy at *Heb.* ix. 23, since, whatever ὑπόδειγμα may mean elsewhere, it is impossible that it can there mean 'pattern,' in our sense of exemplar or original from which a copy or sketch is derived, 'patron' upon whom the client forms and fashions himself. This is inconsistent with, and would indeed entirely defeat, the whole argument of the Apostle. The ὑποδείγματα there can be only the earthly copies and imitations of the heavenly and archetypal originals, ἀντίτυπα τῶν ἀληθινῶν. A passage, however, in the *Homilies* entirely relieves them from any charge of error. All that can be

said is that they have employed 'pattern' in a
somewhat unusual sense, but one which an analogous
use of 'copy' in our own day sufficiently explains.

Which priests serve unto the *patron* [ὑποδείγματι] and shadow
of heavenly things.—*Heb.* viii. 5. Geneva.

It was therefore necessary that the *patterns* of things in the
heavens should be purified with these; but the heavenly things
themselves with better sacrifices than these.—*Heb.* ix. 23.
Authorized Version.

Where most rebellions and rebels be, there is the express
similitude of hell, and the rebels themselves are the very figures
of fiends and devils; and their captain, the ungracious *pattern*
of Lucifer and Satan, the prince of darkness.—*Homilies, Against
Wilful Rebellion.*

PEEVISH,   ⎫ By 'peevishness' we now under-
PEEVISHNESS. ⎭ stand a small but constantly fretting
ill-temper; yet no one can read our old authors, with
whom 'peevish' and 'peevishness' are of constant
recurrence, without feeling that their use of them is
different from ours; although precisely to determine
what their use was is anything but easy. Gifford
(*Massinger*, vol. i. p. 71) says confidently, 'peevish is
foolish;' but upon induction from an insufficient
number of passages. 'Peevish' is rather self-willed,
obstinate. That in a world like ours those who refuse
to give up their own wills should be continually
crossed, and thus should become fretful, and 'peevish'
in our modern sense of the word, is inevitable; and
here is the history of the change of meaning which
it has undergone.

> *Valentine.* Cannot your grace win her to fancy him?
> *Duke.* No, trust me; she is *peevish*, sullen, froward,
> Proud, disobedient, stubborn, lacking duty.
>   SHAKESPEARE, *Two Gentlemen of Verona*, act iii. sc. 1.

We provoke, rail, scoff, calumniate, challenge, hate, abuse (hard-hearted, implacable, malicious, *peevish*, inexorable as we are), to satisfy our lust or private spleen.—BURTON, *Anatomy of Melancholy*, part iii. § 1.

Pertinax hominum genus, a *peevish* generation of men.—Id., *Ib.*, part iii. § 4.

That grand document of keeping to the light within us they [the Quakers] borrow out of St. John's Gospel; and yet they are so frantic and *peevish*, that they would fling away the staff without which they are not able to make one step in religion.— H. MORE, *Grand Mystery of Godliness*, b. viii. c. 12.

In case the Romans, upon an inbred *peevishness* and engraffed pertinacity of theirs, should not hear reason, but refuse an indifferent end, then both God and man shall be witness as well of the moderation of Perseus, as of their pride and insolent frowardness.—HOLLAND, *Livy*, p. 1152.

We must carefully distinguish continuance in opinion from obstinacy, confidence of understanding from *peevishness* of affection, a not being convinced from a resolution never to be convinced.—J. TAYLOR, *Liberty of Prophesying*, § ii. 10.

PENCIL. The distinction between 'pencil' and paint-brush is quite modern. The older use of 'pencil' ('penicillus' or little tail) was etymologically more correct than the modern; the brush being so called because it hung and drooped as does that.

> Heaven knows, they were besmeared and overstained
> With slaughter's *pencil*, where revenge did paint
> The fearful difference of incensed kings.
> > SHAKESPEARE, *King John*, act iii. sc. 1.

Learning is necessary to him [the heretic], if he trades in a critical error; but if he only broaches dregs, and deals in some dull sottish opinion, a trowel will serve as well as a *pencil* to daub on such thick coarse colours.—FULLER, *The Profane State*, b. v. c. 10.

The first thing she did after rising was to have recourse to the *red-pot*, out of which she laid it on very thick with a *pencil*, not only on her cheeks, chin, under the nose, above the eyebrows and edges of the ears, but also on the inside of her hands, her fingers, and shoulders.—*The Lady's Travels into Spain, Letter* 8.

PENITENTIARY. It is curious that this word has possessed three entirely independent meanings, penitent, ordainer of penances in the Church, and place for penitents; only the last is current now.

So Manasseh in the beginning and middle of his reign filled the city with innocent blood, and died a *penitentiary.*—JACKSON, *Christ's Session at God's Right Hand*, b. ii. c. 42.

'Twas a French friar's conceit that courtiers were of all men the likeliest to forsake the world and turn *penitentiaries.*—HAMMOND, *The Seventh Sermon, Works,* vol. iv. p. 517.

Penitentiary, a priest that imposes upon an offender what penance he thinks fit.—PHILLIPS, *New World of Words.*

PENURY. This expresses now no more than the *objective* fact of extreme poverty; an ethical *subjective* meaning not lying in it, as would sometimes of old. This is now retained only in ' penurious,' ' penuriousness.'

God sometimes punishes one sin with another; pride with adultery, drunkenness with murder, carelessness with irreligion, idleness with vanity, *penury* with oppression.—J. TAYLOR, *The Faith and Patience of the Saints.*

PERSEVERANCE. It is difficult to connect the uses of ' perseverance ' whereof examples are given below, and they might easily be multiplied, with its more frequent use of old, and its sole use at present. Indeed I have sometimes doubts whether the word in these instances be the same word at

all, and whether we are not to look to 'sepa-
rare,' 'sevrer,' 'severance' (it might thus be the
power of dividing and distinguishing,) for its root
rather than to 'perseverantia.' None of our Dictionaries give any assistance here; but there is a
good collection of illustrative passages in *Notes and
Queries*, No. 182.

For his diet he [Ariosto] was very temperate, and a great
enemy of excess and surfeiting, and so careless of delicates as
though he had no *perseverance* in the taste of meats.—Sir J.
HARINGTON, *Life of Ariosto*, p. 418.

He [Æmilius Paulus] suddenly fell into a raving (without any
perseverance of sickness spied in him before, or any change or
alteration in him [πρὶν αἰσθέσθαι καὶ νοῆσαι τὴν μεταβολήν]), and
his wits went from him in such sort that he died three days after.
—NORTH, *Plutarch's Lives*, p. 221.

PERSON. We have forfeited the full force of the
statement, 'God is no respecter of *persons*;' from the
fact that 'person' does not mean for us now all that
it once meant. 'Person,' from 'persona,' the mask
constantly worn by the actor of antiquity, is by
natural transfer the part or *rôle* in the play which
each sustains, as πρόσωπον is in Greek. In the great
tragi-comedy of life each sustains a 'person;' one
that of a king, another that of a hind; one must play
Dives, another Lazarus. This 'person' God, for
whom the question is not *what* 'person' each sustains, but *how* he sustains it, does not respect.

 King. What, rate, rebuke, and roughly send to prison
The immediate heir of England! was this easy?
May this be washed in Lethe, and forgotten?
 Chief Justice. I then did use the *person* of your father;
The image of his power lay then in me.
      SHAKESPEARE, 2 *Henry IV.*, act v. sc. 2.

Cæsar also is brought in by Julian attributing to himself the honour (if it were at all an honour to that *person* which he sustained), of being the first that left his ship and took land.— MILTON, *History of England*, b. ii.

> Her gifts
> Were such as under government well seemed;
> Unseemly to bear rule, which was thy part
> And *person*, hadst thou known thyself aright.
>
> <div align="right">Id., <i>Paradise Lost</i>, b. x. 153.</div>

Certain it is, that no man can long put on a *person* and act a part but his evil manners will peep through the corners of his white robe, and God will bring a hypocrite to shame even in the eyes of men.—J. TAYLOR, *Apples of Sodom.*

PERSPECTIVE. 'Telescope' and 'microscope' are both as old as Milton; but for a long while 'perspective' (glass being sometimes understood, and sometimes expressed) did the work of these. It is sometimes written 'prospective.' Our present use of 'perspective' does not, I suppose, date farther back than Dryden.

> A guilty conscience
> Is a black register, wherein is writ
> All our good deeds and bad, a *perspective*
> That shows us hell.
>
> <div align="right">WEBSTER, <i>Duchess of Malfi</i>, act iv. sc. 2.</div>

While we look for incorruption in the heavens, we find they are but like the earth, durable in their main bodies, alterable in their parts; whereof, beside comets and new stars, *perspectives* begin to tell tales; and the spots that wander about the sun, with Phaeton's favour, would make clear conviction.—Sir T. BROWNE, *Hydriotaphia.*

Look through faith's *perspective* with the magnifying end on invisibles (for such is its frame, it lesseneth visibles), and thou wilt see sights not more strange than satisfying.—WHITLOCK, *Zootomia*, p. 535.

> A tiny mite, which we can scarcely see
> Without a *perspective*.
>
> <div align="right">OLDHAM, <i>Eighth Satire of M. Boileau.</i></div>

PESTER. There is no greater discomfort or annoyance than extreme straitness or narrowness of room; out of which in Greek στενοχωρία, signifying this, has come to have a secondary signification of trouble or anguish. In English, 'to pester' bears witness to the same fact, though it has travelled in exactly the opposite direction, and having first the meaning of to vex or annoy, which meaning it still retains, had also once a second meaning of painfully cooping-up in a narrow and confined space; which, however, it now has let go.

Now because the most part of the people might not possibly have a sight of him, they gat up all at once into the theatre, and *pestered* it quite full.—HOLLAND, *Livy*, p. 1055.

They within, though *pestered* with their own numbers, stood to it like men resolved, and in a narrow compass did remarkable deeds.—MILTON, *History of England*, b. ii.

The calendar is filled, not to say, *pestered* with them, jostling one another for room, many holding the same day in copartnership of festivity.—FULLER, *Worthies of England*, c. 3.

PHYSICAL, ⎫ Though 'physical' has not disso-
PHYSICALLY. ⎭ ciated itself from 'physics,' it has from 'physic' and 'physician,' being used now as simply the equivalent for 'natural,' with which the Greek language has supplied us; but it was not always so.

> Is Brutus sick? and is it *physical*
> To walk unbraced and suck up the humours
> Of the dank morning?
> SHAKESPEARE, *Julius Cæsar*, act ii. sc. 1.

Attalus, surnamed Philometer (to say, lover of his mother), would plant and set *physical* herbs, as helleborum.—NORTH, *Plutarch's Lives*, p. 739.

And for physic, he [Lord Bacon] did indeed live *physically*,[*] but not miserably.—Rawley, *Life of Lord Bacon*.

Placard. Formerly used often in the sense of a license or permission, the 'placard' being properly the broad tablet or board on which this, as well as other edicts and ordinances, was exposed.

> Then for my voice I must (no choice)
> Away of force, like posting horse,
> For sundry men had *placards* then
>   Such child to take.
>
>   Tusser, *Author's Life.*

Others are of the contrary opinion, and that Christianity gives us a *placard* to use these sports; and that man's charter of dominion over the creatures enables him to employ them as well for pleasure as necessity.—Fuller, *The Holy State*, b. iii. c. 13.

Plantation. We still 'plant' a colony, but a 'plantation' is now of trees only; and not of men. There was a time when 'The Plantations' was the standing name by which our transatlantic colonies were known. One of Bacon's state-papers has this title, ' Certain Considerations touching the *Plantation* in Ireland.'

It is a shameful and unblessed thing to take the scum of people and wicked condemned men to be the people with whom you plant; and not only so, but it spoileth the *plantation*.— Bacon, *Essays*, 33.

Plantations make mankind broader, as generation makes it thicker.—Fuller, *The Holy State*, b. iii. c. 16.

Plausible,   That is 'plausible' now which pre-
Plausibly,   sents itself as worthy of applause;
Plausibility.   yet always with a subaudition, or at

---

[*] There is allusion here to the Latin proverb, Medice vivere est misere vivere.

least a suggestion, that it is not so really ; it was
once that which obtained applause, with at least the
primâ facie likelihood that the applause which it obtained was deserved.

This John, Bishop of Constantinople, that assumed to himself
the title of Universal Bishop or Patriarch, was a good man,
given greatly to alms and fasting, but too much addicted to
advance the title of his see ; which made a *plausible* bishop seem
to be Antichrist to Gregory the Great.—HACKET, *Life of Archbishop Williams*, part ii. p. 66.

> The Romans *plausibly* did give consent
> For Tarquin's everlasting banishment.
>   SHAKESPEARE, *The Rape of Lucrece.*

He was no sooner in sight than every one received him
plausibly, and with great submission and reverence.—STUBS,
Anatomy of Abuses, p. 17.

Being placed in the upper part of the world, [he] carried on
his dignity with that justice, modesty, integrity, fidelity, and
other gracious *plausibilities*, that in a place of trust he contented
those whom he could not satisfy, and in a place of envy procured
the love of those who emulated his greatness.—VAUGHAN, *Life
and Death of Dr. Jackson.*

POACH, } It sounds strange to say that ' poker '
POACHER. } and ' poacher ' are in fact one and the
same word ; which doubtless they are.   A ' poacher '
is strictly speaking an intruder, the word means
nothing more ;   one who intrudes, ' pokes,' or
' poaches,' into land where he has no business ;
the fact that he does so with intention of spoiling
the game is superadded, not lying in the word.

So that, to speak truly, they [the Spaniards] have rather
poached and offered at a number of enterprises, than maintained
any constantly.—BACON, *Notes of a Speech concerning a War
with Spain.*

It is ill conversing with an ensnarer, delving into the bottom of your mind, to know what is hid in it. I would ask a casuist if it were not lawful for me not only to hide my mind, but to cast something that is not true before such a *poacher*.—HACKET, *Life of Archbishop Williams*, part ii. p. 113.

POLITE, ⎫ Between 'polite' and 'polished' this
POLITELY. ⎭ much of difference has now grown up and established itself, that 'polite' is always employed in a secondary and tropical sense, having reference to the polish of the mind, while it is free to use 'polished' in the literal and figurative sense alike.

Polite bodies, as looking-glasses.—CUDWORTH, *Intellectual System*, p. 731.

Polite ; well-polished, neat.—PHILLIPS, *New World of Words*.

In things artificial seldom any elegance is wrought without a superfluous waste and refuse in the transaction. No marble statue can be *politely* carved, no fair edifice built, without almost as much rubbish and sweeping.—MILTON, *Reason of Church Government*, b. i. c. 7.

POLITICS, ⎫ At the present 'politics' are always
POLITICIAN. ⎭ *things*, but were sometimes *persons* as well in times past. 'Politician' too had an evil sub-audition. One so named was a trickster or underhand self-seeker and schemer in politics, or it might be, as it is throughout in the sermon of South, quoted below, in the ordinary affairs of life. Fuller calls his Life of the wicked usurper Andronicus, 'The Unfortunate Politician.'

It did in particular exasperate Tacitus, and other *politicks* of his temper, to see so many natural Romans renounce their name and country for maintenance of Jewish religion.—JACKSON, *The Eternal Truth of Scriptures*, b. i. c. 20.

Let them [spiritual persons] have the diligence and craft of fishers, the watchfulness and the care of shepherds, the prudence of *politics*, the tenderness of parents.—J. TAYLOR, *Life of Christ*, part 2, § 12.

If this arch-*politician* [the Devil] find in his pupils any remorse, any feeling or fear of God's future judgement, he persuades them that God hath so great need of men's souls that He will accept them at any time and upon any conditions.— Sir W. RALEIGH, *History of the World*, b. i. c. 7, § 9.

Why, look you, I am whipped and scourged with rods,
Nettled and stung with pismires, when I hear
Of this vile *politician* Bolingbroke.
> SHAKESPEARE, 1 *Henry IV.*, act i. sc. 3.

A *politician* is the devil's quilted anvil;
He fashions all sins on him, and the blows
Are never heard.
> WEBSTER, *Duchess of Malfi*, act iii. sc. 2.

The *politician*, whose very essence lies in this, that he is a person ready to do any thing that he apprehends for his advantage, must first of all be sure to put himself in a state of liberty, as free and large as his principles, and so to provide elbow-room enough for his conscience to lay about it, and have its full play in.—SOUTH, *Sermons*, 1744, vol. i. p. 324.

POMP,
POMPOUS,
POMPOUSLY. } 'Pomp' is one of the many words which Milton employs with a strict classical accuracy, so that he is only to be perfectly understood when we keep in mind that a 'pomp' with him is always πομπή, a procession. He is not, however, singular here, as he often is, in the stricter and more rigorous use of a word. It is easy to perceive how 'pomp' obtained its wider application. There is no such favourable opportunity for the display of state and magnificence as a procession; this is almost the inevitable form which they take; and thus the word, first applied to the most frequent display of these, came afterwards to be

transferred to every display. In respect of 'pompous' and 'pompously' there is something else to note. There is in them always now the subaudition of that which is more in show than in substance, or, at any rate, of a magnificence which, if real, is yet vaingloriously and ostentatiously displayed. But they did not convey, and were not intended to convey, any such impression once.

[Antiochus] also provided a great number of bulls with gilt horns, the which he conducted himself with a goodly *pomp* and procession to the very gate of the city [ἄχρι τῶν πυλῶν ἐπόμπευσε].—HOLLAND, *Plutarch's Morals*, p. 417.

> With goddess-like demeanour forth she went,
> Not unattended ; for on her, as queen,
> A *pomp* of winning graces waited still.
> > MILTON, *Paradise Lost*, b. viii.

> The planets in their stations listening stood,
> While the bright *pomp* ascended jubilant.
> > Id., *Ib.*, b. vii.

> What *pompous* powers of ravishment were here,*
> What delicate extremities of pleasure.
> > BEAUMONT, *Psyche*, can. xv. st. 299.

All expresses related that the entertainment [of Prince Charles at Madrid] was very *pompous* and kingly.—HACKET, *Life of Archbishop Williams*, part i. p. 119.

He [Hardecnute] gave his sister Gunildis, a virgin of rare beauty, in marriage to Henry the Alman Emperor ; and to send her forth *pompously*, all the nobility contributed their jewels and richest ornaments.—MILTON, *History of England*, b. vi.

POPULAR, } He was 'popular' once, not who had
POPULARITY. } acquired, but who was laying himself out to acquire, the favour of the people. 'Popu-

---

* In heaven.

larity ' was the wooing, not, as now, the having won, that favour ; exactly the Latin ' ambitio.' The word, which is passive now, was active then.

Of a senator he [Manlius] became *popular*, and began to break his mind and impart his designs unto the magistrates of the commons, finding fault with the nobility.—HOLLAND, *Livy*, p. 224.

> And oft in vain his name they closely bite,
> As *popular* and flatterer accusing.
> > P. FLETCHER, *Purple Island*, c. 10.

Divers were of opinion that he [Caius Gracchus] was more *popular* and desirous of the common people's good will and favour than his brother had been before him. But indeed he was clean contrary.—NORTH, *Plutarch's Lives*, p. 690.

Cato the Younger charged Muræna, and indited him in open court for *popularity* and ambition.—HOLLAND, *Plutarch's Morals*, p. 243.

Harold, lifted up in mind, and forgetting now his former shows of *popularity*, defrauded his soldiers their due and well-deserved share of the spoils.—MILTON, *History of England*, b. vi.

PORTLY, } There lies in ' portly ' a certain sense
PORTLINESS. } of dignity of demeanour still, but always connoted with this a cumbrousness and weight, such as Spenser in his noble *Epithalamion* (see below) would never have ascribed to his bride, as little Shakespeare to the swift-footed Achilles (*Troilus and Cressida*, act iv. sc. 5), or to the youthful Romeo.

The chief and most *portly* person of them all was one Hasdrubal [*Insignis* tamen inter ceteros Hasdrubal erat].—HOLLAND, *Livy*, p. 770.

> He [Romeo] bears him like a *portly* gentleman.
> > SHAKESPEARE, *Romeo and Juliet*, act i. sc. 5.

Rudely thou wrongest my dear heart's desire,
In finding fault with her too *portly* pride ;
For in those lofty looks is close implied
Scorn of base things and 'sdeigne of foul dishonour,
Such pride is praise, such *portliness* is honour.

SPENSER, *Sonnet* 5.

PRAGMATICAL. This is always employed at the present in an ill sense ; the ' pragmatical ' man is not merely busy, but over-busy, officious, meddling; nay, more than this, with an assumption of bustling self-importance. The word's etymology does not require this ill sense, which is merely superinduced upon it, and from which it was not indeed always, but often free in its earli er us

It may appear at the first a new and unwonted argument, to teach men how to raise and make their fortune ; but the handling thereof concerneth learning greatly both in honour and in substance. In honour, because *pragmatical* men may not go away with an opinion that learning is like a lark, that can mount and sing and please herself, and nothing else ; but may know that she holdeth as well of the hawk, that can soar aloft, and also descend and strike upon the prey.—BACON, *Advancement of Learning*, b. ii.

We cannot always be contemplative or *pragmatical* abroad ; but have need of some delightful intermissions, wherein the enlarged soul may leave off her severe schooling.—MILTON, *Tetrachordon.*

PREPOSTEROUS, ⎰ A word nearly or quite unser-
PREPOSTEROUSLY. ⎱ viceable now, being merely an ungraceful and slipshod synonym for absurd. But restore and confine it to its old use and to one peculiar branch of absurdity, the reversing of the true order and method of things, the putting of the last first, and the first last, and of what excellent service it would be capable !

It is a *preposterous* order to teach first, and to learn after.—
The Translators [of the Bible, 1611] *to the Reader.*

King Asa justly received little benefit by them [physicians],
because of his *preposterous* addressing himself to them before he
went to God (2 *Chron.* xvi. 12).—FULLER, *Worthies of England,*
c. ix.

To reason thus, I am of the elect, I therefore have saving
faith, and the rest of the sanctifying qualities, therefore that
which I do is good : thus I say to reason is very *preposterous.*
We must go a quite contrary course, and thus reason : my
life is good . . . I therefore have the gifts of sanctification,
and therefore am of God's elect.—HALES, *Sermon on St. Peter's
Fall.*

Some indeed *preposterously* misplace these, and make us par-
take of the benefit of Christ's priestly office in the forgiveness of
our sins and our reconcilement to God, before we are brought
under the sceptre of his kingly office by our obedience.—SOUTH,
Sermons, 1744, vol. xi. p. 3.

PRETEND,
PRETENCE,
PRETENSION.
To charge one with 'pretending'
anything is now a much more serious
charge than it was once. Indeed it
was not necessarily, and only by accident, a charge at
all. That was 'pretended' which one stretched out
before himself and in face of others ; but whether it
was the thing it affirmed itself to be, or, as at present,
only a deceitful resemblance of this, the word did
not decide. While it was thus with 'to pretend,'
there was as yet no distinction recognized between
' pretence ' and 'pretension ;' they both signified the
act of ' pretending,' or the thing 'pretended ;' but
whether truly or falsely it was left to the context, or
to the judgment of the reader, to decide. ' Pretence '
has since followed the fortunes of ' pretend,' and has
fallen with it ; while 'pretension' has disengaged
itself from being a merely useless synonym of

'pretence,' and, retaining its relation to the earlier uses of the verb, now signifies a claim put forward which may or may not be valid, the word leaving this for other considerations to determine. Louis Napoleon assumed the dictatorship under the 'pretence' of resisting anarchy; the House of Orleans has 'pretensions' to the throne of France. But these distinctions are quite modern.

Being preferred by King James to the bishopric of Chichester, and *pretending* his own imperfectness and insufficiency to undergo such a charge, he caused to be engraven about the seal of his bishopric, those words of St. Paul, Et ad hæc quis idoneus?— ISAACSON, *Life and Death of Lancelot Andrews.*

[The Sabbath] is rather hominis gratiâ quam Dei; and though God's honour is mainly *pretended* in it, yet it is man's happiness that is really intended by it, even of God Himself.—H. MORE, *Grand Mystery of Godliness*, b. viii. c. 13.

> I come no enemy, but to set free
> From out this dark and dismal house of pain
> Both him and thee, and all the heavenly host
> Of Spirits, that, in our just *pretences* armed,
> Fell with us from on high.
> > MILTON, *Paradise Lost*, b. ii.; cf. b. vi. 421.

This is the tree whose leaves were intended for the healing of the nations, not for a *pretence* and palliation for sin.—H. MORE, *Grand Mystery of Godliness*, b. viii. c. 1.

He [the Earl of Pembroke] was exceedingly beloved in the Court, because he never desired to get that for himself which others laboured for; but was still ready to promote the *pretences* of worthy men.—CLARENDON, *History of the Rebellion*, b. i. c. 121.

It is either secret pride, or base faintness of heart, or dull sloth, or some other thing, and not true modesty in us if, being excellently gifted for some weighty employment in every other man's judgment, we yet withdraw ourselves from it with *pretensions* of unsufficiency.—SANDERSON, *Sermons*, 1671, p. 208.

PREVARICATE, ⎱ This verb, often now very loosely
PREVARICATION. ⎰ used, had once a very definite
meaning of its own. 'To prevaricate' is to betray
the cause which one affects to sustain, the prevari-
cator is the feint pleader, as he used to be called,
and, so far as I know, the words are always so used
by our early writers. We have inherited the word
from the Latin law-courts, which borrowed it from
the life. The 'prævaricator' being one who halted
on two unequal legs, the name was transferred to him
who, affecting to prosecute a charge, was in secret
collusion with the opposite party, and so managed
the cause as to ensure his escape. Observe in the
two following passages the accuracy of use which so
habitually distinguishes our writers of the seventeenth century as compared with too many of the
nineteenth.

I proceed now to do the same service for the divines of
England; whom you question first in point of learning and
sufficiency, and then in point of conscience and honesty, as
prevaricating in the religion which they profess, and inclining to
Popery.—CHILLINGWORTH, *Religion of Protestants*, Preface,
p. 11.

If we be not all enemies to God in this kind [in a direct
opposition], yet in adhering to the enemy we are enemies; in
our *prevarications*, and easy betrayings and surrendering of ourselves to the enemy of his kingdom, Satan, we are his enemies.—
DONNE, *On the Nativity*. Sermon 7.

PREVENT, ⎱ One may reach a point before another
PREVENTION. ⎰ to help or to hinder him there; may
anticipate his arrival either with the purpose of
keeping it *for* him, or keeping it *against* him. 'To
prevent' has slipped by very gradual degrees, which

it would not be difficult to trace, from the sense of keeping *for* to that of keeping *against*, from the sense of arriving first with the intention of helping, to that of arriving first with the intention of hindering, and then generally from helping to hindering.

So it is, that if Titus had not *prevented* the whole multitude of people which came to see him, and if he had not got him away betimes, before the games were ended, he had hardly escaped from being stifled amongst them.—North, *Plutarch's Lives*, p. 321.

Gentlemen that were brought low, not by their vices, but by misfortune, poveri vergognosi as the Tuscan calls them, bashful, and could not crave though they perished, he *prevented* their modesty, and would heartily thank those that discovered their commiserable condition to him.—Hacket, *Life of Archbishop Williams*, part i. p. 201.

That poor man had waited thirty and eight years [at the pool of Bethesda], and still was *prevented* by some other.—J. Taylor, *Life of Christ*, part iii. § 13.

> There he beheld how humbly diligent
> New Adulation was to be at hand ;
> How ready Falsehood stept ; how nimbly went
> Base pick-thank Flattery, and *prevents* command.
> > Daniel, *Civil Wars*, b. ii. st. 56.

> Half way he met
> His daring foe, at this *prevention* more
> Incensed.
> > Milton, *Paradise Lost*, b. vi.

PROBABLE. Already in the best classical Latin 'probabilis' had passed over into the secondary meaning of 'probatus;' thus 'probabilis orator' (Cicero) is an approved orator. 'Probable' is often so used by our scholarly writers of the seventeenth century ; though we now use it only in its original sense of 'likely.'

The Lord Bacon would have rewards given to those men who in the quest of natural experiments make *probable* mistakes. An ingenious miss is of more credit than a bungling casual hit.— FULLER, *Mixt Contemplations*, i. 26.

S. Ambrose, who was a good *probable* doctor, and one as fit to be relied on as any man else, hath these words.—J. TAYLOR, *Doctrine and Practice of Repentance*, Preface.

PROBATION. This is strictly speaking=δοκιμή, the process of proving; as ' proof' is=δοκίμιον or δοκιμεῖον, that by which this proving is carried out; thus toil is the δοκίμιον of soldiers (Herodian).; and we now very properly keep the words apart according to this rule ; but formerly this was not so.

> He, sir, was lapped
> In a most curious mantle, wrought by the hand
> Of his queen-mother, which for more *probation*
> I can with ease produce.
> > SHAKESPEARE, *Cymbeline*, act v. sc. 5.

Also Philip the Evangelist had three daughters. Neither can it help to say that these children were born before his election ; for this is but a simple saying, and no *probation*.—FRITH, *Works*, 1572, p. 325.

PRODIGIOUS. This notes little now but magnitude. Truer to its etymology once (' prodigium '='prodicium,' and that from ' prodico '), it signified the ominous or ominously prophetic.

> Blood shall put out your torches, and instead
> Of gaudy flowers about your wanton necks,
> An axe shall hang, like a *prodigious* meteor,
> Ready to crop your loves' sweets.
> > BEAUMONT and FLETCHER, *Philaster*, act v. sc. 1.

Without this comely ornament of hair, their [women's] most glorious beauty appears as deformed, as the sun would be *prodigious* without beams.—FULLER, *The Profane State*, b. v. c. 5.

I began to reflect on the whole life of this *prodigious* man.—
Cowley, *On the Government of Oliver Cromwell.*

Promote, ⎫ ' To promote,' that is, to further or
Promoter, ⎬ set forward, a ' promoter,' a furtherer,
Promotion.⎭ are now words of harmless, often of
quite an honourable, signification. They were once
terms of extremest scorn ; a ' promoter ' being a common informer, and so called because he ' promoted '
charges and accusations against men (promotor
litium : Skinner).

There lack men to *promote* the king's officers when they do
amiss, and to *promote* all offenders.—Latimer, *Last Sermon
before Edward VI.*

> Thou, Linus, that lov'st still to be *promoting*,
> Because I sport about King Henry's marriage,
> Think'st this will prove a matter worth the carriage.
> Sir J. Harington, *Epigrams*, ii. 98.

Aristogiton the sycophant, or false *promoter*, was condemned
to death for troubling men with wrongful imputations.—Holland,
Plutarch's Morals, p. 421.

> His eyes be *promoters*, some trespass to spy.
> Tusser, *Of an envious and haughty Neighbour.*

Promoters be those which in popular and penal actions do
defer the names or complain of offenders, having part of the
profit for their reward.—Cowell, *The Interpreter*, s. v.

Covetousness and *promotion* and such like are that right hand
and right eye which must be cut off and plucked out, that the
whole man perish not.—Tyndale, *Exposition of the Sixth Chap.
of Matthew.*

Propriety. All ' propriety ' is now mental or
moral ; where material things are concerned, we
employ ' property,' at the first no more than a
different spelling or slightly different form of the
same word.

He [the good servant] provides good bounds and sufficient fences betwixt his own and his master's estate (Jacob, *Gen.* xxx. 36, set his flock three days' journey from Laban's), that no quarrel may arise about their *propriety*, nor suspicion that his remnant hath eaten up his master's whole cloth.—FULLER, *The Holy State*, b. i. c. 8.

> Hail, wedded love, mysterious law, true source
> Of human offspring, sole *propriety*
> In Paradise of all things common else.
>
> MILTON, *Paradise Lost*, b. v.

A *propriety* is nothing else but *jus ad rem*, when a man doth claim such a thing as his own, and has a power to use it and dispose of it in a lawful way for his own benefit and advantage. —STRONG, *Of the Two Covenants*, b. iii. c. i.

PROSE,⎫ 'To prose' is now to talk or to write
PROSER.⎭ heavily, tediously, without spirit and without animation; but 'to prose' was once the antithesis of to versify, and a 'proser' of a writer in metre. In the tacit assumption that vigour, animation, rapid movement, with all the precipitation of the spirit, belong to verse rather than to prose, lies the explanation of the changed uses of the words.

It was found that whether ought was imposed me by them that had the overlooking, or betaken to of mine own choice in English or other tongue, *prosing* or versing, but chiefly this latter, the style, by certain vital signs it had, was likely to live. —MILTON, *Reason of Church Government*, b. ii.

> And surely Nash, though he a *proser* were,
> A branch of laurel yet deserves to bear.
>
> DRAYTON, *On Poets and Poesy.*

PRUNE. At present we only 'prune' trees; but our earlier authors use the word where we should use 'preen,' which indeed is but another form of the word; nay, with a wider signification; for with us only birds 'preen' their feathers, while women, as in the example which follows, might 'prune' themselves of old.

> A husband that loveth to trim and pamper his body, causeth his wife by that means to study nothing else but the tricking and *pruning* of herself.—Holland, *Plutarch's Morals*, p. 318.

PUNCTUAL, } 'This word is now confined to the
PUNCTUALLY. } meagre denoting of accuracy in respect to time—fidelity to the precise moment of an appointment. But originally it was just as often and just as reasonably applied to space as to time. Nor only was it applied to time and space, but it had a large and very elegant figurative use' (De Quincey, *Note Book*). Thus a 'punctual' narration was a narration which entered into minuter *points* of detail.

> Truly I thought I could not be too *punctual* in describing the animal life, it being so serviceable for our better understanding the divine.—H. More, *Grand Mystery of Godliness*, Preface, p. x.

> All curious solicitude about riches smells of avarice ; even the very disposing of it with a too *punctual* and artificial liberality is not worth a painful solicitude.—Cotton, *Montaigne's Essays*, b. iii. c. 9.

> Every one is to give a reason of his faith ; but priests or ministers more *punctually* than any.—H. More, *Grand Mystery of Godliness*, b. x. c. 12.

PUNY. The present use of 'puny,' as that which is at once weak and small, is only secondary and inferential. 'Puny' or 'puisne' (puis né) is born after another, therefore younger; and only by inference smaller and weaker.

> It were a sign of ignorant arrogancy, if *punies* or freshmen

should reject the axioms and principles of Aristotle, usual in the schools, because they have some reasons against them which themselves cannot answer.—JACKSON, *The Eternal Truth of Scriptures*, c. i.

[The worthy soldier] had rather others should make a ladder of his dead corpse to scale a city by it, than a bridge of him whilst alive for his *punies* to give him the go-by, and pass over him to preferment.—FULLER, *The Holy State*, b. iv. c. 17.

He is dead and buried, and by this time no *puny* among the mighty nations of the dead; for though he left this world not very many days past, yet every hour, you know, addeth largely unto that dark society.—Sir T. BROWNE, *Letter to a Friend,* p. 1.

PURCHASE. Now always to acquire in exchange for money, to buy; but much oftener in our old writers simply to acquire, being properly to hunt, 'pourchasser,' 'procacciare;' and then to take in hunting; then to acquire; and then, as the commonest way of acquiring is by giving money in exchange, to buy. The word occurs six times in our Version of the New Testament, *Acts* i. 18; viii. 10; xx. 28; *Ephes.* i. 14; 1 *Tim.* iii. 13; 1 *Pet.* ii. 9, margin; in none of these is the notion of buying involved. At *Acts* i. 18, this is especially noteworthy. It is there said: ' This man *purchased* a field with the reward of iniquity.' There will always remain certain difficulties in reconciling the different records of the death of Judas; but if St. Peter had here affirmed that Judas had *bought* this field of blood, these difficulties would be seriously increased, for the chief priests were the actual buyers (*Matt.* xxvii. 7). He affirms no such thing, neither did our Translators understand him to do so, but simply that Judas made that ominous potter's field his own (ἐκτήσατο); he

who had given away a heavenly inheritance, took
fearful handsel and possession of this his earthly,
when there 'falling headlong, he burst asunder in
the midst and all his bowels gushed out.'

And therefore true consideration of estate can hardly find
what to reject, in matter of territory, in any empire, except it be
some glorious acquists obtained sometime in the bravery of wars,
which cannot be kept without excessive charge and trouble, of
which kind were the *purchases* of King Henry VIII., that of
Tournay, and that of Bologne.—BACON, *History of King Henry
VII.*

The *purchases* of our own industry are joined commonly with
labour and strife.—Id., *Colours of Good and Evil*, 9.

Meditation considers anything that may best make us to
avoid the place and to quit a vicious habit, or master and rectify
an untoward inclination, or *purchase* a virtue or exercise one.—
J. TAYLOR, *Life of Christ*, part i. § 5.

[Men] will repent, but not restore; they will say *Nollem
factum*, they wish they had never done it ; but since it is done,
you must give them leave to rejoice in their *purchase.*—Id.,
Sermon preached to the University of Dublin.

As it is a happiness for us to *purchase* friends, so is it misery
to lose them.—REYNOLDS, *God's Revenge against Murther*, b. v.
hist. 21.

PURSUER. 'Pursue' and 'pursuer' are older
words in the language than 'persecute' and 'perse-
cutor'—earlier adoptions of 'persequor' and 'per-
secutor,' and not, as these last, immediately from the
Latin. Besides the meaning which they still retain,
they once also covered the meanings which these
later words have, since their introduction, appropriated as exclusively their own. In Scotch law the
prosecutor is the 'pursuer,' ὁ διώκων.

I first was a blasphemer and *pursuwer.*—1 *Tim.* i. 13.
WICLIF.

If God leave them in this hardness of heart, they may prove as desperate opposites and *pursuers* of all grace, of Christ and Christians, as the most horrible open swine, as we see in Saul and Julian.—Rogers, *Naaman the Syrian*, p. 106.

QUAINT, } In ' quaint,' which is the Latin ' comp-
QUAINTLY. } tus,' the early English ' coint,' there lies always now the notion of a certain curiosity and oddness, however these may be subordinated to ends of beauty and grace, and indeed may themselves be made to contribute to these ends : pretty after some bygone standard of prettiness ; but all this is of late introduction into the word, which had once simply the meaning of elegant, graceful, skilful, subtle. See Earle, *Philology of the English Tongue*, p. 343.

> O brotel joye, O swete poison *queinte,*
> O monstre that so sotilly canst peinte
> Thy giftes, under hewe of stedfastness,
> That thou deceivest bothe more and less.
> > CHAUCER, *The Merchantes Tale.*

> But you, my lord, were glad to be employed
> To show how *quaint* an orator you are.
> > SHAKESPEARE, 2 *Henry VI.*, act iii. sc. 2.

Whom evere I schal kisse, he it is; holde ye him, and lede ye warli, *or queyntly.*—*Mark* xiv. 44. WICLIF.

> A ladder *quaintly* made of cords.
> SHAKESPEARE, *Two Gentlemen of Verona*, act iii. sc. 1.

QUERULOUS. Not formerly, as now, addicted to complaints, but quarrelsome ; perhaps through some confusion between 'querulous' and quarrellous.

There inhabit these regions a kind of people, rude, warlike, ready to fight, *querulous,* and mischievous.—HOLLAND, *Camden's Scotland*, p. 39.

Not *querulous,* or clamorous in his discourse ; ' He shall not

strive nor cry, neither shall any hear his voice in the streets ; '
but meek and quiet.—FULLER, *A Pisgah Sight of Palestine*,
b. iii. c. 6.

RACE. 'Racy' still exists as an epithet applied
to that which, growing out of a strong and vigorous
root, tastes of that root out of which it grows; but
'race,' in the sense of root imparting these qualities,
is not any longer in use.

> But thy vile *race*,
> Though thou didst learn, had that in it which good natures
> Could not abide to be with ; therefore wast thou
> Deservedly confined into this rock,
> Who hadst deserved more than a prison.
>
> SHAKESPEARE, *Tempest*, act i. sc. 2.

I think the Epistles of Phalaris to have more *race*, more spirit,
more force of wit and genius, than any other I have ever seen,
either ancient or modern.—Sir WILLIAM TEMPLE, *Works*, vol. iii.
p. 463.

RAISIN. It is conveniently agreed now that 'raisin'
shall be employed only of the *dried* grape, but this
does not lie in 'racemus,' from which it is descended,
nor yet in its earlier uses; indeed, 'raisins *of the sun*'
(Sir J. Harington) was the phrase commonly employed when the dried fruit was intended.

Nether in the vyneyerd thou schalt gadere *reysyns* and greynes
fallynge doun, but thou schalt leeve to be gaderid of pore men
and pilgryms.—*Lev.* xix. 10.   WICLIF.

RASCAL,   } The lean unseasonable members of
 · RASCALITY. } the herd of deer were originally so
called ; then the common people, the *plebs* as distinguished from the *populus*, although it would be hard
to trace any connexion between the Anglo-Saxon

' rascal ' and the French ' racaille ; ' while it is only in comparatively modern English that the word is one of moral contempt.

And he smoot of the puple seventi men, and fifti thousandis of the *raskeyl* [Et percussit de populo septuaginta viros et quinquaginta millia *plebis* (Vulg.)]—1 *Kin.* vi. 19. WICLIF.

The common priests be not so obedient unto their ordinaryes that they will pay money except they know why. Now it is not expedient that every *rascal* should know the secretes of the very true cause, for many considerations.—TYNDALE, *The Practice of Popishe Prelates.*

> Now shall I tel you which ben bestes of chace ;
> And ye shall, my dere sones, other bestes all,
> Whereso ye hem finde, *rascall* hem call.
> > JULIANA BERNERS, *The Book of St. Albans.*

As one should in reproach say to a poor man, Thou *raskall* knave, where *raskall* is properly the hunter's term given to young deer, lean and out of season, and not to people.—PUTTENHAM, *Art of English Poesy,* 1811, p. 150.

> Both sorts of seasoned deer,
> Here walk the stately red, the freckled fallow there;
> The bucks and lusty stags among the *rascals* strewed,
> As sometimes gallant spirits amongst the multitude.
> > DRAYTON, *Polyolbion,* song 13.

The report which these roving hunters had made to their countrymen of that pleasant land, did invite the chief heads of their clans, with their several *rascalities,* to flock into Europe, like beggars dismissed out of a prison, invited to a solemn banquet.—JACKSON, *A Treatise on the Divine Essence,* b. vi. c. 27, § 6.

RATHER. This survives for us now only as an adverb, that part of speech to which so many others seem to tend ; but meets us often in old English in its prior form, that is as an adjective ; being properly the comparative of ' rathe,' a synonym for early.

This is he that I seide of, aftir me is comen a man, whiche was made bifor me, for he was *rather* than I [quia *prior* me erat, Vulg.].—*John* i. 30. Wiclif.

If the world hatith you, wite ye that it hadde me in hate *rather* than you [me *priorem* vobis odio habuit, Vulg.].—*John* xv. 18. Wiclif.

The Sarazines maden another cytie more far from the see, and clepeden it the newe Damyete, so that now no man dwellethe at the *rathere* town of Damyete.—Sir John Maundeville, *Voyage and Travaile*, p. 46, Halliwell's edition.

Whatsoever thou or such other say, I say that the pilgrimage that now is used is to them that do it, a praisable and a good mean to come the *rather* to grace.—Foxe, *Book of Martyrs ; Examination of William Thorpe.*

> The *rather* lambs been starved with cold.
> Spenser, *The Shepherd's Calendar, February.*

Reclaim. A ' reclamation ' is still sometimes a calling *out against* ; but ' to reclaim ' is never, I think, anything now but to call *back again* ; never to disclaim.

Herod, instead of *reclaiming* what they exclaimed [*Acts* xii. 22], embraced and hugged their praises as proper to himself, and thereupon an angel and worms, the best and basest of creatures, met in his punishment, the one smiting, the other eating him up.—Fuller, *A Pisgah Sight of Palestine*, b. ii. c. 8.

Recognize. This verb means now to revive our knowledge of a person or thing ; to reacquaint oneself with it ; but in earlier usage to review, as in my first quotation, to reconnoitre, as in my second.

In *recognizing* this history I have employed a little more labour, partly to enlarge the argument which I took in hand, partly also to assay, whether by any painstaking I might pacify the stomachs, or to satisfy the judgments of these importune quarrellers.—Foxe, *Book of Martyrs ; Epistle Dedicatory [of the Second Edition] to the Queen's Majesty.*

In quartering either in village, field, or city, he [a commander] ought himself to *recognize* all avenues, whereby his enemies may come to him.—Monro, *His Expedition*, p. 9.

REDUCE. That which is 'reduced' now is brought back to narrower limits, or lower terms, or more subject conditions, than those under which it subsisted before. But nothing of this lies of necessity in the word, nor yet in the earlier uses of it. According to these, that was 'reduced' which was brought back to its former estate, an estate that might be, and in all the following examples is, an ampler, larger, or more prosperous one than that which it superseded.

The drift of the Roman armies and forces was not to bring free states into servitude, but contrariwise, to *reduce* those that were in bondage to liberty.—Holland, *Livy*, p. 1211.

There remained only Britain [*i.e.* Britany] to be reunited, and so the monarchy of France to be *reduced* to the ancient terms and bounds.—Bacon, *History of King Henry VII.*

That he might have these keys to open the heavenly Hades to *reduced* apostates, to penitent, believing, self-devoting sinners, for this it was necessary He should put on man, become obedient to death, even that servile punishment, the death of the cross.—Howe, *The Redeemer's Dominion over the Invisible World.*

> Abate the edge of traitors, gracious Lord,
> That would *reduce* these bloody days again.
> > Shakespeare, *Richard III.*, act v. sc. 5.

REIGN. This is now in the abstract what 'kingdom' is in the concrete, but there was no such distinction once between them.

> And for a little glorie vaine,
> They lesen God, and eke his *raigne.*
> > Chaucer, *Romaunt of the Rose*, 448.

REJOICE. See ' Enjoy.'

Than was mad pes on this manere, that he and his puple schuld frely *rejoyce* all the lond of the othir side of Seyne.—CAPGRAVE, *Chronicle of England*, p. 112.

In special he [Constantine] assigned and bequathe the lord-schip of the west parte, which was Rome, to his eeldist sone Constantyn, which sone *rejoiced* the same parte so to him devysid, and that thorugh al his liif.—PECOCK, *Repressor*, c. xiii.

RELIGION. Not, as too often now, used as equivalent for godliness; but like θρησκεία, for which it stands *Jam.* i. 27, it expressed the outer form and embodiment which the inward spirit of a true or a false devotion assumed.

In the Middle Ages a ' religion' was a monastic order, and they were ' religious' who had entered into one of these.

We would admit and grant them, that images used for no *religion*, or superstition rather, we mean of none worshipped, nor in danger to be worshipped of any, may be suffered.—*Homilies; Against Peril of Idolatry.*

> By falsities and lies the greatest part
> Of mankind they corrupted to forsake
> God their Creator, and the invisible
> Glory of Him that made them to transform
> Oft to the image of a brute, adorned
> With gay *religions* full of pomp and gold.
> MILTON, *Paradise Lost*, b. i.

> *Religious* folke ben full covert,
> Secular folke ben more apert,
> But natheless I woll not blame
> *Religious* folke, ne hem diffame
> In what habite that ever thei go ;
> *Religion* humble and true also
> Woll I not blame ne dispise ;
> But I n'ill love it in no wise,

I mean of false *religious*,
That stout been and malicious,
That wollen in a habit go
And setten not hir herte thereto.
CHAUCER, *Romaunt of the Rose*, 6152–63.

And thus when that thei were counseilled,
In black clothes thei them clothe,
The daughter and the lady both,
And yolde hem to *religion*.
GOWER, *Confessio Amantis*, b. viii.

REMARK. There are no ' remarks ' now but verbal ones. ' To remark ' was once to point out, to designate.

They [the publicans and harlots] are moved by shame, and punished by disgrace, and *remarked* by punishments, and frighted by the circumstances and notices of all the world, and separated from sober persons by laws and an intolerable character.—J. TAYLOR, *Of Lukewarmness and Zeal*, Serm. 13, part ii.

Officer. Hebrews, the prisoner Samson here I seek.
Chorus. His manacles *remark* him ; there he sits.
MILTON, *Samson Agonistes*, 1308.

REMONSTRATE. ⎫ Its present sense, namely to ex-
REMONSTRANCE. ⎭ postulate, was only at a late date superinduced on the word. ' To remonstrate ' is properly to make *any* show or representation in regard to some step that has been taken. It is now only such show or representation *as protests against* this step ; but always assumes this step to have been distasteful ; but this limitation lies not of necessity in the word.

Properties of a faithful servant : a sedulous eye, to observe all occasions within or without, tending to *remonstrate* the habit within.—ROGERS, *Naaman the Syrian*, p. 309.

It [the death of Lady Carbery] was not (in all appearance) of so much trouble as two fits of a common ague ; so careful was God to *remonstrate* to all that stood in that sad attendance that this soul was dear to Him.—J. TAYLOR, *Funeral Sermon on Lady Carbery.*

I consider that in two very great instances it was *remonstrated* that Christianity was the greatest prosecution of natural justice and equality in the whole world.—Id., *Life of Christ*, Preface, § 32.

When Sir Francis Cottington returned with our king's oath, plighted to the annexed conditions for the ease of the Roman Catholics, the Spaniards made no *remonstrance* of joy, or of an ordinary liking to it.—HACKET, *Life of Archbishop Williams*, part i. p. 145.

No ; the atheist is too wise in his generation to make *remonstrances* and declarations of what he thinks. It is his heart and the little council that is held there, that is only privy to his monstrous opinions.—SOUTH, *Sermons*, 1744, vol. ix. p. 78.

REMORSE, } In 'remorseless' and in the phrase
REMORSEFUL. } 'without remorse,' we retain a sense of 'remorse' as equivalent with pity, which otherwise has quite passed away from it. It may thus have acquired this meaning. There is nothing which is followed in natures not absolutely devilish with so swift revulsion of mind as acts of cruelty. Nowhere does the conscience so quickly 'remord,' if one may use the word, the guilty actor as in and after these ; and thus 'remorse,' which is the penitence of the natural man, the penitence not wrought by the spirit of grace, while it means the revulsion of the mind and conscience against any evil which has been done, came to mean predominantly revulsion against acts of cruelty, the pity which followed close on these ; and thus pity in general, and not only as in this way called out.

King Richard by his own experience grew sensible of the miseries which merchants and mariners at sea underwent. Wherefore, now touched with *remorse* of their pitiful case, he resolved to revoke the law of wrecks.—FULLER, *The Holy War*, b. iii. c. 7.

> His helmet, justice, judgment, and *remorse*.
> MIDDLETON, *Wisdom of Solomon*, c. v. 17.

> O Eglamour, thou art a gentleman,
> Valiant, wise, *remorseful*, well accomplished.
> SHAKESPEARE, *Two Gentlemen of Verona*, act iv. sc. 2.

REPEAL. 'To repeal' (rappeler) is to recall, and seldom or never applied now except to some statute or law, but once of far wider use.

> I will *repeal* thee, or, be well assured,
> Adventure to be banishèd myself.
> SHAKESPEARE, 2 *Henry VI.*, act iii. sc. 2.

> Whence Adam soon *repealed*
> The doubts that in his heart arose.
> MILTON, *Paradise Lost*, vii. 59.

> Or else Nepenthe, enemy to sadness,
> Repelling sorrows, and *repealing* gladness.
> DUBARTAS, *Eden, The Second Week*.

REPROVE. Now 'to rebuke,' but once equivalent to 'disprove,' and convertible with it.

As it [the Apology] hath been well allowed of and liked of the learned and godly, so hath it not hitherto, for ought that may appear, been anywhere openly *reproved* either in Latin or otherwise, either by any one man's private writing, or by the public authority of any nation.—JEWEL, *Defence of the Apology*.

> *Reprove* my allegation if you can ;
> Or else conclude my words effectual.
> SHAKESPEARE, 2 *Henry VI.*, act iii. sc. 1.

RESENT,
RESENTMENT. } When first introduced into the language (this was in the seventeenth

century ; ' vox nova in nostrâ linguâ : ' Junius), ' to resent' meant to have a sense or feeling of that which had been done to us ; but whether a sense of gratitude for the good, or of enmity for the evil, the word itself did not decide, and was employed in both meanings. Must we gather from the fact that the latter is now the exclusive employment of it, that our sense of injuries is much stronger and more lasting than our sense of benefits ?

> 'Tis by my touch alone that you *resent*
> What objects yield delight, what discontent.
>
> BEAUMONT, *Psyche*, can. iv. st. 156.

Perchance as vultures are said to smell the earthliness of a dying corpse ; so this bird of prey [the evil Spirit which personated Samuel] *resented* a worse than earthly savour in the soul of Saul, an evidence of his death at hand.—FULLER, *The Profane State*, b. v. c. 4.

The judicious palate will prefer a drop of the sincere milk of the word before vessels full of traditionary pottage, *resenting* of the wild gourd of human invention.—Id., *A Pisgah Sight of Palestine*, b. iii. c. 1.

I *resented* as I ought the news of my mother-in-law's death.— SANCROFT, *Variorum Shakespeare*, vol. i. p. 518.

Sadness does in some cases become a Christian, as being an index of a pious mind, of compassion, and a wise, proper *resentment* of things.—J. TAYLOR, *Sermon* 23, part ii.

The Council taking notice of the many good services performed by Mr. John Milton, their Secretary for foreign languages, particularly for his book in vindication of the Parliament and people of England against the calumnies and invectives of Salmasius, have thought fit to declare their *resentment* and good acceptance of the same, and that the thanks of the Council be returned to Mr. Milton.—*Extract from ' The Council Book,'* 1651, June 18.

RESIDENCE,⎱ It will be seen from the quotations
RESIDENT. ⎰ which follow that ' residence' in the

seventeenth century meant something quite different from ordinary place of habitation, which is all the meaning which now it has.

> Separation in it is wrought by weight, as in the ordinary *residence* or settlement of liquors.—BACON, *Natural History*, § 302.

> Of waters of a muddy *residence* we may make good use and quench our thirst, if we do not trouble them; yet upon any ungentle disturbance we drink down mud, instead of a clear stream.—J. TAYLOR, *Sermon on the Gunpowder Treason.*

> The inexperienced Christian shrieks out whenever his vessel shakes, thinking it always a danger that the watery pavement is not stable and *resident* like a rock.—Id., *Sermon* 11, part 3.

RESTIVE, RESTIVENESS. } Any one now invited to define a 'restive' horse would certainly put into his definition that it was one with *too much* motion ; but in obedience to its etymology 'restive' would have once meant one with *too little*; determined to continue at *rest* when it ought to go forward. Immobile, lazy, stubborn (the Italian ' ritroso '), are the three stages of meaning which the word went through, before it reached the fourth and present.

> Bishops or presbyters we know, and deacons we know, but what are chaplains ? In state perhaps they may be listed among the upper serving-men of some great man's household, the yeomen ushers of devotion, where the master is too *resty* or too rich to say his own prayers, or to bless his own table.—MILTON, *Iconoclastes,* c. **xxiv.**

> *Restive,* or *Resty,* drawing back instead of·going forward, as some horses do,—PHILLIPS, *New World of Words.*

> Nothing hindereth men's fortunes so much as this : Idem manebat, neque idem decebat ; men are where they were, when occasions turn. From whatsoever root or cause this *restiveness* of mind proceedeth, it is a thing most prejudicial.—BACON, *Advancement of Learning,* b. ii.

The snake, by *restiness* and lying still all winter, hath a certain membrane or film growing over the whole body.—HOLLAND, *Pliny*, part i. p. 210.

RETALIATE,　It has fared with 'retaliate' and
RETALIATION.　'retaliation' as it has with 'resent' and 'resentment,' that whereas men could once speak of the 'retaliation' of benefits as well as of wrongs, they only 'retaliate' injuries now.

Our captain would not salute the city, except they would *retaliate.*—*Diary of Henry Teonge*, Aug. 1, 1675.

[The king] expects a return in specie from them [the Dissenters], that the kindness which he has graciously shown them may be *retaliated* on those of his own persuasion.—DRYDEN, *The Hind and the Panther*, Preface.

His majesty caused directions to be sent for the enlargement of the Roman priests, in *retaliation* for the prisoners that were set at liberty in Spain to congratulate the prince's welcome.—HACKET, *Life of Archbishop Williams*, part i. p. 166.

REVOKE. This has now a much narrower range of meaning than the Latin 'revocare;' but some took for granted once that wherever the one word could have been used in Latin, the other might be used in English.

　　　The wolf, who would not be
Revokèd from the slaughter for the sweetness of the blood,
Persisted sharp and eager still, until that as he stood,
Fast biting on a bullock's neck, she turned him into stone.
　　　　　GOLDING, *Ovid's Metamorphosis*, b. xi.

Her knees *revoked* their first strength, and her feet
Were borne above the ground with wings to greet
The long-grieved queen with news her king was come.
　　　　　CHAPMAN, *The Odysseys of Homer*, b. xxiii. l. 5.

RIG. A somewhat vulgar word, with the present use of which, however, we are probably all familiar from its occurrence in *John Gilpin* :

> ' He little guessed when he set out
> Of running such a *rig*.'

But a ' rig ' in its earlier use was not so often a strange uncomely *feat*, as a wanton uncomely *person*.

Let none condemn them [the girls] for *rigs* because thus hoyting with the boys, seeing the simplicity of their age was a patent to privilege any innocent pastime.—FULLER, *A Pisgah Sight of Palestine*, b. iv. c. 6.

RIPPLE. The same word as ' wrimple,' ' rumple,' to make wrinkles on. It is now a poetical word, and nothing is ' rippled ' but the surface of the water ; but once it was otherwise ; and provincially is so still. Thus in a useful *Glossary of Yorkshire Words and Phrases*, Whitby, 1855, p. 140 : ' *To ripple*, to scratch slightly as with a pin upon the skin ; ' which is precisely its use in the following citation.

On a sudden an horseman's javelin, having slightly *rippled* the skin of his [Julian's] left arm, pierced within his short ribs, and stuck fast in the nether lappet or fillet of his liver.—HOLLAND, *Ammianus*, p. 264.

ROGUE. There was a time when ' rogue ' meant no more than wandering mendicant. What of dishonesty is implied now in the word was afterwards superinduced upon it ; as was also the case with ' vagabond.'

> Mine enemy's dog,
> Though he had bit me, should have stood that night
> Against my fire ; and wast thou fain, poor father,

> To hovel thee with swine and *rogues* forlorn
> In short and musty straw ?
> > SHAKESPEARE, *King Lear*, act iv. sc. 7.

Rogue signifieth with us an idle sturdy beggar, that, wandering from place to place without passport, after he hath been by justices bestowed upon some certain place of abode, or offered to be bestowed, is condemned to be so called; who for the first offence is called a *rogue* of the first degree, and punished by whipping, and boring through the gristle of the right ear with a hot iron an inch in compass, and for the second offence is called a *rogue* of the second degree, and put to death as a felon, if he be above eighteen years old.— COWELL, *The Interpreter*, s. v.

The third sort of those that live unprofitably and without a calling are our idle sturdy *rogues* and vagrant towns-end beggars. I mean such as are able to work, yet rather choose to wander abroad the country, and to spend their days in a most base and ungodly course of life. —SANDERSON, *Sermons*, 1671, vol. i. p. 197.

ROOM. In certain connexions we still employ ' room' for place, but in many more it obtains this meaning no longer. Thus one who accepts the words, ' When thou art bidden of any man to a wedding, sit not down in the highest *room* ' (*Luke* xiv. 8), according to the present use of 'room,' will probably imagine to himself guests assembling in various apartments, some more honourable than other; and not, as indeed the meaning is, taking higher or lower *places* at one and the same table.

> Is Clarence, Henry, and his son, young Edward,
> And all the unlooked-for issue of their bodies,
> To take their *rooms*, ere I can place myself?
> > SHAKESPEARE, 3 *Henry VI.*, act iii. sc. 2.

If he have but twelve pence in's purse, he will give it for the best *room* in a playhouse.—Sir T. OVERBURY, *Characters : A Proud Man*.

RUFFIAN, } The Italian 'ruffiano,' the Spanish
RUFFIANLY. } 'rufian,' the French 'rufien,' all
signify the setter-forward of an infamous traffic between the sexes; nor will the passages quoted below
leave any doubt that this is the proper meaning of
'ruffian' in English, others being secondary and derived from it. At the same time the 'ruffian' is not
merely the 'leno,' he is the 'amasius' as well; and
the frequent allusions to long and elaborately curled
hair which go along with the word make one suspect
a connexion with the Spanish 'rufo,' not as it means
red, but crisp or curled. On the possible derivations
see Diez, *Roman. Sprache*, p. 299; and for some
instructive English uses of it, Ascham's *Scholemaster*,
Wright's edit. pp. 44, 215.

Let young men consider the precious value of their time, and
waste it not in idleness, in jollity, in gaming, in banqueting, in
ruffians' company.—*Homilies ; Against Idleness.*

Xenocrates, casting but his eye upon Polemon, who was
come into his school like a *ruffian*, by his very look only redeemed him from his loose life.—HOLLAND, *Plutarch's Morals*,
p. 112.

He [her husband] is no sooner abroad than she is instantly at
home, revelling with her *ruffians*.—REYNOLDS, *God's Revenge
against Murther*, b. iii. hist. 11.

Who in London hath not heard of his [Greene's] dissolute
and licentious living; his fond disguising of a Master of Art
with *ruffianly* hair, unseemly apparel, and more unseemly company?—G. HARVEY, *Four Letters touching Robert Greene*, p. 7.

Some frenchified or outlandish monsieur, who hath nothing
else to make him famous, I should say infamous, but an effeminate, *ruffianly*, ugly, and deformed lock.—PRYNNE, *The Unloveli-
ness of Love-Locks*, p. 27.

RUMMAGE. At present so to look for one thing
as in the looking to overturn and unsettle a great

many others. It is a sea-term, and signified at first to dispose with such orderly method goods in the hold of a ship that there should be the greatest possible room, or 'roomage.' The quotation from Phillips shows the word in the act of transition from its former use to its present.

And that the masters of the ships do look well to the *romaging*, for they might bring away a great deal more than they do, if they would take pain in the *romaging*.—HACKLUYT, *Voyages,* vol. i. p. 308.

To *rummage* (sea-term): To remove any goods or luggage from one place to another, especially to clear the ship's hold of any goods or lading, in order to their being handsomely stowed and placed ; whence the word is used upon other occasions, for to rake into, or to search narrowly.—PHILLIPS, *New World of Words.*

SAD,
SADLY,
SADNESS. } This had once the meaning of earnest, serious, sedate, 'set,' this last being only another form of the same word. The passage from Shakespeare quoted below marks 'sadly' and 'sadness' in their transitional state from the old meaning to the new ; Benvolio using 'sadness' in the old sense, Romeo pretending to understand him in the new.

> O dere wif, o gemme of lustyhede,
> That were to me so *sade*, and eke so trewe.
> > CHAUCER, *The Manciples Tale.*

He may have one year, or two at the most, an ancient and *sad* matron attending on him.—Sir T. ELYOT, *The Governor,* b. i. c. 6.

> For when I think how far this earth doth us divide,
> Alas, meseems, love throws me down ; I feel how that I slide.
> But then I think again, Why should I thus mistrust
> So sweet a wight, so *sad* and wise. that is so true and just ?
> > SURREY, *The Faithful Lover.*

In go the speres *sadly* in the rest.
>   CHAUCER, *The Knightes Tale.*

Therefor ye, britheren, bifor witynge kepe you silf, lest ye be disseyved bi errour of unwise men, and falle awei fro youre owne *sadness* [a propriâ *firmitate*, Vulg.].—2 *Pet.* iii. 17. WICLIF.

> *Benvolio.* Tell me in *sadness* who she is you love?
> *Romeo.* What, shall I groan, and tell you?
> *Ben.*   Groan? why, no;
>   But *sadly* tell me who?
> >   SHAKESPEARE, *Romeo and Juliet,* act i. sc. 1.

SAMPLER. This has now quite dissociated itself in meaning from 'exemplar,' of which it is the popular form, as 'sample' has done from 'example;' not so, however, once.

Job, the *sawmpler* of pacience.—*Preparatory Epistles of St. Jerome to Wiclif's Bible.*

SASH. At present always a belt or girdle *of the loins*; not so, however, when first introduced from the East. By the 'sash,' or 'shash' as it was then always spelt, was understood the roll of silk, fine linen, or gauze, worn about the head; in fact a turban.

Shash : Cidaris seu tiara, pileus Turcicus, ut doct. Th. H. placet, ab It. Sessa, gausapina cujus involucris Turcæ pileos suos adornant.—SKINNER, *Etymologicon.*

So much for the silk in Judea, called Shesh in Hebrew, whence haply that fine linen or silk is called *shashes,* worn at this day about the heads of eastern people.—FULLER, *A Pisgah Sight of Palestine,* b. ii. c. 14.

He [a Persian merchant] was apparelled in a long robe of cloth of gold, his head was wreathed with a huge *shash* or tuli-pant of silk and gold.—HERBERT, *Travels,* 1638, p. 191.

SCARCE, ⎫ Now expressing the fact that the thing
SCARCELY, ⎬ to which this epithet is applied is rare,
SCARCITY. ⎭ not easily to be come by; but in the
time of Chaucer, Wiclif, and Gower, and till a later
day, miserly or stingy. For the derivation see Littré,
Dict. Franc. s. v. Echars.

Ye shuln usen the richesses which ye have geten by youre wit
and by youre travaille, in swiche manere, that men holde ye not
to *scarse* ne to sparing, ne fool-large; for right as men blamen an
avaricious man because of his *scarsitee* and chincherie, in the
same wise is he to blamen that spendeth over largely.—CHAUCER,
Tale of Melibæus.

A man is that is maad riche in doynge *scarsli* [parce agendo,
Vulg.].—*Ecclus.* xi. 18. WICLIF.

For I saye this thing, he that soweth *scarséli* schal also repe
scarseli.—2 *Cor.* xi. 6. Id.

> Both free and *scarce*, thou giv'st and tak'st again;
> Thy womb, that all doth breed, is tomb to all.
>
> DAVISON, *Poetical Rhapsody*, p. 256.

SECURE, ⎫ In our present English the difference
SECURELY, ⎬ between 'safe' and 'secure' is hardly
SECURITY. ⎭ recognized, but once it was otherwise.
'Secure' ('securus'=sine curâ) was *subjective*; it was
a man's own sense, well grounded or not, of the absence
of danger; safe was *objective*, the actual fact of such
absence of danger. A man, therefore, might *not* be
'safe,' just because he was 'secure' (thus see *Judges*
xviii. 7, 10, 27, and *Paradise Lost*, iv. 791). I may
observe that our use of 'secure' at *Matt.* xxviii. 14,
is in fact this early, though we may easily read the
passage as though it were employed in the modern
sense. 'We will *secure* you' of our Version repre-
sents ἀμερίμνους ὑμᾶς ποιήσομεν of the original.

My wanton weakness did herself betray
 With too much play.
I was too bold; he never yet stood safe
 That stands *secure*.

       QUARLES, *Emblems*, ii. 14.

We cannot endure to be disturbed or awakened from our
pleasing lethargy. For we care not to be safe, but to be *secure*.
—J. TAYLOR, *Of Slander and Flattery*.

   Man may *securely* sin, but safely never.
       BEN JONSON, *The Forest*, xi.

  We see the wind sit sore upon our sails,
  And yet we strike not, but *securely* perish.
     SHAKESPEARE, *Richard II.*, act ii. sc. 1.

 He means, my lord, that we are too remiss,
 While Bolingbroke, through our *security*,
 Grows strong and great in substance and in friends.
      Id. *Ibid.*, act iii. sc. 2.

The last daughter of pride is delicacy, under which is contained gluttony, luxury, sloth, and *security*.—NASH, *Christ's
Tears over Jerusalem*, p. 137.

      How this man
 Bears up in blood; seems fearless! Why 'tis well:
 Security some men call the suburbs of hell,
 Only a dead wall between.
    WEBSTER, *Duchess of Malfi*, act v. sc. 2.

SEDITION,⎫ There was an attempt on the part of
SEDITIOUS.⎭ some scholarly writers at the beginning of the seventeenth century to keep ' sedition '
true to its etymology, and to the meaning which
' seditio ' bears in the Latin. This is the explanation
of its employment as a rendering of διχοστασίαι, Gal.
v. 21, as quoted below; which in our present English
would be more accurately rendered, secessions, dis-
sensions, or divisions; in exactly which sense ' seditious ' is there used by our Translators. So too,

when Satan addresses Abdiel 'seditious Angel,' this
is to find the same explanation, as is plain from the
words which immediately follow. He the one faithful,
taking the Lord's side, had in so doing divided the
ranks of those who adhered to the fallen Archangel,
and separated from them, being therein 'seditious.'
The quotation from Bishop Andrews not less evidently
shows how distinct in his mind 'seditions' were from
those overt acts of petty treason which we now call
by this name; however, they might often lead to
such.

Whom you find thus magnifying of changes and projecting
new plots for the people, be sure they are in the way to *sedition*.
For (mark it) they do *sedire*, that is *scorsim ire*, go aside; they
have their meetings apart about their new alterations. Now of
sedire comes *sedition*, side-going. For if that be not looked to
in time, the next news is, the blowing of a trumpet, and Sheba's
proclamation, We have no part in David. It begins in Shimei;
it ends in Sheba.—ANDREWS, *Of the Gunpowder Treason*,
Serm. 6.

Now the works of the flesh are manifest, which are these,
. . *seditions.*—*Gal.* v. 20, 21. Authorized Version.

> Ill for thee, but in wished hour
> Of my revenge, first sought for, thou returnest
> From flight, *seditious* Angel, to receive
> Thy merited reward.
> MILTON, *Paradise Lost*, vi. 150.

SEE. Not always confined as now to the *seat* or
residence of a bishop; nor indeed did it necessarily
involve the notion of a seat *of authority* at all.

> At Babiloine was his soveraine *see*.
> CHAUCER, *The Monkes Tale*.

> And small harpers with hir glees
> Sate under hem in divers *sees*.
> Id., *The House of Fame*, b. iii.

The Lord smoot all the fyrst gotun in the loond of Egipte, fro the fyrst gotun of Pharao, that sat in his *sce*, unto the fyrst gotun of the caitiff woman that was in prisoun.—*Exod.* xii. 29. WICLIF.

> Not that same famous temple of Diane
> Might match with this by many a degree;
> Nor that which that wise King of Jewry framed
> With endless cost to be the Almighty's *see*.
>
> SPENSER, *Fairy Queen*, iv. 10, 30.

SENSUAL, } 'Sensual' is employed now only in
SENSUALITY. } an ill meaning, and implies ever a predominance of sense in provinces where it ought not so to predominate. Milton, feeling that we wanted another word affirming this predominance where no such fault was implied by it, and that ' sensual' only imperfectly expressed this, employed, I know not whether he coined, 'sensuous,' a word which, if it had rooted itself in the language, might have proved of excellent service. 'Sensuality' has had always an ill meaning, but not always the same ill meaning which it has now. Any walking by sense and sight rather than by faith was 'sensuality' of old.

Hath not the Lord Jesus convinced thy *sensual* heart by *sensual* arguments? If thy *sense* were not left-handed, thou mightest with thy right hand bear down thine infidelity; for God hath given assurance sufficient by his Son to thy very *sense*, if thou wert not brutish (1 *John* i. 1).—ROGERS, *Naaman the Syrian*, p. 493.

There cannot always be that degree of *sensual*, pungent, or delectable affections towards religion as towards the desires of nature and sense.—J. TAYLOR, *Life of Christ*, part ii. § 12.

> Far as creation's ample range extends,
> The scale of *sensual*, mental powers ascends.
>
> POPE, *Essay on Man*, b. i.

I do take him to be a hardy captain; but yet a man more meet to be governed than to govern; for all his enterprizes be made upon his own *sensuality*, without the advice and counsel of those that been put in trust by the King's Majesty.—*State Papers*, 1538, vol. iii. p. 95.

He who might claim this absolute power over the soul to be believed upon his bare word, yet seeing the *sensuality* of man and our woful distrust, is willing to allow us all the means of strengthening our souls in his promise, by such seals and witnesses as confirm it.—ROGERS, *Naaman the Syrian*, p. 483.

A great number of people in divers parts of this realm, following their own *sensuality*, and living without knowledge and due fear of God, do wilfully and schismatically abstain aud refuse to come to their own parish churches.—*Act of Uniformity*, 1661.

SERVANT. A wooer, follower, admirer, lover, not of necessity an accepted one, was a 'servant' in the chivalrous language of two or three centuries ago.

Valentine. Madam and mistress, a thousand good morrows.
Silvia. Sir Valentine and *servant*, to you two thousand.
    SHAKESPEARE, *Two Gentlemen of Verona*, act. ii. sc. 1.

SERVILITY. The *subjective* abjectness and baseness of spirit of one who is a slave, or who acts as one, is always implied by this word at the present; while once it did but express the *objective* fact of an outwardly servile condition in him of whom it was predicated, leaving it possible that in spirit he might be free notwithstanding.

Such *servility* as the Jews endured under the Greeks and Asiatics, have they endured under the Saracen and the Turk.—JACKSON, *The Eternal Truth of Scriptures*, b. i. c. 26.

We are no longer under the *servility* of the law of Moses, but are all the children of God by faith in Christ Jesus.—HENRY MORE, *On Godliness*, b. viii. c. 6.

The same [faith] inclined Moses to exchange the dignities and delights of a court for a state of vagrancy and *servility*.—BARROW, *Sermon* 3, *On the Apostles' Creed*.

SHED. There are two A. S. verbs, 'scedan,' our present 'to shed,' and 'sceadan,' the modern German 'scheiden,' to separate or divide. To this last, not surviving as a verb, we owe ' shed ' and 'watershed,' or water-divider. How strongly this of partition or division was felt to be the central meaning of ' shed ' the quotations which follow will show. ' To shed ' is still used in the North in this sense.

They say also that the manner of making the *shed* [διακρί-νεσθαι] of new-wedded wives' hair with the iron head of a javelin came up then likewise.—NORTH, *Plutarch's Lives*, p. 22.

They were never so careful to comb their heads as when they should to the battle ; for then they did noint their selves with sweet oils, and did *shed* their hair.—Id., *Ibid.* p. 45.

SHEER. It is curious that Christopher Sly's declaration that he was ' fourteen pence on the score for *sheer* ale ' (*Taming of the Shrew, Induction,* sc. 2) should have given so much trouble to some of the early commentators upon Shakespeare. ' Sheer,' which is pure, unmixed, was used of things concrete once, although mostly of things abstract now.

They had scarcely sunk through the uppermost course of sand above, when they might see small sources to boil up, at the first troubled, but afterward they began to yield *sheer* and clear water in great abundance.—HOLLAND, *Livy*, p. 1191.

> Thou *sheer*, immaculate, and silver fountain,
> From whence this stream through muddy passages
> Hath held his current.
> >   SHAKESPEARE, *King Richard II.*, act v. sc. 3.

> Thou never hadst in thy house, to stay men's stomachs,
> A piece of Suffolk cheese, or gammon of bacon,
> Or any esculent, but *sheer* drink only,
> For which gross fault I here do damn thy license.
> >   MASSINGER, *A New Way to pay Old Debts*, act iv. sc. 2.

SHELF. 'To shelve' as to shoal, still remains; but not so, except in mariners' charts, 'shelf' as=shallow or sandbank.

I thought fit to follow the rule of coasting maps, where the *shelves* and rocks are described as well as the safe channel.—DAVENANT, *Preface to Gondibert.*

> God wisheth none should wreck on a strange *shelf*;
> To Him man's dearer than t' himself.
>   BEN JONSON, *The Forest*, iii.

> The watchful hero felt the knocks, and found
> The tossing vessel sailed on shoaly ground.
> Sure of his pilot's loss, he takes himself
> The helm, and steers aloof, and shuns the *shelf.*
>   DRYDEN, *Virgil's Æneid*, b. v.

SHREW. There are at the present no 'shrews' save female ones; but the word, like so many others which we have met with, now restrained to one sex, was formerly applied to both. It conveyed also of old a much deeper moral reprobation than now or in the middle English it did. Thus Lucifer is a 'shrew' in *Piers Ploughman*, and two murderers are 'shrews' in the quotation from Chaucer which follows.

> And thus accorded ben this *shrewes* tweye
> To slea the thridde, as ye han herd me seye,
>   CHAUCER, *The Pardoneres Tale.*

If I schal schewe me innocent, He schal preve me a *schrewe* [*pravum* me comprobabit, Vulg.].—*Job* ix. 20. WICLIF.

I know none more covetous *shrews* than ye are, when ye have a benefice.—FOXE, *Book of Martyrs; Examination of William Thorpe.*

SHREWD, } The weakness of the world's moral
SHREWDNESS. } indignation against evil causes a multitude of words which once conveyed intensest

moral reprobation gradually to convey none at all, or
it may be even praise. 'Shrewd' and 'shrewdness'
must be numbered among these.

Is he *shrewd* and unjust in his dealings with others ?—SOUTH,
Sermons, 1737, vol. vi. p. 106.

Forsothe the erthe is corupt before God, and is fulfilled with
shrewdnes [iniquitate, Vulg.].— *Gen.* vi. 12. WICLIF.

The prophete saith : Flee *shrewdnesse* [declinet *a malo*, Vulg.],
and do goodnesse ; seek pees, and folwe it.—CHAUCER, *The Tale
of Melibeus.*

SIEGE. A 'siege' is now *the sitting down* of an
army before a fortified place with the purpose of
taking it ; and has no other meaning but this. It
had once the double meaning, abstract and concrete,
of the French 'siége,' a seat.

Whanne mannes sone schal come in his *majeste* and alle hiso
aungelis with him, thanne he schal sitte on the *sege* of his ma·
jeste, and alle folkis schal be gaderide bifore hym.—*Matt.* xxv
3, 321. WICLIF.

A stately *siege* of soveraine majesty,
And thereon sat a woman gorgeous gay.
SPENSER, *Fairy Queen*, ii. 7, 44.

Besides, upon the very *siege* of justice
Lord Angelo hath to the common ear
Professed the contrary.
SHAKESPEARE, *Measure for Measure*, act iv. sc. 2.

SIGHT. The use of 'sight' to signify a multitude,
a many, that is, to see, has now a touch of vulgarity
about it, which once it was very far from possessing.

Ye are come unto the mounte Sion, and to the citie of the
livinge God, the celestiall Jerusalem, and to an innumerable
sight of angels.—*Heb.* xii. 22. TYNDALE.

Clodius was ever about him in every place and street he went, having a *sight* of rascals and knaves with him.— NORTH, *Plutarch's Lives*, p. 722.

SILLY, } A deep conviction of men that he who
SILLINESS.} departs from evil will make himself a prey, that none will be a match for the world's evil who is not himself evil, has brought to pass the fact that a number of words, signifying at first goodness, signify next well-meaning simplicity; the notions of goodness and foolishness, with a strong predominance of the last, for a while interpenetrating one another in them; till at length the latter quite expels the former, and remains as the sole possessor of the word. I need hardly mention the Greek ἄκακος, εὐήθης, εὐήθεια: while the same has happened in regard of our own 'silly,' which (the same word as the German 'selig') has successively meant, (1) blessed, (2) innocent, (3) harmless, (4) weakly foolish.

> O *sely* woman, full of innocence.
> > CHAUCER, *Legend of Fair Women*, 1252.

Holofernes, a valiant and mighty captain, being overwhelmed with wine, had his head stricken from his shoulders by that *silly* woman Judith.—*Homilies ; Against Gluttony and Drunkenness.*

This Miles Forest and John Dighton about midnight (the *silly* children lying in their beds) came into the chamber, and suddenly lapped them up among the clothes.—Sir T. MORE, *History of King Richard III.*

> Oh God, quod she, so worldly *selinesse,*
> Which clerkes callen false felicite,
> Ymeddled is with many bitternesse.
> > CHAUCER, *Troilus and Cressida*, 3, 800.

SINCERE, } The etymology of 'sincerus' being
SINCERITY.} uncertain, it is impossible to say what is the primary notion of our English 'sincere.' These

words belong now to an ethical sphere exclusively,
and even there their meaning is not altogether what
once it was; but the absence of foreign admixture
which they predicate might be literal once.

> The mind of a man, as it is not of that content or receipt to
> comprehend knowledge without helps and supplies, so again, it is
> not *sincere*, but of an ill and corrupt tincture.—BACON, *Of the
> Interpretation of Nature,* c. xvi.

> The Germans are a people that more than all the world, I
> think, may boast *sincerity*, as being for some thousands of years
> a pure and unmixed people.—FELTHAM, *A brief Character of
> the Low Countries,* p. 59.

SKELETON. Now the framework of bones as entirely denuded of the flesh ; but in early English, and
there in stricter agreement with its etymology, the
dried mummy.

> *Scelet*; the dead body of a man artificially dried or tanned for
> to be kept or seen a long time.—HOLLAND, *Plutarch's Morals ;
> An Explanation of certain obscure Words.*

SMUG. One of many words which have been spoilt
through being drawn into our serio-comic vocabulary.
It still means *adorned*, being connected with the German 'schmucken;' but seeks to present the very
adornment and smoothness which it implies in a
ridiculous ignoble point of view. Any such intention
was very far from it once.

> And here the *smug* and silver Trent shall run
> In a new channel, fair and evenly.
> > SHAKESPEARE, 1 *Henry IV.*, act iii. sc. 1.

> Twelve sable steeds, *smug* as the old raven's wing,
> Of even stature and of equal pride,
> Sons of the wind, or some more speedy thing,
> To his fair chariot all abreast were tied.
> > BEAUMONT, *Psyche*, ix. 176.

SNAIL. It is curious what different objects men will be content for long to confuse under a common name. Thus in some provincial dialects of Germany they have only one name, ' padde' (compare our 'paddock '), for frog and toad. So too ' snail ' (cochlea) and 'slug ' (limax) with us were both to a comparatively recent period included under the former name. ' Slug ' indeed, as=sluggard, is an old word in the language; but only at the end of the seventeenth or beginning of the eighteenth century was it transferred to that familiar pest of our gardens which we now call by this name. Indeed up to the present day in many of our provincial dialects slugs and snails are invariably both included under the latter name. See an interesting discussion in the Philological Society's *Transactions*, 1860-1, pp. 102–106.

There is much variety even in creatures of the same kind. See these two *snails*. One hath a house, the other wants it; *yet both are snails*, and it is a question whether case is the better. That which hath a house hath more shelter, that which wants it hath more freedom.—Bishop HALL, *Occasional Meditations*.

Snails, a soft and exosseous animal, whereof in the *naked* and greater sort, as though she would requite the loss of a shell on their back, nature near the head hath placed a flat white stone. Of the great gray *snails* I have not met with any that wanted it.—Sir T. BROWNE, *Vulgar Errors*, b. iii. c. 13.

SNUB. Another form of ' snip,' ' sneap,' ' snape,' to nip with cold, and so to check or cut short. It is now never used save in a figurative sense; but this formerly was not so.

If we neglect them [the first stirrings of corruption] but a little, out of a thought that they can do no great harm yet, or that we shall have time enough to *snub* them hereafter, we do it to our own certain disadvantage, if not utter undoing.— SANDERSON, *Sermons*, 1671, vol. ii. p. 241.

SOFT,
SOFTNESS. It is not an honourable fact that ' soft' and ' softness ' should now be terms of slight, almost of contempt, when ethically employed; although indeed it is only a repetition of what we find in χρηστός, εὐήθης, ' gutig,' ' bonhomie,' and other words not a few.

That they speak evil of no man, that they be no fighters, but *soft* [ἐπιεικεῖς], showing all meekness unto all men.—*Titus* iii. 2. TYNDALE.

The meek or *soft* shall inherit the earth ; even as we say, Be still, and have thy will.—TYNDALE, *Exposition on the Fifth Chapter of Matthew.*

Let your *softness* [τὸ ἐπιεικὲς ὑμῶν] be known unto all men.— *Phil.* iv. 5. CRANMER.

SONNET. A ' sonnet ' now must consist of exactly fourteen lines, neither more nor less ; and these with a fixed arrangement, though admitting a certain re- laxation, of the rhymes ; but ' sonnet ' used often to be applied to *any* shorter poem, especially of an amatory kind.

He [Arion] had a wonderful desire to chaunt a *sonnet* or hymn unto Apollo Pythius.—HOLLAND, *Plutarch's Morals*, p. 343.

If ye will tell us a tale, or play a jig, or show us a play and fine sights, or sing *sonnets* in our ears, there we will be for you. —ROGERS, *Naaman the Syrian*, p. 492.

SOT,
SOTTISH,
SOTTISHNESS. He only is a ' sot' now whose stupor and folly is connected with, and the result of, excessive drink; but *any* fool would once bear this name.

> In Egypt oft has seen the *sot* bow down,
> And reverence some deified baboon.
>
> OLDHAM, *Eighth Satire of Boileau.*

I do not here speak of a legal innocence (none but *sots* and Quakers dream of such things), for as St. Paul says, ' By the works of the law shall no flesh living be justified ; ' but I speak of an evangelical innocence.—SOUTH, *Sermons*, vol. ii. p. 427.

He [Perseus] commanded those poor divers to be secretly murdered, that no person should remain alive that was privy to that *sottish* commandment of his.—HOLLAND, *Livy*, p. 1177.

> A leper once he lost, and gained a king,
> Ahaz his *sottish* conqueror, whom he drew
> God's altar to disparage and displace
> For one of Syrian mode.
>
> MILTON, *Paradise Lost*, b. i.

Sottishness and dotage is the extinguishing of reason in phlegm or cold.—H. MORE, *Grand Mystery of Godliness*, b. viii. c. 14.

SPARKLE.   Water ' sparkles ' most when it is scattered.   This must explain the transition of the word from its former meaning, as indicated in the passages given below, to its present.

The Lansgrave hath *sparkled* his army without any further enterprise.—*State Papers*, vol. x. p. 718.

> Cassandra yet there sawe I, how they haled
> From Pallas' house with *spercled* tresse undone.
>
> SACKVILLE, *Induction to a Mirror for Magistrates.*

And awhile chawing all those things in his mouth, he spitteth it upon him whom he desireth to kill ; who being *sparkled* therewith, dieth by force of the poison within the space of half an hour.—*Purchas's Pilgrims*, part ii. p. 1495.

SPECIOUS.   Like the Latin ' speciosus,' it simply signified beautiful once ; it now means always presenting a deceitful appearance of that beauty which

is not really possessed, and is never used in any but
an ethical sense.

> This prince hadde a dowter dere, Asneth was her name,
> A virgine ful *specious*, and semely of stature.
>> *Metrical Romance of the Fourteenth Century.*

And they knew him, that it was he which sate for alms at the
specious gate of the temple.—*Acts* iii. 10.   Rheims.

> His mind as pure and neatly kept
> As were his nurseries, and swept
> So of uncleanness or offence
> That never came ill odour thence;
> And add his actions unto these,
> They were as *specious* as his trees.
>> BEN JONSON, *Epitaph on Master Vincent Corbet.*

Which [almug-trees], if odoriferous, made that passage as
sweet to the smell as *specious* to the sight.—FULLER, *A Pisgah
Sight of Palestine*, b. iii. c. 2, § 5.

SPICE.   We have in English a double adoption of
the Latin 'species,' namely 'spice' and 'species.'
'Spice,' the earlier form in which we made the word
our own, is now limited to certain aromatic drugs,
which, as consisting of various *kinds*, have this name
of 'spices.'   But 'spice' was once employed as
'species' is now.

Absteyne you fro al yvel *spice* [ab omni *specie* malâ, Vulg.].—
1 *Thess.* v. 22. WICLIF.

The *spices* of penance ben three.   That on of hem is solempne,
another is commune, and the thridde privie.—CHAUCER, *The
Persones Tale.*

Justice, although it be but one entire virtue, yet is described
in two kinds of *spices*.   The one is named justice distributive,
the other is called commutative.—Sir T. ELYOT, *The Governor*,
b. iii. c. 1.

SPINSTER. A name that was often applied to women of evil life, in that they were set to enforced labour of spinning in the Spittle or House of Correction (it is still called ' The *Spinning* House ' at Cambridge), and thus were 'spinsters.' None of our Dictionaries, so far as I have observed, take note of this use of the word.

Many would never be indicted *spinsters*, were they spinsters indeed, nor come to so public and shameful punishments, if painfully employed in that vocation.—FULLER, *Worthies of England, Kent.*

> *Geta.*　　　These women are still troublesome ;
> 　　There be houses provided for such wretched women,
> 　　And some small rents to set ye a spinning.
> *Drusilla.*　　　　　Sir,
> 　　We are no *spinsters*, nor if you look upon us,
> 　　So wretched as you take us.
> 　　　　　　　BEAUMONT and FLETCHER, *The Prophetess,*
> 　　　　　　　act iii. sc. 1.

SQUANDER. The examples which follow will show that ' to squander ' had once, if not a different, yet a much wider use than it now, at least in our classical English, retains. In the northern dialects it is still used as equivalent to ' disperse.'

He hath an argosy bound to Tripolis, another to the Indies ; . . . he hath a third at Mexico, a fourth for England, and other ventures he hath, *squandered* abroad.—SHAKESPEARE, *Merchant of Venice*, act i. sc. 3.

The minister is not to come into the pulpit, as a fencer upon the stage, to make a fair flourish against sin, but rather as a captain into the field, to bend his forces specially against the strongest troops of the enemy, and to *squander* and break through the thickest ranks.—SANDERSON, *Sermon 2, ad Clerum.*

> They charge, recharge, and all along the sea
> They chase and *squander* the huge Belgian fleet.
> 　　　　　　　DRYDEN, *Annus Mirabilis*, st. 67.

STAPLE. A curious change has come over this word. We should now say, Cotton is the great 'staple,' that is, the established merchandize, of Manchester; our ancestors would have reversed this and said, Manchester is the great 'staple,' or established mart, of cotton. We make the goods prepared or sold the 'staple' of the place; they made the place the 'staple' of the goods. See Cowell, *The Interpreter*, s. v.

Men in all ages have made themselves merry with singling out some place, and fixing the *staple* of stupidity and stolidity therein.—FULLER, *Worthies of England, Nottinghamshire.*

Staple; a city or town, where merchants jointly lay up their commodities for the better uttering of them by the great; a public storehouse.—PHILLIPS, *New World of Words.*

STARVE. The A.-S. 'steorfan,' the German 'sterben,' to die, it is only by comparatively modern use restricted to dying *by cold or by hunger*; in this restriction of use, resembling somewhat the French 'noyer,' to kill *by drowning*, while 'necare,' from which it descends, is to kill by any manner of death. But innumerable words are thus like rivers, which once pouring their waters through many channels, have now left dry and abandoned them all, save one, or, as in the present instance it happens, save two.

> For wele or wo she n'ill him not forsake :
> She n'is not wery him to love and serve,
> Though that he lie bedrede til that he *sterve*.
> > CHAUCER, *The Merchantes·Tale.*

> But, if for me ye fight, or me will serve,
> Not this rude kind of battle, nor these arms
> Are meet, the which do men in bale to *sterve*.
> > SPENSER, *Fairy Queen*, ii. 6, 34.

STATE. Used often by our old writers for a raised dais or platform, on which was placed a chair or throne with a canopy (the German ' Thronhimmel ') above it; being the chiefest seat of honour ; thus in Massinger's *Bondman*, act i. sc. 3, according to the old stage-direction Archidamus ' offers Timoleon the *state*.' But there is another use of ' state ' not unfrequent in the seventeenth century, though altogether unknown in our own. A ' state ' was a republic, as contradistinguished from a monarchy. This usage, which the States of Holland may have contributed to bring about, does not seem to have lasted very long.

> But for a canopy to shade her head,
> No *state* which lasts no longer than 'tis stayed,
> And fastened up by cords and pillars' aid.
> > BEAUMONT, *Psyche*, can. xix. st. 170.

Their majesties were seated as is aforesaid under their canopies or *states*, whereof that of the Queen was somewhat lesser and lower than that of the King, but both of them exceeding rich.—*History of the Coronation of King James II.*, 1687, p. 61.

When he went to court, he used to kick away the *state*, and sit down by his prince cheek by jowl. Confound these *states*, says he, they are a modern invention.—SWIFT, *History of John Bull*, part ii. c. 1.

What say some others ? A government of *states* would do much better for you than a monarchy.—ANDREWS, *Sermon* 6, *Of the Gunpowder Treason*.

> Dull subjects see too late
> Their freedom in monarchal reign ;
> Finding their freedom in a *state*
> Is but proud strutting in a chain.
> > DAVENANT, *The Dream*.

Those very Jews who at their very best
Their humour more than loyalty expressed,
Thought they might ruin him; they could create
Or melt him to that golden calf, a *state*.
DRYDEN, *Absalom and Achitophel*, 66.

STATIONER. There was a time when 'stationer,' meaning properly no more than one who had his *station*, that is, in the market-place or elsewhere, included the bookseller and the publisher, as well as the dealer in the raw material of books. But when, in the division of labour, these became separate businesses, the name was restrained to him who dealt in the latter articles alone.

I doubt not but that the Animadverter's *stationer* doth hope and desire that he hath thus pleased people in his book, for the advancing of the price and quickening the sale thereof.—FULLER, *Appeal of Injured Innocence*, p. 38.

The right of the printed copies (which the *stationer* takes as his own freehold), was dispersed in five or six several hands.— OLEY, *Preface to Dr. Jackson's Works*.

Quarles, Chapman, Heywood, Wither had applause,
And Wild, and Ogilby in former days;
But now are damned to wrapping drugs and wares,
And cursed by all their broken *stationers*.
OLDHAM, *A Satire*.

STICKLE, } Now to stand with a certain pertinacity
STICKLER. } to one's point, refusing to renounce or go back from it; but formerly equivalent to the emphatic 'décharpir,' a word which the French language has now let go, to interpose between combatants and separate them, when they had sufficiently satisfied the laws of honour; some deriving it from the wands, sceptres, or *sticks* with which the heralds

engaged in this office separated the combatants. Our present meaning of the word connects itself with the past in the fact that the 'sticklers,' or seconds, as we should call them now, often fulfilled another function, being ready to maintain in their own persons and by their own arms the quarrel of their principals, and thus to 'stickle' for it.

> Betwixt which three a question grew,
> Which should the worthiest be;
> Which violently they pursue,
> And would not *stickled* be.
>
> DRAYTON, *Muses' Elysium, Nymph.* 6.

The same angel [in Tasso], when half of the Christians are already killed, and all the rest are in a fair way of being routed, *stickles* betwixt the remainders of God's hosts and the race of fiends; pulls the devils backwards by the tails, and drives them from their quarry.—DRYDEN, *Dedication of Translations from Juvenal*, p. 122.

> The dragon wing of night o'erspreads the earth,
> And, *stickler*-like, the armies separates.
>
> SHAKESPEARE, *Troilus and Cressida*, act v. sc. 9.

> Our former chiefs, like *sticklers* of the war,
> First fought to inflame the parties, then to poise;
> The quarrel loved, but did the cause abhor,
> And did not strike to hurt, but make a noise.
>
> DRYDEN, *On the Death of Oliver Cromwell.*

STOMACH. Already in classical Latin 'stomachus' had all the uses, courage, pride, indignation, ill-will, which 'stomach' may be seen in the following quotations to have once possessed, but which at this day have nearly or quite departed from it.

And sence we herde therof oure hert hath failed us, neither is there a good *stomache* more in eny man, by the reason of youre commynge.—*Josh.* ii. 11. COVERDALE.

He was a man
Of an unbounded *stomach*, ever ranking
Himself with princes.
SHAKESPEARE, *Henry VIII.*, act iv. sc. 2.

Arius, discontented that one should be placed before him in honour, whose superior he thought himself in desert, became through envy and *stomach* prone unto contradiction, and bold to broach that heresy wherein the Deity of our Lord Jesus Christ was denied.—HOOKER, *Ecclesiastical Polity*, b. v. § 42.

STOUT, } The temptation to the strong to be
STOUTNESS. } also the proud is so natural, so diffi-
cult to resist, and resisted by so few, that it is nothing wonderful when words, first meaning the one, pass over into the sense of the other. 'Stout,' however, has not retained, except in some provincial use, the sense of proud, nor ' stoutness ' of pride.

Commonly it is seen that they that be rich are lofty and *stout*.
—LATIMER, *Sermons*, p. 545.

I *stout* and you *stout*,
Who will carry the dirt out ?
Old Proverb.

Come all to ruin ; let
Thy mother rather feel thy pride, than fear
Thy dangerous *stoutness* ; for I mock at death
With as big heart as thou.
SHAKESPEARE, *Coriolanus*, act iii. sc. 2.

STOVE. This word has much narrowed its mean ing. Bath, hothouse, any room where air or water was artificially heated, was a ' stove' once.

When a certain Frenchman came to visit Melancthon, he found him in his *stove*, with one hand dandling his child in the swaddling-clouts, and the other holding a book and reading it.—FULLER, *The Holy State*, b. ii. c. 9.

How tedious is it to them that live in *stoves* and caves half a

year together, as in Iceland, Muscovy, or under the pole!—
BURTON, *Anatomy of Melancholy*, part i. sect. 2.

When most of the waiters were commanded away to their
supper, the parlour or *stove* being nearly emptied, in came a
company of musketeers, shot every one his man, and so pro-
ceeded to an apothecary's house, where Wallenstein lay.—
Letters and Despatches of Thomas Earl of Strafford, vol. i. p.
226.

STREET. This, one of the words which the Romans
left behind them when they quitted Britain, and
which the Saxons learned from the Britons, is more
properly a road or causeway ('via *strata*') than a
street, in our present sense of the word; and as late
as Coverdale was so used.

For they soughte them thorow every *strete*, and yet they founde
them not.—*Josh.* ii. 22. COVERDALE.

But when one sawe that all the people stode there still, he
removed Amasa from the *strete* unto the felde.—1 *Sam.* xx. 12.
COVERDALE.

SUBLIME. There is an occasional use of 'sublime'
by our earlier poets, a use in which it bears much
the meaning of the Greek ὑπερήφανος, or perhaps
approaches still more closely to that of μετέωρος, high
and lifted up, as with pride; which has now quite
departed from it.

> For the proud Soldan, with presumptuous cheer
> And countenance *sublime* and insolent,
> Sought only slaughter and avengément.
> >   SPENSER, *Fairy Queen*, v. 8, 30.

> Their hearts were jocund and *sublime*,
> Drunk with idolatry, drunk with wine.
> >   MILTON, *Samson Agonistes.*

SUE. One now ' sues ' or *follows* another into the courts of law, being, as in the legal language of Greece, ὁ διώκων, the 'pursuer;' but 'to sue' was once to follow, without any such limitation of meaning.

If thou wolt be perfite, go, and sille alle thingis that thou hast, and come, and *sue* me.—*Matt.* xix. 21. WICLIF.

And anoon, the nettes forsaken, thei *sueden* hym.—*Mark* i. 19. Id.

SURE. Used once in the sense of affianced, or, as it would be sometimes called, ' hand-fasted,' See ' Assure,' ' Ensure.'

The king was *sure* to dame Elizabeth Lucy, and her husband before God.—Sir T. MORE, *History of King Richard III.*

SUSPECT, ⎱ To 'suspect' is properly to look under,
SUSPICION. ⎰ and out of this fact is derived our present use of the word; but in looking *under* you may also look *up,* and herein lies the explanation of an occasional use of ' suspect ' and ' suspicion ' which we find in our early writers.

Pelopidas being sent the second time into Thessaly, to make accord betwixt the people and Alexander, the tyrant of Pheres, was by this tyrant (not *suspecting* the dignity of an ambassador, nor of his country) made prisoner.—NORTH, *Plutarch's Lives,* p. 927.

If God do intimate to the spirit of any wise inferiors that they ought to reprove, then let them *suspect* their own persons, and beware that they make no open contestation, but be content with privacy.—ROGERS, *Naaman the Syrian,* p. 330.

Cordeilla, out of mere love, without the *suspicion* of expected reward, at the message only of her father in distress, pours forth true filial tears.—MILTON, *History of England,* b. i.

SYCOPHANT. The early meaning of 'sycophant,' when it was employed as equivalent to informer, delator, calumniator, 'promoter' (which see), agreed better with its assumed derivation, and undoubted use, in the Greek, than does our present. Employing it now in the sense of false and fawning flatterer, we might seem at first sight to employ it in a sense not merely altogether unconnected with, but quite opposite to, its former. Yet indeed there is a very deep inner connexion between the two uses. It is not for nothing that Jeremy Taylor treats of these two, namely 'Of Slander and Flattery,' in one and the same course of sermons; for, as the Italian proverb has taught us, 'He who flatters me before, spatters me behind.'

The poor man, that hath nought to lose, is not afraid of the *sycophant* or promoter.—HOLLAND, *Plutarch's Morals*, p. 261.

He [St. Paul] in peril of the wilderness, that is of wild beasts; they [rich men] not only of the wild beast called the *sycophant*, but of the tame beast too, called the flatterer.—ANDREWS, *Sermon preached at the Spittle*.

Sanders, that malicious *sycophant*, will have no less than twenty-six wain-load of silver, gold, and precious stones to be seized into the king's hands by the spoil of that monument.— HEYLIN, *History of the Reformation*, 1849, vol. i. p. 20.

SYMBOL. The employment of 'symbol' in its proper Greek sense of contribution thrown into a common stock, as in a pic-nic or the like, is frequent in Jeremy Taylor, and examples of it may be found in other scholarly writers of the seventeenth century.

The consideration of these things hath oft suggested, and at length persuaded me to make this attempt, to cast in my mite to this treasury, my *symbolum* toward so charitable a work.— HAMMOND, *A Paraphrase on the Psalms*, Preface.

Christ hath finished his own sufferings for expiation of the world; yet there are 'portions that are behind of the sufferings' of Christ, which must be filled up by his body the Church; and happy are they that put in the greatest *symbol*; for ' in the same measure you are partakers of the sufferings of Christ, in the same shall ye be also of the consolation.'—J. TAYLOR, *The Faith and Patience of the Saints.*

There [in Westminster Abbey] the warlike and the peaceful, the fortunate and the miserable, the beloved and the despised princes, mingle their dust and pay down their *symbol* of mortality.—Id., *Holy Dying*, c. i. § 2.

TABLE. The Latin 'tabula' had for one of its meanings picture or painting; and this caused that 'table' was by our early writers used often in the same meaning.

The *table* wherein Detraction was expressed, he [Apelles] painted in this form.—Sir T. ELYOT, *The Governor*, b. iii. c. 27.

You shall see, as it were in a *table* painted before your eyes, the evil-favouredness and deformity of this most detestable vice. —*Homilies ; Against Contention.*

Learning flourished yet in the city of Sicyon, and they esteemed the painting of *tables* in that city to be the perfectest for true colours and fine drawing, of all other places.—NORTH, *Plutarch's Lives*, p. 843.

TALENT. The original meaning, as of 'talento' in Italian, 'talante' in Spanish, was will, inclination, from 'talentum' (τάλαντον), balance, scales, and then inclination of balance; thus in Spenser (*Fairy Queen*, iii. 4, 61), 'maltalent' is grudge or ill will. It is probably under the influence of the Parable of the Talents (*Matt.* xxv.) that it has travelled to its present meaning. Clarendon still employs it very distinctly in its older sense.

Whoso then wold wel understonde these peines, and bethinke him wel that he hath deserved these peines for his sinnes, certes he shold have more *talent* for to sighe and to wepe than for to singe and playe.—CHAUCER, *The Persone's Tale.*

The meaner sort rested not there, but creating for their leader Sir John Egremond, a factious person and one who had of a long time borne an ill *talent* towards the king, entered into open rebellion.—BACON, *History of King Henry VII.*

Though the nation generally was without any ill *talent* to the Church, either in the point of the doctrine or the discipline, yet they were not without a jealousy that Popery was not enough discountenanced.—CLARENDON, *History of the Rebellion*, b. i. e. 194.

TALL. Our ancestors superinduced on the primary meaning of ' tall ' a secondary, resting on the assumption that tall men would be also brave, and this often with a dropping of the notion of height altogether.

His [the Earl of Richmond's] companions being almost in despair of victory were suddenly recomforted by Sir William Stanley, which came to succours with three thousand *tall* men.— GRAFTON, *Chronicle.*

Tamburlaine. Where are my common soldiers now, that fought
    So lionlike upon Asphaltis' plains ?
Soldier. Here, my lord.
Tamburlaine. Hold ye, *tall* soldiers, take ye queens apiece.
   MARLOWE, *Tamburlaine the Great*, part ii. act iv. sc. 4.

He [Prince Edward] would proffer to fight with any mean person, if cried up by the volge for a *tall* man.—FULLER, *The Holy War*, b. iv. c. 29.

TARPAULIN. Not any longer used except in the shorter form of ' tar ' for sailor. See the quotation from Smollett, *s. v.* ' Companion.'

The Archbishop of Bordeaux is at present General of the French naval forces, who though a priest, is yet permitted to turn *tarpaulin* and soldier.—*Turkish Spy*, Letter 2.

TAWDRY. 'Tawdry' laces and such like were cheap and showy articles of finery bought at St. Etheldreda's or St. Awdrey's fair ; but it is only in later times that this cheapness, showiness, with a further suggestion of vulgarity, made themselves distinctly felt in the word.

> Bind your fillets fast,
> And gird in your waist
> For more fineness with a *tawdry* lace.
> SPENSER, *Shepherd's Calendar, Fourth Eclogue.*

Come, you promised me a *tawdry* lace and a pair of sweet gloves.—SHAKESPEARE, *Winter's Tale,* act iv. sc. 3.

TEMPER. What has been said under 'humour' will also explain 'temper,' and the earlier uses of it which we meet. The happy 'temper' would be the happy mixture, the blending in due proportions, of the four principal 'humours' of the body.

> The exquisiteness of his [the Saviour's] bodily *temper* increased the exquisiteness of his torment, and the ingenuity of his soul added to his sensibleness of the indignities and affronts offered to him.—FULLER, *A Pisgah Sight of Palestine,* vol. i. p. 345.

> Concupiscence itself follows the crasis and temperature of the body. If you would know why one man is proud, another cruel, another intemperate or luxurious, you are not to repair so much to Aristotle's ethics, or to the writings of other moralists, as to those of Galen, or of some anatomists, to find the reason of these different *tempers.*—SOUTH, *Sermons,* 1744, vol. ii. p. 5.

TEMPERAMENT. The Latin 'temperamentum' had sometimes very nearly the sense of our English 'compromise' or the French 'transaction,' and signified, as these do, a middle term reached by mutual concession, by a *tempering* of the extreme claims upon either side. This same use of 'temperament'

appears from time to time in such of our writers as
have allowed their style to be modified by their Latin
studies.

> Safest, therefore, to me it seems that none of the Council be
> moved unless by death, or just conviction of some crime. How-
> ever, I forejudge not any probable expedient, any *temperament*
> that can be found in things of this nature, so disputable on
> either side.—MILTON, *The Ready and Easy Way to establish a
> Free Commonwealth.*

> Many *temperaments* and explanations there would have been,
> if ever I had a notion that it ['Observations on the Minority']
> should meet the public eye.—BURKE, *Letter to Lawrence.*

TERMAGANT.   A name at this time applied only to
women of fierce temper and ungoverned tongue, but
formerly to men and women alike; and indeed predominantly to the first; 'Termagant' in the popular
notion being the name of the false god of the Maho-
metans.

> Art thou so fierce, currish, and churlish a Nabal, that even
> when thou mightest live in the midst of thy people (as she told
> Elisha [2 *Kin.* iv. 13]), thou delightest to play the tyrant and
> *termagant* among them?—ROGERS, *Naaman the Syrian,* p. 270.

> This would make a saint swear like a soldier, and a soldier
> like *Termagant.*—BEAUMONT and FLETCHER, *King or No King.*

THEWS.   It is a remarkable evidence of the influence of Shakespeare upon the English language,
that while, so far as yet has been observed, every
other writer, one single instance excepted, employs
'thews' in the sense of manners, qualities of mind
and disposition, his employment of it in the sense of
nerves, muscular vigour, has quite overborne the
other; which, once so familiar in our literature, has

now quite past away. See a valuable note in Craik's
English of Shakespeare, p. 117.

> To all good *thewes* born was she ;
> As liked to the goddes or she was born,
> That of the shefe she should be the corne.
>> CHAUCER, *The Legend of Hypermestre.*

> For every thing to which one is inclined
> Doth best become and greatest grace doth gain ;
> Yet praise likewise deserve good *thewes* enforced with pain.
>> ᛫ SPENSER, *Fairy Queen*, ii. 2.

> The mother of three daughters, well upbrought
> In goodly *thewes* and godly exercise.
>> Id. *Ib.*, i. 10, 4.

THINK,
THOUGHT,
THOUGHTFUL.
Many, as they read or hear in our
English Bible these words of our
Lord, 'Take no *thought* for your
life' (*Matt.* vi. 25 ; cf. 1 *Sam.* ix. 5), are perplexed,
for they cannot help feeling that there is some exagge-
ration in them, that He is urging here something
which is impossible, and which, if possible, would not
be desirable, but a forfeiting of the true dignity of
man. Or perhaps, if they are able to compare the
English with the Greek, they blame our Translators
for having given an emphasis to the precept which it
did not possess in the original. But neither is the
fact. 'Thought' is constantly *anxious* care in our
earlier English, as the examples which follow will
abundantly prove ; and 'to think,' though not so frequently, is to take *anxious* care. To this day they
will say in Yorkshire, 'It was *thought* that did for
her,' meaning that it was care that killed her.

> *Cleopatra.* What shall we do, Enobarbus?
> *Enobarbus.*   *Think* and die.
>> SHAKESPEARE, *Antony and Cleopatra*, act iii. sc. 13.

> Yet, for his love that all hath wrought,
> Wed me, or else I die for *thought.*
>> SKELTON, *Manerly Margery.*

He so plagued and vexed his father with injurious indignities, that the old man for very *thought* and grief of heart pined away and died.—HOLLAND, *Camden's Ireland*, p. 120.

In five hundred years only two queens have died in childbirth. Queen Catherine Parr died rather of *thought.*—*Somers' Tracts* (*Reign of Elizabeth*), vol. i. p. 172.

Harris, an alderman of London, was put in trouble, and died of *thought* and anxiety before his business came to an end.— BACON, *History of Henry VII.*

> O *thoughtful* herte, plungyd in dystres.
>> LYDGATE, *Lyf of our Lady.*

THRIFTY. The 'thrifty' is on the way to be the thriving; yet 'thrifty' does not mean thriving now, as once it did. It still indeed retains this meaning in provincial use; as I have heard a newly-transplanted tree which was doing well, described as 'thrifty.' See 'Unthrifty.'

No grace hath more abundant promises made unto it than this of mercy, a sowing, a reaping, a *thrifty* grace.—Bishop REYNOLDS, *Sermon* 30.

TIDY. This, identical with the German 'zeitig,' has lost that reference to *time* which in 'noon*tide*,' 'even*tide*,' and some other compounds still survives.

> Seven eares wexen fette of coren
> On an busk ranc and wel *tidi.*
>> *Story of Genesis and Exodus*, 2104.

Lo an erthetilier abideth preciouse fruyt of the erthe, paciently suffrynge til he resseyve tymeful and lateful fruit— that is *tidi* and ripe.—*James* v. 7. WICLIF.

TINSEL. This is always now *cheap* finery, glistering (étincelant) like silver and gold, but at the same time pretending a value and a richness which it does not really possess. There lay no such insinuation of pretentious splendour in its earlier uses. A valuable note in Keightley's *Milton*, vol. i. p. 126, makes it, I think, clear that by 'tinsel' was commonly meant 'a *silver* texture, less dense and stout than cloth of silver;' yet not always, for see my first quotation.

Under a duke, no man to wear cloth of gold *tinsel.*—*Literary Remains of King Edward VI.*, 1551, 2.

Every place was hanged with cloth of gold, cloth of silver, *tinsel*, arras, tapestry, and what not.—STUBBS, *Anatomy of Abuses*, p. 18.

> [He] never cared for silks or sumptuous cost,
> For cloth of gold, or *tinsel* figurie,
> For baudkin, broidery, cutworks, nor conceits.
> > GASCOIGNE, *The Steel Glass.*

> Her garments all were wrought of beaten gold,
> And all her steed with *tinsel*-trappings shone.
> > SPENSER, *Fairy Queen*, iii. 1, 15.

TOBACCONIST. Now the seller, once the smoker, of tobacco.

Germany hath not so many drunkards, England *tobacconists*, France dancers, Holland mariners, as Italy alone hath jealous husbands.—BURTON, *Anatomy of Melancholy*, part iii. sect. 3.

Hence is it that the lungs of the *tobacconist* are rotted.—BEN JONSON, *Bartholomew Fair.*

> But let it be of any truly said,
> He's great, religious, learned, wise or staid,
> But he is lately turned *tobacconist*,
> Oh what a blur! what an abatement is't!
> > SYLVESTER, *Tobacco Battered.*

TORY. It is curious how often political parties have
ended by assuming to themselves names first fastened
on them by their adversaries in reproach and scorn.
The ' Gueux' or ' Beggars ' of Holland are perhaps the
most notable instance of all ; so too 'tories' was a name
properly belonging to the Irish bogtrotters, who during
our Civil War robbed and plundered, professing to be
in arms for the maintenance of the royal cause ; and
from them transferred, about the year 1680, to those
who sought to maintain the extreme prerogatives
of the Crown. There is an Act of the 6th of Anne
with this title : ' For the more effectual suppressing
Tories and Rapparees ; and for preventing persons
becoming *Tories* or resorting to them.' For the best
account of the ' tories ' see Prendergast, *Cromwellian
Settlement of Ireland*, pp. 163–183 ; and compare
Carte's *Life of the Duke of Ormonde*, vol. ii. p. 481.

That Irish Papists who had been licensed to depart this
nation, and of late years have been transplanted into Spain,
Flanders and other foreign parts, have nevertheless secretly
returned into Ireland, occasioning the increase of *tories* and
other lawless persons.—*Irish State Papers*, 24th January, 1656.

Let such men quit all pretences to civility and breeding.
They are ruder than *tories* and wild Americans.—GLANVILLE,
Sermons, p. 212.

In the open or plain countries the peasants are content to live
on their labour ; the woods, bogs, and fastnesses fostering and
sheltering the robbers, *tories*, and woodkerns, who are usually
the offspring of gentlemen, that have either misspent or forfeited
their estates ; who, though having no subsistance, yet contemn
trade, as being too mean and base for a gentleman reduced never
so low.—*MS. Account of the State of the County of Kildare*, of
date 1684, in Trinity College Library, Dublin.

Mosstroopers, a sort of rebels in the northern part of Scotland,
that live by robbery and spoil, like the *tories* in Ireland, or the
banditti in Italy.—PHILLIPS, *New World of Words*, ed. 1706.

TRADE. Properly that path which we 'tread,' and thus the ever recurring habit and manner of our life, whatever this may be.

> A postern with a blinde wicket there was,
> A common *trade* to passe through Priam's house.
> > Lord SURREY, *Translation of the Æneid*, b. ii. l. 592.

For him that lacketh nothing necessary, nor hath cause to complain of his present state, it is a great folly to leave his old acquainted *trade* of life, and to enter into another new and unknown.—NORTH, *Plutarch's Lives*, p. 53.

Teach a child in the *trade* of his way, and when he is old, he shall not depart from it.—*Proverbs* xxii. 6. Geneva.

> There those five sisters had continual *trade*,
> And used to bathe themselves in that deceitful shade.
> > SPENSER, *Fairy Queen*, ii. 12, 30.

TREACLE. This at present means only the sweet syrup of molasses, but was once of far wider reach and far nobler significance, having come to us from afar, and by steps which are curious to trace. They are these. The Greeks, in anticipation of modern homœopathy, called a fancied antidote to the viper's bite, which was composed of the viper's flesh, θηριακή, —from θηρίον, a name often given to the viper (*Acts* xxviii. 5); of this came the Latin 'theriaca,' and our 'theriac,' of which, or rather of the Latin form, 'triacle' and 'treacle' are but popular corruptions. See the *Promptorium Parvulorum*, p. 500.

For a most strong *treacle* against these venomous heresies wrought our Saviour many a marvellous miracle.—Sir T. MORE, *A Treatise on the Passion, Works*, p. 1357.

There is no more *triacle* at Galaad, and there is no phisician that can heale the hurte of my people.—*Jer.* viii. 22. COVERDALE.

At last his body [Sir Thomas Overbury's] was almost come by use of poisons to the state that Mithridates' body was by the use of *treacle* and preservatives, that the force of the poisons was blunted upon him.—BACON, *Charge against Robert, Earl of Somerset.*

The saints' experiences help them to a sovereign *treacle* made of the scorpion's own flesh (which they through Christ have slain), and that hath a virtue above all other to expel the venom of Satan's temptations from the heart.—GURNALL, *The Christian in Complete Armour,* c. ix. § 2.

Wonderful therefore is the power of a Christian, who not only overcomes and conquers and kills the viper, but like the skilful apothecary makes antidote and *triacle* of him.—HALES, *Sermon on Christian Omnipotence.*

Treacle; a physical composition, made of vipers and other ingredients.—PHILLIPS, *New World of Words.*

TREE. This might once have been used of the dead timber, no less than of the living growth; thus ' rood*tree*,' ' axle*tree*,' ' saddle*tree*.'

In a greet hous ben not oneli vessels of gold and of silver, but also of *tree* [lignea, Vulg.] and of erthe.—2 *Tim.* ii. 20. WICLIF.

He had a castel of *tre*, which he cleped Mategrifon.—CAP-GRAVE, *Chronicle of England*, p. 145.

> Take down, take down that mast of gowd,
> Set up a mast of *tree*,
> Ill sets it a forsaken lady
> To sail sae gallantlie.
>
> *Old Ballad.*

TRIUMPH. A name often transferred by our early writers to any stately show or pageantry whatever, not restricted, as now, to one celebrating a victory. See Lord Bacon's Essay, the 37th, with the heading, ' Of Masks and *Triumphs*,' passim.

Our daughter,
In honour of whose birth these *triumphs* are,
Sits here, like beauty's child.

Pericles, Prince of Tyre, act ii. sc. 2.

You cannot have a perfect palace except you have two several
sides, the one for feasts and *triumphs*, the other for dwelling.—
BACON, *Essays*, 45.

This day to Dagon is a solemn feast,
With sacrifices, *triumph*, pomp and games.

MILTON, *Samson Agonistes.*

TRIVIAL. A 'trivial' saying is at present a slight
one; it was formerly a well-worn or often-repeated
one, or, as we should now say, one that was trite;
but this, it might be, on the ground of the weight
and wisdom which it contained; as certainly the
maxim quoted by Hacket is anything but 'trivial' in
our sense of the word. Gradually the notion of
slightness was superadded to that of commonness,
and thus an epithet once of honour has become one of
dishonour rather.

Others avouch, and that more truly, that he [Duns Scotus]
was born in Downe, and thereof they guess him to be named
Dunensis, and by contraction Duns, which term is so *trivial* and
common in schools, that whoso surpasseth others either in cavil-
ling sophistry or subtle philosophy is forthwith nicknamed a
Duns.—STANYHURST, *Description of Ireland*, p. 2.

Æquitas optimo cuique notissima, is a *trivial* saying, A very
good man cannot be ignorant of equity.—HACKET, *Life of Archbishop Williams*, part i. p. 57.

These branches [of the divine life] are three, whose names
though *trivial* and vulgar, yet, if rightly understood, they bear
such a sense with them, that nothing more weighty can be pronounced by the tongue of men or seraphims, and in brief they
are these, Charity, Humility, and Purity.—H. MORE, *Grand
Mystery of Godliness*, b. ii. c. 12.

TRUMPERY. That which is deceitful is without any worth; and ' trumpery,' which was at first deceit, fraud (tromperie), is now anything which is worthless and of no account. Was Milton's use of the word in his well-known line, ' Black, white and gray, with all their *trumpery*,' our present, or that earlier ?

> When truth appeared, Rogero hated more
> Alcyna's *trumperies*, and did them detest,
> Than he was late enamourèd before.
> <div align="right">Sir J. HARINGTON, <i>Orlando Furioso</i>, b. vii.</div>

Britannicus was now grown to man's estate, a true and worthy plant to receive his father's empire ; which a grafted son by adoption now possessed by the injury and *trumpery* of his mother. —GREENWEY, *Tacitus*, p. 182.

TURK. It is a remarkable evidence of the extent to which the Turks and the Turkish assault upon Christendom had impressed themselves on the minds of men, of the way in which they stood as representing the entire Mahometan world, that ' Turk,' being in fact a national, is constantly employed by the writers of the sixteenth and seventeenth centuries as a religious, designation, as equivalent to, and coextensive with, Mahometan ; exactly as "Ελλην in the New Testament means continually not of Greek nationality, but of Gentile religion.

Have mercy upon all Jews, *Turks*, infidels, and heretics.— *Collect for Good Friday.*

It is no good reason for a man's religion, that he was born and brought up in it; for then a *Turk* would have as much reason to be a *Turk* as a Christian to be a Christian.—CHILLINGWORTH, *The Religion of Protestants*, part i. c. 2.

TUTOR, } The ' tutor ' of our forefathers was
TUITION. } rather a caretaker and guardian than an

instructor ; but seeing that one defends another most effectually who imparts to him those principles and that knowledge whereby he shall be able to defend himself, our modern use of the word must be taken as a deeper than the earlier.

This is part of the honour that the children owe to their parents and *tutors* by the commandment of God, even to be bestowed in marriage as it pleaseth the godly, prudent and honest parents or *tutors* to appoint.—BECON, *Catechism*, Parker Soc. ed., p. 871.

Tutors and guardians are in the place of parents ; and what they are in fiction of law they must remember as an argument to engage them to do in reality of duty.—J. TAYLOR, *Holy Living*, iii. 2.

As though they were not to be trusted with the king's brother, that by the assent of the nobles of the land were appointed, as the king's nearest friends, to the *tuition* of his own royal person. —Sir T. MORE, *History of King Richard III.*, p. 36.

Afterwards turning his speech to his wife and his son, he [Scanderbeg] commended them both with his kingdom to the *tuition* of the Venetians.—KNOLLES, *History of the Turks*, vol. i. p. 274.

UMBRAGE, ⎱ ' To take umbrage ' is, I think, the
UMBRAGEOUS. ⎰ only phrase in which the word ' umbrage ' is still in use among us, the only one at least in which it is ethically employed; but 'umbrage' in its earlier use coincides in meaning with the old French ' ombrage ' (see the quotation from Bacon), and signifies suspicion, or rather the disposition to suspect ; and ' umbrageous,' as far as I know, is constantly employed in the sense of suspicious by our early authors ; having now no other but a literal sense. Other uses of ' umbrage,' as those of Fuller and Jeremy Taylor which follow, must be explained from

the classical sympathies of these writers; out of which the Latin etymology of the word gradually made itself felt in the meaning which they ascribed to it, namely as anything slight and *shadowy*.

I say, just fear, not out of *umbrages*, light jealousies, apprehensions afar off, but out of clear foresight of imminent danger.—BACON, *Of a War with Spain.*

To collect the several essays of princes glancing on that project [a new Crusade], were a task of great pains and small profit; especially some of them being *umbrages* and state representations rather than realities, to ingratiate princes with their subjects, or with the oratory of so pious a project to woo money out of people's purses.—FULLER, *The Holy War*, b. v. c. 25.

You look for it [truth] in your books, and you tug hard for it in your disputations, and you derive it from the cisterns of the Fathers, and you inquire after the old ways; and sometimes are taken with new appearances, and you rejoice in false lights, or are delighted with little *umbrages* or peep of day.—J. TAYLOR, *Sermon preached to the University of Dublin.*

There being in the Old Testament thirteen types and *umbrages* of this Holy Sacrament, eleven of them are of meat and drink.—Id., *The Worthy Communicant*, c. ii. § 2.

At the beginning some men were a little *umbrageous*, and startling at the name of the Fathers; yet since the Fathers have been well studied, we have behaved ourselves with more reverence toward the Fathers than they of the Roman persuasion have done.—DONNE, *Sermons*, 1640, p. 557.

That there was none other present but himself when his master De Merson was murdered, it is *umbrageous*, and leaves a spice of fear and sting of suspicion in their heads.—REYNOLDS, *God's Revenge against Murther*, b. iii. hist. 13.

UNCOUTH. Now unformed in manner, ungraceful in behaviour; but once simply unknown. The change in signification is to be traced to the same causes which made ' barbarous,' meaning at first only foreign, to have afterwards the sense of savage and wild.

Almost all nations regard with disfavour and dislike that which is outlandish, and generally that with which they are unacquainted; so that words which at first did but express this fact of strangeness, easily acquire a further unfavourable sense.

The vulgar instruction requires also vulgar and communicable terms, not clerkly or *uncouth*, as are all these of the Greek and Latin languages.—PUTTENHAM, *Art of English Poesy*, b. iii. c. 10.

> Wel-away the while I was so fond,
> To leave the good that I had in hond,
> In hope of better that was *uncouth* ;
> So lost the dog the flesh in his mouth.
>> SPENSER, *The Shepherd's Calendar, September.*

' *Uncouth*, unkist,' said the old famous poet, Chaucer ; which proverb very well taketh place in this our new poet, who for that he is *uncouth* (as said Chaucer) is unkist ; and, *unknown* to most men, is regarded but of a few.—E. K., *Epistle Dedicatory prefixed to Spenser's Shepherd's Calendar.*

UNEQUAL. From the constant use made of ' unequal ' by our early writers, for whom it was entirely equivalent to unjust, unfair, one might almost suppose they saw in it ' iniquus ' rather than 'inæqualis.' At any rate they had no scruple in using it in a sense, which ' inæqualis' never has, but 'iniquus' continually.

> To punish me for what you make me do
> Seems most *unequal.*
>> SHAKESPEARE, *Antony and Cleopatra*, act ii. sc. 5.

> These imputations are too common, sir,
> And easily stuck on virtue, when she's poor :
> You are *unequal* to me.
>> BEN JONSON, *The Fox*, act iii. sc. 1.

Jerome, a very *unequal* relator of the opinion of his adversaries.—WORTHINGTON, *Life of Joseph Mede*, p. xi.

UNHANDSOME.   See 'Handsome.'

A narrow straight path by the water's side, very *unhandsome* [οὐ ῥᾳδίαν] for an army to pass that way, though they found not a man to keep the passage.—NORTH, *Plutarch's Lives*, p. 317 ; cf. p. 378.

The ships were unwieldy and *unhandsome.*—HOLLAND, *Livy*, p. 1188.

UNHAPPY,   }   A very deep truth lies involved in
UNHAPPINESS. }   the fact that so many words, and I suppose in all languages, unite the meanings of wicked and miserable, as the Greek σχέτλιος, our own 'wretch' and 'wretched.'   So, too, it was once with 'unhappy,' although its use in the sense of ' wicked ' has now passed away.

Fathers shall do well also to keep from them [their children] such schoolfellows as be *unhappy*, and given to shrewd turns ; for such as they are enough to corrupt and mar the best natures in the world.—HOLLAND, *Plutarch's Morals*, p. 16.

> Thou old *unhappy* traitor,
> Briefly thyself remember; the sword is out
> That must destroy thee.
>
> SHAKESPEARE, *King Lear*, act iv. sc. 6.

The servants of Dionyse, king of Sicily, which although they were inclined to all *unhappiness* and mischief, yet after the coming of Plato, perceiving that for his doctrine and wisdom the king had him in high estimation, they thus counterfeited the countenance and habit of the philosopher.—Sir T. ELYOT, *The Governor*, b. ii. c. 14.

[Man] from the hour of his birth is most miserable, weak, and sickly : when he sucks, he is guided by others ; when he is grown great, practiseth *unhappiness* and is sturdy ; and when old, a child again and repenteth him of his past life.—BURTON, *Anatomy of Melancholy ; Democritus to the Reader.*

UNION.   The elder Pliny (*H. N.* ix. 59) tells us that the name 'unio' had not very long before his time begun to be given to a pearl in which all chiefest excellencies, size, roundness, smoothness, whiteness, weight, met and, so to speak, were *united*; and as late as Jeremy Taylor the word 'union' was often employed of a pearl of a rare and transcendent beauty.

> And in the cup an *union* shall he throw,
> Richer than that which four successive kings
> In Denmark's crown have worn.
>
> SHAKESPEARE, *Hamlet*, act v. sc. 2.

Pope Paul II. in his pontifical vestments outwent all his predecessors, especially in his mitre, upon which he had laid out a great deal of money in purchasing at vast rates diamonds, sapphires, emeralds, crysoliths, jaspers, *unions*, and all manner of precious stones.—Sir PAUL RYCAUT, *Platina's History of the Popes*, p. 114.

Perox, the Persian king, [hath] an *union* in his ear worth an hundred weight of gold.—BURTON, *Anatomy of Melancholy*, mem. ii. sect. 3.

UNKIND, } ' Unkind ' has quite forfeited now its
UNKINDNESS. } primary meaning, namely that which violates the law of kind, thus ' *unkind* abominations ' (Chaucer), meaning incestuous unions and the like ; and has taken up with the secondary, that which does not recognize the duties flowing out of this kinship. In its primary meaning it moves in a region where the physical and ethical meet ; in its secondary· in a purely ethical sphere. How soon it began to occupy this the passages which follow will show ; for out of a sense that nothing was so unnatural or ' unkind ' as ingratitude, the word early obtained use as a special designation of this vice.

Unkynde [ingrati,Vulg.], cursid, withouten affeccioun.—2 *Tim.* iii. 2, 3. WICLIF.

It is all one to sey *unkinde,*
As thing whiche doone is againe kinde,
For it with kinde never stoode
A man to yelde evill for goode.

GOWER, *Confessio Amantis,* b. v.

Whar-for ilk man, bathe lered and lewed,
Suld thinke on that love that He man shewed,
And love Hym and thank Hym als he can,
And elles es he an *unkynd* man.

RICHARD ROLLE DE HAMPOLE, *Prick of Conscience,* 117.

The most damnable vice and most against justice, in mine opinion, is ingratitude, commonly called *unkindness.* He is *unkind* that denieth to have received any benefit, that indeed he hath received; he is *unkind* that dissimuleth; he is *unkind* that recompenseth not; but he is most *unkind* that forgetteth.— Sir T. ELYOT, *The Governor,* b. ii. c. 13.

God might have made me even such a foule and unreasonable beast as this is; and yet was I never so *kynde* as to thancke Him that He had not made me so vile a creature; which thing I greatly bewayle, and my *unkindenesse* causeth me now thus to weepe.—FRITH, *Works,* 1573, p. 90.

We have cause also in England to beware of *unkindnesse,* who have had in so fewe yeares the candel of Goddes woorde, so oft lightned, so oft put out; and yet will venture by our unthankfulnesse in doctrine, and sinfull life, to leese againe lighte, candle, candlesticke, and all.—ASCHAM, *The Scholemaster,* b. i.

UNTHRIFTY, } As the 'thrifty' will probably be
UNTHRIFTINESS. } the thriving, so the 'unthrifty'
the unthriving; but the words are not synonymous
any more, as once they were. See 'Thrifty.'

What [is it] but this self and presuming of ourselves causes grace to be *unthrifty,* and to hang down the head? what but our ascribing to ourselves in our means-using, makes them so unfruitful?—ROGERS, *Naaman the Syrian,* p. 146.

Staggering, non-proficiency, and *unthriftiness* of profession is the fruit of self.—ID., *Index.*

UNVALUED. This and 'invaluable' have been usefully desynonymized; so that 'invaluable' means now having a value greater than can be estimated, 'unvalued' esteemed to have no value at all. Yet it was not so once; though in Shakespeare (see *Hamlet*, act i. sc. 3) our present use of 'unvalued' occasionally obtained.

> Two golden apples of *unvalued* price.
>> SPENSER, *Sonnet* 77.

>> Go, *unvalued* book,
> Live, and be loved; if any envious look
> Hurt thy clear fame, learn that no state more high
> Attends on virtue than pined envy's eye.
>> CHAPMAN, *Dedication of Poems.*

>> Each heart
> Hath from the leaves of thy *unvalued* book
> Those Delphic lines with deep impression took.
>> MILTON, *An Epitaph on Shakespeare.*

USURY, } This, which is now the lending of money
USURER. } upon inordinate interest, was once the lending it upon any. The man who did not lend his money for nothing was then a 'usurer,' not he, as now, who makes unworthy profit by the necessities of the needy or the extravagance of the foolish. It is true that the word was as dishonourable then as it is now; and it could not be otherwise, so long as all receiving of interest was regarded as a violation at once of divine and of natural law. When at length the common sense of men overcame this strange but deep-rooted prejudice, the word was too deeply stained with dishonour to be employed to express the lawful receiving of a measurable interest; but 'usury,' taking up a portion only of its former meaning, was

now restricted to that which still remained under a moral ban, namely the exacting of an excessive interest for money lent.

On the other side, the commodities of *usury* are: first, that howsoever *usury* in some respect hindereth merchandizing, yet in some other it advanceth it; for it is certain that the greatest part of trade is driven by young merchants upon *borrowing at interest*; so as if the *usurer* either call in or keep back his money, there will ensue presently a great stand of trade.—Bacon, *Essays*.

Wherefore then gavest not thou my money into the bank, that at my coming I might have required mine own with *usury* [σὺν τόκῳ]?—*Luke* xix. 23. Authorized Version.

Brokers, takers of pawns, biting *usurers* I will not admit; yet because we converse here with men, not with gods, and for the hardness of men's hearts, I will tolerate some kind of *usury*.—Burton, *Anatomy of Melancholy; Democritus to the Reader*.

VARLET. Littré, dealing with this very word, has truly said, 'Les mots, soit en changeant de pays, soit en changeant de siècle, s'ennoblissent ou s'avilissent d'une façon singulière' (*Hist. de la Langue Française*, vol. ii. p. 166). There could be no more signal proof of this than that which the word 'varlet' supplies. I continue to quote his words, '*Vaslet*, ou, par une substitution non rare de l'*r* à l'*s*, *varlet*, est un diminutif de *vassal*; *vassal* signifiait un vaillant guerrier, et *varlet* un jeune homme qui pouvait aspirer aux honneurs de la chevalerie.' From this it fell to the use in which we find it in the passage quoted below from Shakespeare of squire or attendant, which is also the continually recurring use in the old English translation of Froissart. In this sense it survives as 'valet;' but not pausing here, it is now tinged with contempt, and implies moral worthlessness in him to whom it is applied.

> Call here my *varlet*; I'll unarm myself.
> > SHAKESPEARE, *Troilus and Cressida,* act i. sc. 1.

Right so there came in a *varlet*; and told Sir Tristram how there was come an errant knight into the town with such colours upon his shield.—Sir T. MALORY, *Morte D'Arthur,* b. x. c. 56.

VASSALAGE. This had once the meaning of courage, prowess, superiority. See in explanation the quotation from Littré under ' Varlet.'

> And certainly a man hath most honour
> To dien in his excellence and flour,
> Than whan his name appalled is for age;
> For all foryetten is his *vassalage.*
> > CHAUCER, *The Knightes Tale.*

> And Catoun seith is noon so great encress
> Of worldly tresour, as for to live in pees,
> Which among vertues hath the *vasselage.*
> > LYDGATE, *Minor Poems,* Halliwell's ed., p. 176.

VERMIN. Now always noxious offensive animals of the *smaller* kind; but employed formerly with no such limitation.

But he shouke of the *vermen* into the fyre and felt no harme. —*Acts* xxviii. 5. Geneva Version.

This crocodile is a mischievous four-footed beast, a dangerous *vermin* used to both elements.—HOLLAND, *Ammianus,* p. 212.

Wherein were all manner of four-footed beasts of the earth, and *vermin* [καὶ τὰ θηρία], and worms, and fowls of the air.— *Acts* x. 12. Geneva.

The Lord rectifies Peter, and frames him to go by a vision of all crawling *vermin* in a clean sheet.—ROGERS, *Naaman the Syrian,* p. 42.

VILIFY. This now implies a great deal more than to hold morally cheap, which was all that in the seventeenth century it involved.

Can it be imagined that a whole people would ever so *vilify* themselves, depart from their own interests to that degree as to place all their hopes in one man.—MILTON, *Defence of the People of England*, c. 7.

The ears of all men will be filled with deceitful figments and gainful lies, the merits of Christ's passion will be *vilified* and maimed.—H. MORE, *The Mystery of Iniquity*, b. ii. c. 7, § 11.

The more I magnify myself, the more God *vilifies* me.—ROGERS, *Naaman the Syrian*, p. 469.

VILLAIN,
VILLANY. } A word whose story is so well known that one may be spared the necessity of repeating it. It was, I think, with ' villany ' that there was first a transfer into an ethical sphere, though it is noticeable how ' villany' till a very late day expressed *words* foul and disgraceful to the utterer much oftener than *deeds*.

Pour the blood of the *villain* in one basin, and the blood of the gentleman in another ; what difference shall there be proved ? —BECON, *The Jewel of Joy*.

We yield not ourselves to be your *villains* and slaves [non *in servitutem* nos tradimus], but as allies to be protected by you.— HOLLAND, *Livy*, p. 935.

[He] was condemned to be degraded of all nobility, and not only himself, but all his succeeding posterity declared *villains* and clowns, taxable and incapable to bear arms.—FLORIO, *Montaigne*, b. i. c. 15.

In our modern language it [foul language] is termed *villany*, as being proper for rustic boors, or men of coarsest education and employment, who, having their minds debased by being conversant in meanest affairs, do vent their sorry passions in such strains.—BARROW, *Of Evil-speaking in general*, Sermon 16.

VIRTUOUS. Virtue is still occasionally used as equivalent to might or potency, but ' virtuous ' has quite abdicated the meaning of valorous or potent which it once had, and which its etymology justified.

With this all strengths and minds he moved ; but young Dei-
    phobus,
Old Priam's son, amongst them all was chiefly *virtuous.*
                CHAPMAN, *Homer's Iliad,* xiii. 147.

> Or call up him that left half told
> The story of Cambuscan old,
> Of Camball and of Algarsife,
> And who had Canace to wife,
> That owned the *virtuous* ring and glass.
>   MILTON, *Il Penseroso.*

> Tho lifting up his *vertuous* staff on high
> He smote the sea, which calmèd was with speed.
>   SPENSER, *Fairy Queen,* ii. 12, 26.

VIVACIOUS,⎫ ' Longevity,' as one might expect to
VIVACITY. ⎰ find it, is a comparatively modern word in the language. ' Vivacity,' which has now acquired the mitigated sense of liveliness, served instead of it ; keeping in English the original sense which ' vivacitas ' had in the Latin.

James Sands, of Horborn in this county, is most remarkable for his *vivacity,* for he lived 140 years.—FULLER, *Worthies of England, Staffordshire.*

Fables are raised concerning the *vivacity* of the deer ; for neither are their gestation nor increment such as may afford an argument of long life.—Sir T. BROWNE, *Vulgar Errors.*

Hitherto the English bishops had been *vivacious* almost to wonder. For, necessarily presumed of good years before entering on their office in the first year of Queen Elizabeth, it was much that but five died for the first twenty years of her reign.— Id., *Church History of Britain,* b. ix. § 27.

VOLUBLE. This epithet always insinuates of him
to whom it is now applied that his speech is freer and
faster than is meet ; but it once occupied that region
of meaning which ' fluent' does at present, without
any suggestion of the kind. Milton (*P. L.* ix. 436)
recalls the word, as he does so many, to its primary
meaning.

He [Archbishop Abbott] was painful, stout, severe against bad
manners, of a grave and a *voluble* eloquence.—HACKET, *Life of
Archbishop Williams*, part i. p. 65.

WAINSCOT. I transcribe a correction of the brief
and inaccurate notice of this word in my first edition,
which a correspondent, with the best opportunity of
knowledge, has kindly sent me : ' " Wainscot " is
always in the building trade applied to oak only, but
not to all kinds of oak. The wainscot oak grows
abroad, chiefly, I think, in Holland, and is used for
wainscoting, or wood lining, of walls of houses,
because it works very freely under the tool, and is
not liable to " cast " or rend, as English oak will do.
It is consequently used for all purposes where expense
is no object. Formerly all panelling to walls was
done in wainscot, and was called " wainscoting." It
was never painted. In modern times it was imitated
in deal, and was painted to represent real wainscot,
or of any other colour, while the name of " wainscoting " adhered to it, though the material was no
longer wainscot. At present, however, the word
" wainscot " is always used to designate the real
wainscot oak.' It will be seen from this very interesting explanation that within the narrow limits of a
particular trade, the old meaning of ' wainscot,' which

has everywhere else disappeared, still survives. It would be curious to trace how much in this way of earlier English within limited technical circles lives on, having everywhere else died out.

A wedge of *wainscot* is fittest and most proper for cleaving of an *oaken* tree.—Sir T. URQUHART, *Tracts*, p. 153.

Being thus arrayed, and enclosed in a chest of *wainscot*, he [Edward the Confessor] was removed into the before-prepared feretry.—DART, *History of St. Peter's, Westminster*, b. ii. c. 3.

WANT. Among other differences between 'carere' and 'egere,' this certainly is one, that the former may be said of things evil as well as good, as well of those whose absence is desirable as of those whose absence is felt as a loss, while 'egere' always implies not merely the absence but the painful sense of the absence. 'To want' which had once the more colourless use of 'carere,' has passed now, nearly though not altogether, into this latter sense, and is ='egere.'

If he be lost, and *want*, thy life shall go for his life.—I *Kings* xx. 39. Geneva.

In a word, he [the true gentleman] is such, that could we *want* him, it were pity but that he were in heaven ; and yet I pity not much his continuance here, because he is already so much in heaven to himself.—CLEMENT ELLIS, *Character of a True Gentleman*.

> Friend of my life, which did you not prolong,
> The world had *wanted* many an idle song.
> POPE, *Lines to Arbuthnot*.

WHIRLPOOL. Dr. Latham, in his edition of Johnson, is the first to notice the use of 'whirlpool' to designate some huge sea-monster of the whale kind,

the sperm whale or cachalot has been suggested.
Thus in the margin of our Bible, there is on *Job* xli. 1,
('Canst thou draw out *leviathan*?') a gloss, 'that is,
a whale or *whirlpool*.'

The Indian Sea breedeth the most and the biggest fishes that
are; among which the whales and *whirlpools*, called balænæ,
take up in length as much as four acres or arpens of land.—
HOLLAND, *Pliny*, vol. i. p. 235.

The ork, *whirlpool*, whale, or huffing physeter.
SYLVESTER, *Dubartas, First Day of the Week.*

About sunset, coming near the Wild Island, Pantagruel spied
afar off a huge monstrous physeter, a sort of whale, which some
call a *whirlpool*.—RABELAIS, *Pantagruel*, b. iv. c. 33.

WHISPERER,   There lay in 'whisperer' once, as
WHISPERING.   in the ψιθυριστής of the Greeks, the
susurro of the Latins, the suggestion of a slanderer
or false accuser, which has now quite passed away
from the word.

Now this Doeg, being there at that time, what doeth he?
Like a *whisperer* or man-pleaser goeth to Saul the king, and told
him how the priest had refreshed David in his journey, and had
given unto him the sword of Goliath.—LATIMER, *Sermons*,
Parker edit., p. 486.

A *whisperer* separateth chief friends.—*Prov.* xvi. 28. Authorized Version.

Kings in ancient times were wont to put great trust in eunuchs.
But yet their trust towards them hath rather been as to good
whisperers than good magistrates and officers.—BACON, *Essays,
Of Deformity.*

Lest there be debates, envyings, wraths, strifes, backbitings,
whisperings, swellings, tumults.—2 *Cor.* xii. 20. Authorized
Version.

WHITEBOY.   Formerly a cockered favourite (compare Barnes's use of 'white son,' Works, 1572, p. 192),

but in later years one of the many names which the perpetrators of agrarian outrages in Ireland either assumed to themselves, or had given to them by others.

His first address was An humble Remonstrance by a dutiful son of the Church, almost as if he had said her *whiteboy.*—MILTON, *Prose Works,* vol. i. p. 172.

The Pope was loath to adventure his darlings into danger. Those *whiteboys* were to stay at home with his Holiness, their tender father.—FULLER, *Holy War,* i. 13.

WIFE. It is a very profound testimony, yielded by language, to the fact that women are intended to be wives, and only find the true completion of their being when they are so, that in so many languages there is a word which, meaning first a woman, means afterwards a wife, as γυνή, 'mulier,' 'femme,' 'weib,' and our English 'wife.' With us indeed the secondary use of the word has now overborne and swallowed up the first, which only survives in a few such combinations as 'mid*wife*,' 'fish*wife*,' 'hus*wife*,' and the like; but it was not always so; nor in our provincial dialects is it so now. An intelligent correspondent who has sent me a ' Glossary of Words used in Central Yorkshire ' writes as follows: 'In rural districts a grown woman is a young wife, though she be unmarried.'

> And with that word upstart this olde *wife.*
> CHAUCER, *The Wife of Bath's Tale*

Like as a *wife* with childe, when hir travaile commeth upon her, is ashamed, crieth, and suffreth the payne, even so are we, O Lorde, in thy sight.—*Isai.* xxvi. 17. COVERDALE,

WIGHT. The best discussion on this interesting word is in Grimm's *Deutsche Mythologie,* pp. 408-410, who has a chapter, On *Wights* and Elves. 'Wight' has for us lost altogether its original sense of a preternatural or supernatural being, and is used, but always slightingly, of men. It is easy to see how, with the gradual contempt for the old mythology, the dying-out of the superstitions connected with it, words such as 'elf' and 'wight' should have lost their weight and honour as well.

> I crouche thee from elves and from *wights.*
>
> CHAUCER, *The Miller's Tale.*

The poet Homer speaketh of no garlands and chaplets but due to the celestial and heavenly *wights.*—HOLLAND, *Pliny*, vol. i. p. 456.

A black horse cometh, and his rider hath a balance, and a voice telleth among the four *wights* that corn shall be dear [*Rev.* vi. 6].—BROUGHTON, *Of Consent upon Apocalypse.*

When the four *wights* are said to have given glory, honour, and thanks to Him that sate upon the throne [*Rev.* v. 14], what was their ditty but this?—MEDE, *Sermons.*

WILFUL.⎫ 'Wilful' and 'willing,' 'wilfully' and
WILFULLY.⎭ 'willingly,' have been conveniently desynonymized by later usage in our language; so that in 'wilful' and 'wilfully' there now lies ever the sense of will capriciously exerted, deriving its motives merely from itself; while the examples which follow show there was once no such implication of *self*-will in the words.

Alle the sones of Israel halewiden *wilful* thingis to the Lord. —*Exod.* xxxv. 29. WICLIF.

A proud priest may be known when he denieth to follow Christ and his apostles in *wilful* poverty and other virtues.— FOXE, *Book of Martyrs ; Examination of William Thorpe.*

Fede ye the flok of God, that is among you, and purvey ye, not as constreyned, but *wilfulli.*—1 *Pet.* v. 2. WICLIF.

And so, through his pitiful nailing, Christ shed out *wilfully* for man's life the blood that was in his veins.—Foxe, *Book of Martyrs ; Examination of William Thorpe.*

WINCE. Now to shrink or start away as in pain from a stroke or touch ; but, as far as I know, used always by our earlier authors in the sense of to kick.

Poul, whom the Lord hadde chosun, long tyme *wynside* agen the pricke.—WICLIF, *Prolog on the Dedis of Apostlis.*

For this flower of age, having no forecast of thrift, but set altogether upon spending, and given to delights and pleasures, *winseth* and flingeth out like a skittish and frampold horse in such sort that it had need of a sharp bit and short curb.— HOLLAND, *Plutarch's Morals,* p. 14.

WIT, ⎫ The present meaning of ' wit ' as com-
WITTY. ⎭ pared with the past, and the period when it was in the act of transition from one to the other, cannot be better marked than in the quotation from Bishop Reynolds which is given below. It is a protest, an impotent one, as such invariably are, against a change in the word's meaning, going on before his eyes. Cowley's Ode, *Of Wit,* is another very important document, illustrating the history of the word.

Who knewe the *witte* of the Lord, or who was his counceilour ? —*Rom.* xi. 34. WICLIF.

I take not *wit* in that common acceptation, whereby men understand some sudden flashes of conceit whether in style or conference, which, like rotten wood in the dark, have more shine than substance, whose use and ornament are, like themselves, swift and vanishing, at once both admired and forgotten. But I understand a settled, constant, and habitual sufficiency of the understanding, whereby it is enabled in any kind of learning, theory, or practice, both to sharpness in search, subtilty in expression, and despatch in execution.—REYNOLDS, *Passions and Faculties of the Soul,* c. xxxix.

For the world laghes on man and smyles,
Bot at the last it him bygyles ;
Tharfor I hald that man noght *witty*
That about the world is over bysy.
RICHARD ROLLE DE HAMPOLE, *Pricke of Conscience*, 1092.

I confess notwithstanding, with the *wittiest* of the school divines, that if we speak of strict justice God could no way have been bound to requite man's labours in so large and ample manner.—HOOKER, *Ecclesiastical Polity*, b. i. c. 11.

WITCH. This was not once restrained, as it now is, to the *female* exerciser of unlawful magical arts, but would have been as freely applied to Balaam or Simon Magus as to her whom we call the ' Witch of Endor.' ' She-witch ' was not uncommon in our Elizabethan literature, when such was intended. In the dialect of Northumbria ' witches ' are of both sexes still (Atkinson).

There was a man in that citie whose name was Symount, a *wicche.—Acts* viii. 9. WICLIF.

Item, he is a *witch*, asking counsel at soothsayers.—FOXE, *Book of Martyrs ; Appeal against Boniface.*

Then the king commanded to call together all the soothsayers, charmers, *witches*, and Caldees, for to shew the king his dream. —*Dan.* ii. 2. COVERDALE.

Who can deny him a wisard or *witch*, who in the reign of Richard the Usurper foretold that upon the same stone where he dashed his spur riding toward Bosworth field he should dash his head in his return ?—COTTA, *The Trial of Witchcraft*, p. 49.

WIZARD. A title not necessarily used in times past with any dishonourable subaudition of *perverted* wisdom on his part to whom it was given, as is now the case.

Then Herod, calling the *wisards* privily, did narrowly search of them the time of the star's appearing.—*Matt.* ii. 7. Sir J. CHEKE.

> When Jeremy his lamentation writ,
> They thought the *wizard* quite out of his wit.
> > DRAYTON, *Elegies, To Mr. G. Sandys.*

> See how from far upon the eastern road
> The star-led *wizards* haste with odours sweet.
> > MILTON, *On the Nativity.*

WOMB. This is now only the ὑστέρα, but once could be ascribed to both sexes, having as wide a meaning as the κοιλία of the Greeks.

And he coveitide to fille his *wombe* of the coddis that the hoggis eeten, and no man gaf hym.—*Luke* xv. 16. WICLIF.

> Of this matere, o Poule, well canst thou trete ;
> Mete unto *wombe*, and *wombe* eke unto mete.
> > CHAUCER, *Canterbury Tales.*

Falstaff. An I had but a belly of any indifferency, I were simply the most active fellow in Europe. My *womb*, my *womb*, my *womb* undoes me.—SHAKESPEARE, 2 *Henry IV.*, act iv. sc. 3.

WORM. This, which designates at present only smaller and innoxious kinds of creeping and crawling things, once, as the German 'wurm,' was employed of all the serpent kind ; and indeed in some of our northern dialects all snakes and serpents are ' worms ' to the present day. In 'blind*worm*,' 'slow*worm*,' ' hag*worm*,' we have tokens of the earlier use.

There came a *viper* out of the heat and leapt on his hand. When the men of the country saw the *worm* hang on his hand, they said, This man must needs be a murderer.—*Acts* xxviii. 3, 4. TYNDALE.

> 'Tis slander,
> Whose edge is sharper than the sword ; whose tongue
> Outvenoms all the *worms* of Nile.
> > SHAKESPEARE, *Cymbeline*, act iii. sc. 4.

T

O Eve, in evil hour thou didst give ear
To that false *worm*, of whomsoever taught
To counterfeit man's voice.

MILTON, *Paradise Lost*, b. ix.

WORSHIP. At present we 'worship' none but God; there was a time when the word was employed in so much more general a sense that it was not profane to say that God 'worshipped,' that is honoured, man. This, of course, is the sense of the word in the Marriage Service, 'with my body I thee *worship*.'

If ony man serve me, my fadir schal *worschip* hym.—*John* xii. 26. WICLIF.

That they show all good faithfulness, that they may do *worship* to the doctrine of our Saviour God in all things.—*Tit.* ii. 10. TYNDALE.

Man, that was made after the image and likeness of God, is full worshipful in his kind; yea, this holy image that is man God *worshippeth.*—FOXE, *Book of Martyrs; Examination of William Thorpe.*

WRETCHED. What has been observed on 'Unhappy' explains and accounts also for the use of 'wretched' as = wicked. 'Wretch' still continues to cover the two meanings of one miserable and one wicked, though 'wretched' does so no more.

Nero regned after this Claudius, of alle men *wrechidhest*, redy to alle maner vices.—CAPGRAVE, *Chronicle of England*, p. 62.

To do evil gratis, to do evil for good, is the *wretchedest* wickedness that can be.—ANDREWS, *Of the Conspiracy of the Gowries*, serm. 4.

YOUNKER. Now, as far as it is used at all, equivalent to 'youngster;' but the 'younker' of our Elizabethan and earlier literature was much more nearly the German 'junker,' or Jung Herr, the young lord or youthful gallant.

Yf some of them can get a fox tale or two, or that he may have a capons feder or a goose feder, or any long feder on his cap, than he is called a *yonker.*—BORDE, *The Boke of the Introduction of Knowledge,* 1513.

> How like a *younker* or a prodigal
> The scarfèd bark puts from her native bay,
> Hugged and embracèd by the strumpet wind.
> > SHAKESPEARE, *Merchant of Venice,* act ii. sc. 6.

> See how the morning opes her golden gates,
> And takes her farewell of the glorious sun!
> How well resembles it the prime of youth,
> Trimmed like a *younker,* prancing to his love.
> > Id., 3 *Henry VI.,* act ii. sc. 1.

Venus loved the *younker* Adonis better than the warrior Mars. —DODOEN, *History of Plants,* p. 656.

As Rehoboam's *yonkers* carried that weighty business of his kingdom and overthrew it, so do the unruly and rebellious humours of most youth miscarry this.—ROGERS, *Matrimonial Honour,* p. 31.

Milton Keynes UK
Ingram Content Group UK Ltd.
UKHW040623141024
2164UKWH00007B/11